Status Survey and Conservation

Palms

Their Conservation and Sustained Utilization

Edited by Dennis Johnson

IUCN/SSC Palm Specialist Group

with parts written by the following authors:
Henk J. Beentje (Chapter 8)
Rodrigo Bernal (Chapter 3: Colombia)
Neela de Zoysa (Chapter 7: Sri Lanka; Box 7.2)
John Dowe (Chapters 5 (in part),11; Box 5.1)
Francis Friedmann (Chapter 9: Seychelles)
Dennis Johnson (Chapters 1,2,3,4,5,7,12 (all in part);
Boxes 1.1,3.1,6.1,8.1,9.1,11.1)
Francis Kahn (Chapter 6: 1st part)
Ruth Kiew (Box 7.1)
Markus Meier (Chapters 1,2,4,6,7,10,12 (all in part))
Bertrand de Montmollin (Chapter 10: *Phoenix theophrasti*)
Monica Moraes (Chapter 6: Bolivia)
Kit Pearce (Chapter 7: Sarawak)
Leng Guan Saw (Chapter 7: Peninsular Malaysia)
Wendy Strahm (Chapter 9: Mascarene and Comoros islands)
Paul Tuley (Chapter 9: African Mainland)
Andrew P. Vovides (Box 4.1)

and contributions from
Michael Ataroff (Venezuela)
Anders Barfod (Thailand)
John Dransfield (Old World)
Michael Ferrero (Papua New Guinea)
Maria Luisa Garcia (Venezuela)
Chrissen Gemmill (Hawaii)
Jean-Jacques de Granville (Guianas)
William Hahn (Paraguay, *Coccothrinax*)
Andrew Henderson (New World)
David Lorence (Hawaii)
Domingo Madulid (Philippines)
Judas Tadeu de Medeiros-Costa (Brazil)
Sven Nehlin (Venezuela)
Fred Stauffer (Venezuela)

IUCN
The World Conservation Union

SPECIES SURVIVAL COMMISSION

Sultanate of Oman

Chicago Zoological Society

WWF

Published by: IUCN, Gland, Switzerland and Cambridge, UK

Citation: Johnson, D. (ed.) and the IUCN/SSC Palm Specialist Group. 1996. *Palms: Their Conservation and Sustained Utilization. Status Survey and Conservation Action Plan.* IUCN, Gland, Switzerland and Cambridge, UK. 116 + viii pp.

ISBN: 2-8317-0352-2

Cover photo: *Dictyosperma album* var. *conjugatum*, Round Island hurricane palm, the last individual in the wild, Mauritius. Endangered. (Wendy Strahm)

Produced by: The Nature Conservation Bureau Limited, Newbury, UK.

Printed by: Press 70, Salisbury, UK.

Available from: IUCN Publications Services Unit
219c Huntingdon Road, Cambridge CB2 0DL, United Kingdom
Tel: +44 1223 277894, Fax +44 1223 277175
E-mail: iucn-psu@wcmc.org.uk
WWW: http://www.iucn.org
A catalogue of IUCN publications is also available.

The text of this book is printed on 115 gsm Grandeur Pure Velvet, which is rated as 5-star under the Eco-Check system and is made from 100% sustainable fiber sources using chlorine-free processes.

Contents

Foreword v

Acknowledgements vi

ExecutiveSummary vii

Résumé viii

Chapter 1. Introduction 1
  The diversity of palms 1
    Systematics 1
    Morphology 4
    Habitats 4
    Distribution 5
  Taxonomy and conservation 5
  Threats 6
  Structure of the Action Plan 6

**Chapter 2. *In situ* Conservation Status of Palms
and Related Issues** 7
  The most highly threatened palms of the world 7
  Monotypic palms 8
  Endemic palms of Unknown conservation status 8
  Palm Floras 10

Chapter 3. Protected Areas 13
  Palms in existing protected areas 13
    Sarawak, East Malaysia 13
    Colombia 13
  Discussion and recommendations 14

Chapter 4. Economic and Ornamental Palms 15
  Major economic palms 15
    Not threatened species 15
    Unknown or threatened species 16
  Major ornamental palms 16
    Not threatened species 17
    Unknown or threatened species 17
    Chamaedoreas 18
  General recommendations 19

Chapter 5. *Ex situ* Conservation 24
  Major limiting factors 24
  Field genebanks 25
  Highly threatened palms in botanic gardens 25
  Priority activities and recommendations 25

Chapter 6. Regional Priorities in the Americas 29
  Amazonian forest ecosystems and their palms 29
  Palm diversity and palm-rich areas in the
    Amazon Basin 31

Palm frequency, density, and response
  to deforestation 32
Palms as keystone species 33
Case study I: palms of the Peruvian Amazon 33
Case study II: the genus *Astrocaryum*
  in Amazonia 34
  Discussion 35
Island species 35
  Threatened island species 35
  Discussion 35
Conservation action 36
  Tropical forests 36
  Islands 39
Specific recommendations for palm
conservation in South American countries 40
  Argentina 40
  Bolivia 40
  Brazil 41
  Colombia 42
  Ecuador 44
  French Giuana, Guyana, Surinam 44
  Meso-America 45
  Mexico 45
  Paraguay 46
  Peru 46
  Venezuela 46

Chapter 7. Regional Priorities in Asia 48
  Palms in Asia 48
  Rattans 48
  Asian palms with economic development
    potential 50
  In situ palm conservation 50
  Research 51
  Specific recommendations for Asian countries 52
    Pakistan 52
    India 52
    Sri Lanka 53
    Bangladesh, Bhutan, Laos, Myanmar,
      Kampuchea, Vietnam, Thailand 57
    China 57
    Philippines 57
    Malaysia 58
    Indonesia 62
    Papua New Guinea 63

Chapter 8. Priorities in Madagascar 66
  Palm flora 66
  Threats 66
  Conservation needs 66

Chapter 9. Regional Priorities in Africa and Indian Ocean Islands 69
  The African mainland 69
    Palms in habitat 69
  Indian Ocean Islands 71
    Mascarene Islands 71
    The Comoros 76
    Seychelles 76

Chapter 10. The Mediterranean Basin 77
  Conservation of Theophrastus's date palm,
  Phoenix theophrasti 77
    Ecology and distribution 77
    Vulnerability, threats, and present
      protection measures 77
  Conservation of the dwarf palm,
  Chamaerops humilis 78

Chapter 11. Regional Priorities in Australia and the Pacific Islands 79
  Australia 79
    Status of Endangered and Vulnerable taxa 79
  New Zealand 80
  South-west Pacific Islands 81
    Conservation status 82
  Hawaii 83
  Other Pacific Islands 85

Chapter 12. Action Plan for Palm Conservation and Utilization 86
  Priorities 86
  Palm Secretariat 86
  Overview of recommendations made in this
  Action Plan 87
    Research 87
    In situ conservation 87
    Ex situ conservation 87
    Economic and ornamental palms 88
    Education and involvement of local people 88
    Implementation 88

References 93

Appendix 1. Definitions of the IUCN Red List conservation categories 99

Appendix 2. Highly endangered palms 100
  2A. By region 100
  2B. By genus 102

Appendix 3. Endemic palms with Unknown conservation status 106

Appendix 4. Citations of selected palm Floras (since 1900) and other references 111

Appendix 5. Contacts 113

Foreword

Palms, with their graceful architecture, often dominate the landscape of tropical habitats, providing many of the essentials for human life. Depending on the area, palms can be the most important of the plant families, as their impact on people's lives is so significant. Many palm populations, even those apparently "wild", have been managed for decades or longer by the local inhabitants, who recognized early on their importance as food, fiber, animal feed, handicrafts, thatch, and construction material.

Good conservation initiatives depend on the involvement and support of local people, rather than their exclusion, and this document reveals an interesting facet of the palm/people relationship: of the 83 "major economic palms" cited in this report, only one species is listed as Endangered (although several others are Unknown or Indeterminate, or are not known in the wild). One reason for this is that, more often than not, local people recognize the value of their natural resources, and have even been able to manage their extraction in sustainable fashion. Exceptions do exist and often outside pressures have resulted in the destruction of the delicate balance of centuries of such plant/people partnerships.

How, then, can conservation be most effectively carried out in a group such as the palms, that often require decades to mature and yield viable propagates? This Action Plan for palms gives the conservation community, for the first time, an answer to this important question. Dennis Johnson and his colleagues have gathered copious information about what is known, and unknown as well, about palm distribution, abundance, and vulnerability. Based on this compilation of available information, they have:

- set crucial taxonomic and geographical priorities for research and rescue of palms,

- proposed the establishment of a more effective coordination body—a Palm Secretariat for the Palm Specialist Group,
- suggested other actions such as the development of *in situ* and *ex situ* conservation activities,
- where needed, determined extraction levels for economically important species that can be sustained over time,
- involved local people in the conservation enterprise through education and economic empowerment,
- encouraged the implementation of the proposed actions via a more proactive program that includes funding for these global endeavours.

As one of the first of the plant conservation Action Plans published by IUCN/SSC, this important effort is a model for furthering similar studies as well as a challenge to the conservation community. Can we make a significant difference in the erosion of palm biodiversity? Will this document and the program it details be adopted by conservationists, palm enthusiasts, farmers, and others interested in plants? Dennis Johnson and his colleagues involved in the production of this document are to be congratulated for their extraordinary efforts in producing an Action Plan for palms. This plan has provided a biologically sound strategy for palm conservation, indeed a map of the journey that will be necessary. It is now up to the conservation community, led by the IUCN/SSC to commit to understanding that journey, navigating its difficult path, and safeguarding the future existence of this wondrous and important plant family.

Dr. Michael J. Balick
Chair, IUCN/SSC Palm Specialist Group
The New York Botanical Garden

Acknowledgements

This Action Plan is the product of the collective knowledge of the IUCN/SSC Palm Specialist Group and other palm specialists who have collaborated in generating and assembling the data and in preparing specific sections of the report.

I wish to offer sincere thanks to the authors who wrote various parts of this document. The individual recommendations they made afford a broad perspective on the subject of palm conservation from region to region. The global recommendations in Chapter 12 represent a synthesis of those views and my own, but the contents are totally my responsibility.

A debt of gratitude is also owed to other individuals who contributed in various ways to the Action Plan by updating lists of species, sharing reference material and providing comments and suggestions: Michael Ataroff, Michael Balick, Anders Barfod, Henrik Balslev, S.K. Basu, Leonor Cusato, John Dransfield, Fred Essig, Randy Evans, Michael Ferrero, Gloria Galeano, Chrissen Gemmill, Jean-Jacques de Granville, William Hahn, Andrew Henderson, Donald Hodel, Charles Hubbuch, David Lorence, Domingo Madulid, Markus Meier, Judas Tadeu de Medeiros-Costa, Johanis Mogea, Bertrand de Montmollin, Sven Nehlin, Larry Noblick, Robin Sears, Fred Stauffer, Jane Villa-Lobos, Natalie Uhl, Trevor Williams, and Scott Zona.

For guidance and moral support in the compilation of this Action Plan, I thank Simon Stuart, Wendy Strahm, and Tim Sullivan of IUCN, as well as Alan Hamilton of WWF. A large debt is owed to WCMC for the special attention given to updating the palm database; Kerry Walter especially helped keep the process moving. Brian Groombridge helped in producing the maps. I also thank Beverley Lewis and Harriet Gillett for diligently handling a large volume of data entry and responding to my requests for printouts. Thanks go to Peter Wyse Jackson and Etelka Leadlay of Botanic Gardens Conservation International (BGCI) for generating a printout of palms in botanic gardens. WWF US provided some funding for this project as well. Final thanks to my wife and fellow conservationist Jane MacKnight who acted as a sounding board for my ideas, assisted with data gathering, and critically read the entire manuscript.

Dr. Dennis Johnson
Deputy Chair, IUCN/SSC Palm Specialist Group

Executive Summary

The palm family (Palmae, or more recently Arecaceae), comprising some 2200 species, is distributed throughout the tropics and subtropics. While exhibiting a tremendous morphological diversity, palms are mainly found in the understory of cloud and rain forests, occurring mostly in tropical Asia and America.

The objectives of this Action Plan are to identify the most threatened palm species, to present recommendations for conservation that cater to their specific requirements, and to provide strategic guidelines for the conservation and sustainable utilisation of the many palms that provide food, construction materials, and an important source of revenue for many people.

The increasing demands on the world's natural resources pose a serious threat to palm biodiversity. The two main threats are over-exploitation and habitat destruction. For example, the use of rattan palms in furniture making has caused dramatic population decline for numerous species which, in turn, has had severe impacts on local and international markets, not to mention local biodiversity. Species used for edible palm hearts, timber and fiber, and ornamental plants are others whose populations are in serious decline. This Action Plan identifies where extraction is sustainable and where, on the contrary, over-exploitation may lead to extinction.

Habitat destruction poses a more permanent and widespread threat to palms throughout the world, but particularly in tropical cloud and rain forests. Species whose habitat range is limited to a small area are most at risk. The situation is particularly alarming for those species restricted to islands. Of the 224 Endangered palm species identified in this Action Plan, 141 are restricted to islands (including 69 species from Madagascar and 19 from Borneo). Eleven of these are representatives of distinct monotypic genera and therefore are of special concern. Invasive species pose a distinct threat to numerous island palms as well.

Chapters one through five of this Action Plan give background information on the palm family including the taxonomy, distribution patterns, and references to the important literature on the family. The importance of taxonomic knowledge, habitat protection, and *ex situ* conservation is discussed in the context of the overall conservation of palms.

Regional overviews with specific country accounts are presented in chapters six through eleven. These accounts highlight the most endangered species, provide specific recommendations for conservation action, and indicate where more research is urgently needed before even remedial action can be taken. Chapter twelve summarizes and prioritizes the conservation actions discussed earlier. Among the top priorities are:

- Compilation of conservation checklists for the Atlantic Forest of Brazil and the forests of Irian Jaya and Papua New Guinea, followed by the establishment of appropriate conservation management plans;
- Implementation of management plans for endangered palms in Madagascar and the Mascarenes, as well as on the islands of Vanuatu, Fiji, and Hawaii;
- Rescue actions for other palms on the verge of extinction in Cuba, India, Sri Lanka, and Malaysia;
- Field studies to assess conservation status and requirements of a large number of palms with Unknown or Indeterminate status.

The Palm Action Plan is intended for use by conservationists in all sectors of society including scientists, policy makers, government officials, educators, planners, and grant awarding bodies. Scientists are encouraged to use this Action Plan in direct consultation with policy makers, government officials, and grant awarding bodies when developing their research projects. Government officials and policy makers in turn may use the project ideas to develop plans for high-profile (and effective) conservation initiatives. Many of the projects presented in the Plan have the potential for student involvement as well.

While members of the Palm Specialist Group will endeavour to stimulate the implementation of the recommendations made here, they would encourage readers to share this Action Plan with others who have an interest in palms and their conservation.

Résumé

La famille des palmiers (Palmae ou, plus récemment, Arecaceae) comprend quelque 2200 espèces réparties dans toutes les régions tropicales et subtropicales du globe. Malgré leur très grand diversité morphologique, les palmiers croissent de préférence sous le couvert des forêts tropicales humides d'Asie et d'Amérique.

Les objectifs de ce Plan d'action sont: d'identifier les espèces de palmiers les plus menacées; de formuler des recommandations pour leur conservation en assuront leurs besoins spécifiques; et, d'établir de lignes directrices pour la conservation ainsi que pour l'exploitation durable des nombreuses espèces de palmiers qui sont utilisées pour l'alimentation ou comme matériaux de construction et qui constituent ainsi une source de revenu importante pour de nombreuses populations.

L'augmentation constante de l'exploitation des ressources naturelles mondiales met sérieusement en danger l'existence de bien des palmiers. Les deux principaux facteurs qui les menacent sont la surexploitation et la destruction de leurs habitats. Par exemple, l'utilisation du rotin pour la construction de meubles a entraîné un déclin dramatique des populations de nombreuses espèces de palmiers, ce qui a eu de graves répercussions non seulement sur la biodiversité locale mais aussi les marchés locaux et internationaux. D'autre part, les espèces utilisées pour la production de 'coeurs de palmiers' destinés à l'alimentation, de bois de construction, de fibres ou comme plantes ornementales ont vu leurs populations naturelles décliner sérieusement. Ce Plan d'action identifie les régions où l'exploitation durable de certaines espèces des palmiers est encore possible et celles où, au contraire, leur surexploitation risque d'entraîner leur extinction.

La destruction de leurs habitats est une menace constante et très répandue pour l'existence des palmiers à travers le monde, particulièrement dans les forêts tropicales humides. Les espèces dont l'aire de répartitiion est réduite courent le plus de risques. La situation est particulièrement alarmante pour les endémiques des îles. Des 224 espèces menacées d'extinction identifiées dans ce Plan d'action, 141 sont des endémiques insulaires, (y compris les 49 espèces de Madagascar et les 19 de Bornéo). Onze d'entre elles font parties de genres monotypiques et méritent donc une attention toute particulière. Les plantes invasives représentent également une menace spécifique pour de nombreuses espèces de palmiers insulaires.

Les cinq premiers chapitres de ce Plan d'action donnent des informations de base sur la famille des palmiers, notamment sur leur taxonomie et leur répartition et présentent la bibliographie existant à leur le sujet. L'importance des connaissances sur la taxonomie, sur la protection des habitats et sur la conservation *ex situ* des palmiers est examinée dans le contexte général de leur protection.

Les chapitres 6 à 11 donnent une vue d'ensemble de différentes régions avec des informations spécifiques sur certains pays. Pour chaque région, les espèces les plus menacées sont mises en évidence, des recommandations pour des actions de conservation sont proposées et des indications sont données sur les espèces pour lesquelles des investigations complémentaires urgentes doivent êtres réalisées avant de pouvoir mettre en oeuvre des actions de restauration. Le douzième chapitre récapitule et établit un ordre de priorité pour les actions de conservation proposées dans les chapitres précédents.

Les principales priorités sont :

- l'analyse des listes d'actions de conservation concernant les Forêts Atlantiques du Brésil ainsi que celles de l'Irian Jaya et de la Papouasie-Nouvelle Guinée, suivie de l'établissement de plans de gestion et de conservation appropriés;
- la mise en oeuvre de plans de gestion pour la conservation des palmiers menacés d'extinction à Madagascar, dans les îles Mascareignes ainsi que dans les îles de Vanuatu, Fiji et Hawaii;
- la mise en oeuvre d'actions de sauvetage des palmiers sur le point d'éteindre à Cuba, aux Indes, au Sri Lanka et en Malaisie;
- la réalisation d'études de terrain pour déterminer les statuts et les besoins de conservation d'un grand nombre de palmiers actuellement classés dans les catégories 'Non évalué' ou 'Données insuffisantes' des Listes Rouges de l'UICN.

Le Plan d'action pour les Palmiers est destiné à être utilisé par des acteurs de la conservation dans tous les secteurs de la société, notamment par les scientifiques, les décideurs, les hommes politiques, les enseignants, les planificateurs et les organismes de subventionnement. Il est particulièrement souhaitable que les scientifiques utilisent ce Plan d'action en coordination directe avec les décideurs, l'administration et les organismes de subventionnement lors du développement de projets de recherche. Les propositions de ce Plan d'action pourront être directement utilisées par les décideurs pour planifier et mettre en oeuvre des actions de conservation importantes et efficaces. De plus, bien des projets présentés dans ce Plan offrent la possibilité de faire participer, et donc de sensibiliser, des étudiantes.

Les membres du Groupe de spécialistes des Palmiers s'efforceront de stimuler la mise en oeuvre des recommandations figurant dans ce Plan d'action et encouragent les lecteurs de ce document à le communiquer à tous ceux qui sont concernés par les palmiers et leur conservation.

Trad. Paul H. Strahm

"Of all land plants, the palm is the most distinguished."
E.J.H. Corner (1966)

"Palms provide one of the tallest trees (*Ceroxylon*), the largest woody climber (*Calamus*), the largest leaf (*Raphia*), the largest inflorescence (*Corypha*) and the largest seed (*Lodoicea*) in the plant kingdom."
J.W. Purseglove (1972)

"The versatility of palms in the hands of man is astonishing. Houses, baskets, mats, hammocks, cradles, quivers, packbaskets, impromptu shelters, blowpipes, bows, starch, wine, protein from insect larvae, fruit beverages, flour, oil, ornaments, loincloths, cassava graters, medicines, magic, perfume—all are derived from palms ... to whatever extent man has been involved in the tropical ecosystem, palms have certainly been a major factor in making possible this involvement ..."
H.E. Moore, Jr. (1973)

Chapter 1

Introduction

The palm family (Palmae, or more recently Arecaceae) is the world's third most useful plant family, after grasses and legumes. Therefore, palm conservation has very

Coco de Mer, Vallée du Mai, Praslin, Seychelles.

Wendy Strahm

practical applications, and conservation recommendations must strike a balance between conservation and utilization. In most cases palm conservation cannot be successful without seriously taking into account utilization, and palm utilization cannot continue unabated without adopting certain measures of conservation.

The diversity of palms

Systematics

The palms are a large family. Although taxonomic opinions are diverse, the contributors to this Action Plan reviewed about 2300 accepted palm taxa, representing nearly 200 genera. The preeminent palm publication of the past decade is the comprehensive treatment of the Palmae at the generic level, and the formal recognition of six subfamilies, each representing a separate line of evolution (Uhl and Dransfield 1987). Within these subfamilies, the authors designated 14 tribes and 37 subtribes. Table 1.1 gives an overview of palm systematics, although the number of palm genera and species are still approximate due to on-going palm research. Taxonomy and species numbers given are based on Uhl and Dransfield (1987), with major updates from Henderson *et al.* (1995) for the Americas and Dransfield and Beentje (1995) for Madagascar. Conservation categories are based on the threatened plants database maintained at WCMC (World Conservation Monitoring Centre). The old IUCN Red List categories of threat (E, V, R, etc., see Appendix 1; IUCN 1980) are used here, as recategorizing all the species following the revised system would have significantly delayed this publication. In future editions of the Palm Action Plan, the revised IUCN categories (CR, EN, VU, etc.; IUCN 1994) for all palm taxa will be applied.

Table 1.1 Systematics of Palmae, with data on distribution and threats

Genus	total	Endangered	Threatened	Unknown	Not threatened	Meso-America	S. America	Africa, W. Asia	Indian Ocean	Indomalaya	Australasia	SW Pacific
CORYPHOIDEAE												
CORYPHEAE												
Trithrinacinae												
Trithrinax	3	.	1	2	.	.	x	.	.	.	.	.
Chelyocarpus	4	.	2	2	.	x	x	.	.	.	.	.
Cryosophila	9	2	3	4	.	x	.	.	.	.	.	.
Itaya	1	.	1	.	.	.	x	.	.	.	.	.
Schippia	1	1	.	.	.	x	.	.	.	.	.	.
Thrinax	7	1	2	.	4	x	.	.	.	.	.	.
Coccothrinax	14	1	3	3	7	x	.	.	.	.	.	.
Zombia	1	.	.	.	1	x	.	.	.	.	.	.
Trachycarpus	4	.	1	2	1	.	.	.	.	x	.	.
Rhapidophyllum	1	.	.	.	1	x	.	.	.	.	.	.
Chamaerops	1	.	.	.	1	.	.	x	.	.	.	.
Maxburretia	3	1	2	.	.	.	.	.	.	x	.	.
Guihaia	2	.	.	2	.	.	.	.	.	x	.	.
Rhapis	11	.	1	1	.	.	.	.	.	x	.	.
Livistoninae												
Livistona	30	.	14	9	7	.	.	x	.	x	x	.
Pholidocarpus	5	.	2	3	.	.	.	.	.	x	x	.
Johannesteijsm	4	2	2	.	.	.	.	x	.	.	.	.
Licuala	111	6	26	74	5	.	.	.	.	x	x	.
Pritchardiopsis	1	.	1	.	.	.	.	.	.	.	.	x
Pritchardia	24	6	6	1	11	.	.	.	.	.	x	.
Colpothrinax	2	.	1	1	.	x	.	.	.	.	.	.
Acoelorraphe	1	.	.	.	1	x	.	.	.	.	.	.
Serenoa	1	.	.	.	1	x	.	.	.	.	.	.
Brahea	9	1	7	.	1	x	.	.	.	.	.	.
Copernicia	13	1	2	1	9	x	x	.	.	.	.	.
Washingtonia	2	.	1	1	.	x	.	.	.	.	.	.
Coryphinae												
Corypha	9	1	3	3	2	.	.	.	.	x	x	.
Nannorrhops	1	.	.	1	.	.	.	x	.	.	.	.
Chuniophoenix	2	2	.	.	.	.	.	.	.	x	.	.
Kerriodoxa	1	.	1	.	.	.	.	.	.	x	.	.
Sabalinae												
Sabal	16	2	3	1	10	x	.	.	.	.	.	.
PHOENICEAE												
Phoenix	17	.	3	5	9	.	x	.	x	.	.	.
BORASSEAE												
Borassodendron	2	.	1	1	.	.	.	.	.	x	.	.
Latania	3	2	1	.	.	.	.	.	x	.	.	.
Borassus	5	1	1	1	2	.	.	x	x	x	x	.
Lodoicea	1	.	1	.	.	.	.	.	x	.	.	.
Hyphaeninae												
Hyphaene	17	.	3	12	2	.	.	x	x	x	.	.
Medemia	2	1	1	.	.	.	.	x	.	.	.	.
Bismarckia	1	.	.	1	.	.	.	.	x	.	.	.
Satranala	1	1	.	.	.	.	.	.	x	.	.	.
CALAMOIDEAE												
CALAMEAE												
Ancistrophyllinae												
Laccosperma	8	.	.	6	2	.	.	x	.	.	.	.
Eremospatha	4	.	.	2	2	.	.	x	.	.	.	.
Eugeissoninae												
Eugeissona	6	.	1	3	2	.	.	.	.	x	.	.
Metroxylinae												
Metroxylon	5	.	3	1	1	.	.	.	.	x	x	.
Korthalsia	26	.	4	19	3	.	.	.	.	x	x	.
Eleiodoxa	1	.	.	.	1	.	.	.	.	x	.	.
Calamineae												
Salacca	23	2	9	6	6	.	.	.	.	x	x	.
Daemonorops	95	2	12	67	14	.	.	.	.	x	x	.
Calamus	360	15	77	236	32	.	.	x	.	x	x	.
Calospatha	1	.	1	.	.	.	.	.	.	x	.	.
Pogonotium	3	1	.	2	.	.	.	.	.	x	.	.
Ceratolobus	6	2	12	1	.	.	.	.	.	x	.	.
Retispatha	1	.	.	1	.	.	.	.	.	x	.	.

Genus	total	Endangered	Threatened	Unknown	Not threatened	Meso-America	S. America	Africa, W. Asia	Indian Ocean	Indomalaya	Australasia	SW Pacific
Plectocomiinae												
Myrialepis	2	.	.	.	2	.	.	.	.	x	.	.
Plectocomiopsis	6	.	1	4	1	.	.	.	.	x	.	.
Plectocomia	16	1	5	8	2	.	.	.	.	x	.	.
Pigafettinae												
Pigafetta	1	.	.	.	1	.	.	.	.	.	x	.
Raphiinae												
Raphia	19	.	.	18	1	x	x	x	x	.	.	.
Oncocalaminae												
Oncocalamus	2	.	.	2	.	.	.	x	.	.	.	.
LEPIDOCARYAE												
Mauritia	2	.	1	.	1	.	x	.	.	.	.	.
Mauritiella	3	.	.	.	3	.	x	.	.	.	.	.
Lepidocaryum	1	.	.	.	1	.	x	.	.	.	.	.
NYPOIDEAE												
Nypa	1	.	.	.	1	.	.	.	.	x	x	.
CEROXYLOIDEAE												
CYCLOSPATHEAE												
Pseudophoenix	4	1	1	1	1	x	.	.	.	.	.	.
CEROXYLEAE												
Ceroxylon	11	1	2	7	1	.	x	.	.	.	.	.
Oraniopsis	1	.	.	1	.	.	.	.	.	.	x	.
Juania	1	.	1	.	.	.	x	.	.	.	.	.
Ravenea	17	8	9	.	.	.	.	.	x	.	.	.
HYOPHORBEAE												
Gaussia	5	1	3	.	1	x	.	.	.	.	.	.
Hyophorbe	5	4	1	.	.	.	.	.	x	.	.	.
Synechanthus	2	.	.	2	.	x	.	.	.	.	.	.
Chamaedorea	76	12	47	7	10	x	x	.	.	.	.	.
Wendlandiella	1	.	.	1	.	.	x	.	.	.	.	.
ARECOIDEAE												
CARYOTEAE												
Arenga	24	.	8	8	8	.	.	.	.	x	x	.
Caryota	10	.	1	5	4	.	.	.	.	x	x	.
Wallichia	6	.	1	4	1	.	.	.	.	x	.	.
IRIARTEEAE												
Iriarteinae												
Dictyocaryum	3	.	.	1	2	x	x	.	.	.	.	.
Iriartella	2	.	.	.	2	.	x	.	.	.	.	.
Iriartea	1	.	.	.	1	x	x	.	.	.	.	.
Socratea	5	.	.	1	4	x	x	.	.	.	.	.
Wettiniinae												
Wettinia	22	2	5	6	9	x	x	.	.	.	.	.
PODOCOCCEAE												
Podococcus	1	.	.	.	1	.	.	x	.	.	.	.
ARECEAE												
Oraniinae												
Orania	18	1	3	14	.	.	.	.	.	x	x	x
Manicariinae												
Manicaria	1	.	.	.	1	x	x	.	.	.	.	.
Leopoldiniinae												
Leopoldinia	3	.	.	1	2	.	x	.	.	.	.	.
Malortieinae												
Reinhardtia	6	1	2	3	.	x	.	.	.	.	.	.
Dypsidinae												
Dypsis	139	71	55	4	9	.	.	.	x	.	.	.
Euterpeinae												
Euterpe	7	.	1	3	3	x	x	.	.	.	.	.
Prestoea	11	.	3	5	3	x	x	.	.	.	.	.
Neonicholsonia	1	.	.	.	1	x	.	.	.	.	.	.
Oenocarpus	9	.	3	3	3	x	x	.	.	.	.	.
Hyospathe	2	.	.	1	1	x	x	.	.	.	.	.
Roystoneinae												
Roystonea	10	.	4	3	3	x	x	.	.	.	.	.

Table 1.1 ... continued. Systematics of Palmae, with data on distribution and threats

Genus	total	Endangered	Threatened	Unknown	Not threatened	Meso-America	S. America	Africa, W. Asia	Indian Ocean	Indomalaya	Australasia	SW Pacific
Archantophoenicinae												
Archontophoenix	2	1	1	.	.	.	.	.	.	.	x	.
Chambeyronia	2	.	2	.	.	.	.	.	.	.	.	x
Hedyscepe	1	.	1	.	.	.	.	.	.	.	.	x
Rophalostylis	2	.	2	.	.	.	.	.	.	.	.	x
Kentiopsis	1	1	.	.	.	.	.	.	.	.	.	x
Mackeea	1	.	1	.	.	.	.	.	.	.	.	x
Actinokentia	2	.	2	.	.	.	.	.	.	.	.	x
Cyrtostachydinae												
Cyrtostachys	10	.	1	8	1	.	.	.	.	x	x	.
Linospadicinae												
Calyptrocalyx	29	.	.	29	.	.	.	.	.	.	x	.
Linospadix	10	.	2	5	3	.	.	.	.	.	x	.
Laccospadix	1	.	1	.	.	.	.	.	.	.	x	.
Howea	2	.	2	.	.	.	.	.	.	.	x	.
Ptychospermatinae												
Drymophloeus	11	1	4	6	.	.	.	.	.	.	x	.
Carpentaria	1	.	1	.	.	.	.	.	.	.	x	.
Veitchia	14	5	7	.	2	.	.	.	.	x	x	.
Balaka	9	.	8	1	.	.	.	.	.	.	x	.
Normanbya	1	.	1	.	.	.	.	.	.	.	x	.
Wodyetia	1	.	1	.	.	.	.	.	.	.	x	.
Ptychosperma	32	1	2	25	4	.	.	.	.	.	x	.
Ptychococcus	8	.	.	7	1	.	.	.	.	.	x	.
Brassiophoenix	2	.	.	2	.	.	.	.	.	.	x	.
Arecinae												
Loxococcus	1	1	.	.	.	.	.	.	x	.	.	.
Gronophyllum	25	.	.	1	24	.	.	.	.	.	x	.
Siphokentia	2	.	.	2	.	.	.	.	.	.	x	.
Hydriastele	9	.	.	8	1	.	.	.	.	.	x	.
Gulubia	9	.	2	4	3	.	.	.	.	.	x	x
Nenga	5	1	2	1	1	.	.	.	.	x	.	.
Pinanga	108	4	37	55	12	.	.	.	.	x	x	.
Areca	53	10	12	29	2	.	.	.	.	x	x	.
Iguanurinae												
Neoveitchia	1	1	.	.	.	.	.	.	.	.	.	x
Pelagodoxa	1	.	1	.	.	.	.	.	.	.	.	x
Iguanura	18	3	11	4	.	.	.	.	.	x	.	.
Brongiartikentia	2	.	2	.	.	.	.	.	.	.	.	x
Lepidorrhachis	1	.	1	.	.	.	.	.	.	.	x	.
Heterospathe	36	.	3	33	.	.	.	.	.	.	x	.
Sommieria	3	.	.	3	.	.	.	.	.	x	x	.
Bentinckia	2	.	2	.	.	.	.	.	.	x	.	.
Clinosperma	1	.	1	.	.	.	.	.	.	.	.	x
Cyphokentia	1	.	1	.	.	.	.	.	.	.	.	x
Moratia	1	.	1	.	.	.	.	.	.	.	.	x
Clinostigma	12	.	5	6	1	.	.	.	.	.	x	x
Satakentia	1	.	1	.	.	.	.	.	.	.	.	x
Rhopaloblaste	8	.	3	5	.	.	.	.	.	x	x	.
Dictyosperma	1	1	.	.	.	.	.	.	x	.	.	.
Actinorhytis	2	.	.	2	.	.	.	.	.	.	x	.
Lavoixia	1	1	.	.	.	.	.	.	.	.	.	x
Alloschmidia	1	.	1	.	.	.	.	.	.	.	.	x
Cyphophoenix	2	1	1	.	.	.	.	.	.	.	.	x
Campecarpus	1	.	1	.	.	.	.	.	.	.	.	x
Basselina	11	.	11	.	.	.	.	.	.	.	.	x
Cyphosperma	4	.	4	.	.	.	.	.	.	.	.	x
Veillonia	1	.	1	.	.	.	.	.	.	.	.	x
Burretiokentia	2	.	2	.	.	.	.	.	.	.	.	x
Physokentia	7	.	4	3	.	.	.	.	.	.	x	x
Goniocladus	1	.	.	1	.	.	.	.	.	.	.	x
Lemurophoenicinae												
Lemurophoenix	1	1	.	.	.	.	.	.	x	.	.	.
Oncospermatinae												
Deckenia	1	.	1	.	.	.	.	.	x	.	.	.
Acanthophoenix	1	.	1	.	.	.	.	.	x	.	.	.
Oncosperma	5	.	2	1	2	.	.	.	.	x	.	.
Tectiphiala	1	1	.	.	.	.	.	.	x	.	.	.
Verschaffeltia	1	.	1	.	.	.	.	.	x	.	.	.
Roscheria	1	.	1	.	.	.	.	.	x	.	.	.
Phoenicophorium	1	.	1	.	.	.	.	.	x	.	.	.
Nephrosperma	1	.	1	.	.	.	.	.	x	.	.	.
Sclerospermatinae												
Sclerosperma	1	.	.	1	.	.	.	x	.	.	.	.
Masoalinae												
Marojejya	2	1	1	.	.	.	.	.	x	.	.	.
Masoala	2	1	1	.	.	.	.	.	x	.	.	.
COCOEAE												
Beccariophoenicinae												
Beccariophoenix	1	1	.	.	.	.	.	.	x	.	.	.
Butiinae												
Voanioala	1	1	.	.	.	.	.	.	x	.	.	.
Paschalococos	1	1	.	.	.	.	.	.	.	.	.	x
Butia	8	1	3	1	3	.	x	.	.	.	.	.
Jubaea	1	.	1	.	.	.	x	.	.	.	.	.
Jubaeopsis	1	.	1	.	.	.	.	x	.	.	.	.
Cocos	1	.	.	.	1	x	x	x	x	x	x	x
Syagrus	30	.	15	4	10	x	x	.	.	.	.	.
Lytocaryum	2	1	.	1	.	.	x	.	.	.	.	.
Parajubaea	2	1	1	.	.	.	x	.	.	.	.	.
Allagoptera	4	.	2	.	2	.	x	.	.	.	.	.
Polyandrococos	1	.	.	.	1	.	x	.	.	.	.	.
Attaleinae												
Attalea	27	2	8	7	10	x	x	.	.	.	.	.
Elaeidinae												
Barcella	1	.	.	1	.	.	x	.	.	.	.	.
Elaeis	2	.	.	.	2	x	x	x	.	.	.	.
Bactridinae												
Acrocomia	2	.	.	1	1	x	x	.	.	.	.	.
Gastrococos	1	.	.	.	1	.	x	.	.	.	.	.
Aiphanes	25	2	13	8	2	x	x	.	.	.	.	.
Bactris	65	1	6	27	31	x	x	.	.	.	.	.
Desmoncus	7	.	2	2	3	x	x	.	.	.	.	.
Astrocaryum	18	.	3	3	12	x	x	.	.	.	.	.
GEONOMEAE												
Pholidostachys	4	.	.	1	3	x	x	.	.	.	.	.
Welfia	1	.	.	.	1	x	.	.	.	.	.	.
Calyptronoma	3	.	1	.	2	x	.	.	.	.	.	.
Calyptrogyne	8	.	2	6	.	x	.	.	.	.	.	.
Asterogyne	5	.	4	.	1	x	x	.	.	.	.	.
Geonoma	51	1	11	16	23	x	x	.	.	.	.	.
PHYTELEPHOIDEAE												
Aphandra	1	.	.	.	1	.	x	.	.	.	.	.
Phytelephas	6	1	.	4	1	x	x	.	.	.	.	.
Ammandra	2	.	.	2	.	x	x	.	.	.	.	.

Summary:
Genera: 192, Species: 2117

Conservation Categories[1] (see Appendix 1):
Endangered or Extinct (E, Ex, E/Ex)
otherwise threatened (V, R, I, K)
Unknown (?)
Not threatened (nt)

Distribution:
Meso-America (including mainland USA, the Caribbean, Meso-America and the coastal areas of Ecuador, Colombia, and Venezuela)
South America (excluding the coastal areas of Ecuador, Colombia, and Venezuela)
Africa, Europe and West Asia (extending to Pakistan)
Indian Ocean islands (Madagascar, Mascarenes, Comoros, Seychelles)
Indomalaya (India, Indochina, China, Malaysia, the Philippines, and Indonesia west of "Wallace's line")
Australasia (including Sulawesi, the Moluccas, New Guinea, Bismarck and Solomon Islands, Australia, and the Pacific Islands)
South-west Pacific (New Zealand, Fiji, Vanuatu, New Caledonia, and Hawaii)

[1] Formal conservation categories are capitalized whenever used in the text. See Appendix 1 for IUCN definitions.

Morphology

The Palmae is a distinctive and ancient family of woody plants with tremendous morphological diversity. Palms may be trees or shrubs varying in size from as much as 60 m to as little as 25 cm; several hundred species are climbing rattans. The palm leaf, root, inflorescence, fruit and seed are also extremely variable. Palms may be solitary or clustering, spiny or smooth, erect or prostrate, unbranched or (rarely) dichotomously branching, pleonanthic (flowering continuously) or less commonly hapaxanthic (flowering then dying). Morphology can be of great conservation significance, as in the case of *Corypha taliera*, a single-stemmed, hapaxanthic palm endemic to India. The risk of extinction for such a palm is especially high, as total predation of the single crop of seed and the subsequent death of the parent plant precludes reproductive success. Indeed, *Corypha taliera* is now Extinct in the Wild because of this.

Habitats

Palms occur in every habitat in the tropics: rain forest, semideciduous forest, montane forest, freshwater swamp, saline swamp, river valley, savanna, desert and mountain. This factor makes palm conservation an issue with very broad geographic dimensions. Palms may occur in dense, virtually pure stands and be principal constituents of the forest, whereas in other cases they are common or uncommon plants of the understory vegetation in rain forests. In some desert oases palms are the predominant trees. Certain palms are adapted to specialized niches within their larger habitats, such as the rheophytes (see Box 1.1), and as a consequence have very restricted geographic distributions and normally are uncommon in nature. Although it is clear that palms occur in every tropical habitat, information is not yet available that would provide reliable global data on the numbers of palm species occurring in each different habitat, and the

---

Box 1.1 Palms with a very specialized habitat: the rheophytes

Palms grow in a wide range of habitats, often in association with water bodies, but one of the most unusual habitats is in the beds and along the banks of swiftly-flowing rivers and streams, up to flood-level. One of the distinctive characteristics of rheophytic palms is their narrow leaves that offer minimal resistance to flowing water. Also, rheophytes usually branch profusely as an apparent adaptation to recovery after flood damage; they are also firmly anchored to the soil and not easily uprooted.

Only a few palms have been described as rheophytes, but that may be because the habitat has been overlooked. Two species of *Pinanga* (*P. rivularis* and *P. tenella* var. *tenella*), and *Areca rheophytica*, are clearly rheophytes; all are endemic to the island of Borneo. In the Americas there are two confirmed rheophytic species: *Chamaedorea cataractarum* in Mexico and *Geonoma linearis* which occurs in Colombia and Ecuador. *Dypsis crinita* (formerly *Vonitra crinita*), a dichotomously branching palm, and the newly-described *Ravenea musicalis*, a solitary palm, both Madagascar endemics, are candidate rheophytes.

The conservation status of these rheophytic palms is poorly known and many aspects of their natural history remain to be studied. Some rheophytes in nature also occur in other habitats, an adaptability that may explain for example the successful cultivation of *Chamaedorea cataractarum* in gardens and pots. But the fact remains that for *in situ* rheophyte conservation a unique habitat must be protected.

Chamaedorea cataractarum in its riverine habitat, Chiapas, Mexico, one of the few rheophytes in the palm family. Vulnerable.

Donald R. Hodel

percentage of those under threat. Thus far, this level of information is only known for a few places, such as Peru (see Kahn and Moussa 1994a). When such information is compiled on a world scale, it will be possible to determine the degree to which the degradation or destruction of a particular habitat represents a threat to palm biodiversity.

Distribution

The overwhelming majority of palm species are native to the tropics, although palm diversity and frequency are unevenly distributed. The Asian tropics have the greatest number of species, with Indonesia leading with about 477 species (Mogea 1991). Next are the American tropics, with Colombia estimated to have at least 227 species (Henderson *et al.* 1995). Africa is a distant third, where the entire mainland is reported to have only about 50 species. However, Madagascar alone has at least 176 species (Dransfield and Beentje 1995). Outside the tropics palms are not very common. Dowe (1992) estimated that only about 130 species occur naturally beyond the tropical latitudes (23.5°N and S). The maximum ranges extend from 44°N in France (*Chamaerops humilis*) to 44°S in New Zealand (*Rhopalostylis sapida*), but most extratropical species are found within the subtropics (see also Figure 2.1).

Table 1.1 shows the distribution of all palm genera. Seven informal regions are recognized here, each with a distinct palm flora which only slightly overlaps with other regions. The Neotropics can be divided into two regions: Southern America (including the Andean range, the Amazon Basin, the Guianas, and the dryer parts of South America) and Meso-America (including the Caribbean and the lowland and montane forests of Meso-America extending to the coastal areas of Venezuela, Colombia, and Ecuador). Africa has a few systematically and geographically isolated palm species and additionally four widespread genera extending to East and South Asia. Only two genera are shared with the Americas. The islands of the western Indian Ocean (Madagascar, the Mascarene Islands, Comoro Islands, and Seychelles) each have many endemic and highly threatened palms. In Asia, the subtropics and tropics of India, Indochina, and China have some endemic genera (many restricted to limestone areas), but the flora of the perhumid Sundashelf (Malaysia, western Indonesia) is much more diverse and distinct. These two areas, together with the Philippines, constitute the Indomalayan Realm. A major separation mark is Wallace's Line: many species occur exclusively either westward (Indomalaya) or eastward (Sulawesi, Moluccas, New Guinea, Bismarck and Solomon Islands, Australia and the Pacific). Here the latter region is called Australasia. New Zealand, the Vanuatu, and Fiji Islands additionally each have distinct endemic genera, and New Caledonia in particular has a very old endemic relict flora. Most genera of these islands belong to the Iguanurinae subtribe and many are Endangered.

Taxonomy and conservation

On-going palm research makes compilation of an Action Plan challenging. Each revision of a palm group leads to changes in species names and numbers, and sometimes even to changes at a higher taxonomic level (genus, subtribe). Therefore in dealing with such a dynamic subject, certain assumptions must be made with the qualification that assessments and recommendations contained in the Action Plan may change according to changes in taxonomy, although the general framework for action will remain valid. However, an adequate body of scientific information on which to base an Action Plan now exists, which was not the case when the Palm Specialist Group was formed in 1984.

The recognition of species as a basic unit is fundamental for all conservation work. Red Lists, legislation, assessments of conservation status, and priorities are all based on species as basic units. Therefore a sound and modern classification of palms is essential, and many recommendations in this Action Plan promote further taxonomic research.

Hundreds of species were described early in this century based on single collections. Species were then considered as well defined and completely constant entities. Modern approaches now take into account natural variation, and many previously described species are now being lumped together, becoming synonymous with more comprehensive and variable species. Extensive field studies and research on molecular genetics, cladistics, population, and reproductive biology are needed to solve many of the arising problems.

However, whatever the outcome, species concepts have important implications for conservation action. By using a wider species concept, many populations of palms are no longer accepted as distinct species, and, even if formerly considered as Rare or Endangered, will consequently disappear from Red Lists. However, as these populations are still important repositories of the species' genetic variability, they still merit protection. Moreover, these populations are often isolated or at the margin of the species range, and may form an important part of the ecosystem. It is therefore important to establish and pay attention to national and local Red Lists, as well as to list varieties, subspecies, and isolated populations also on a global level.

On the other hand, a wider species concept helps to define priorities. Taxonomic distinctness is considered an important element in setting priorities for conservation action. With a narrow species concept, all populations (called 'species') get the same attention, while with a wider species concept, close relatives are grouped together and only this group as a whole (forming the 'species') is of importance.

In the case of the Americas, it was decided to follow the new *Field Guide to the Palms of the Americas* (Henderson *et al.* 1995), which applies a rather wide species concept. The decision was not only made because of the modern approach, but also because the guide constitutes a useful tool for palm conservation for a wide audience, as it includes discussions of the present status of taxonomy for all groups, synonyms, distribution maps, and useful references.

Table 1.2 shows the implication of this *Field Guide* on species numbers. Of the about 1000 accepted species recorded in the threatened plant database at WCMC, more than 500 have been lumped, but partly retained as (newly established) subspecies or varieties, and some new species were also added, resulting in a new list of about 600 taxa. It is remarkable that lumping occurred in palms of all categories of threat, but with the highest percentage in the group of Unknown (?), Insufficiently known but suspected to be threatened (K), and Rare (R) palms. Many of these palms are known from their type collection only, or are otherwise rare and taxonomically not well defined.

Table 1.2 Changes of numbers of American palms in different categories of threat due to changes in nomenclature (see text)

Status	Nomenclature Old[1]	Nomenclature New[2]	Reduction in species no. (%)
E	55	40	27
V	104	75	28
R	110	59	46
I	84	56	33
K	29	4	86
?	356	191	46
nt	263	170	35
Total	1032	601	40

[1] According to the threatened plant database, maintained at WCMC, as of October 1995.
[2] Using the same source for conservation status, but adopting the nomenclature of Henderson *et al.* (1995).

Threats

Tropical deforestation is by far the principal threat to palm biodiversity because the greatest diversity of palm species occurs in the understory of tropical rain forests, examples of which are given later in this document. According to Myers (1993) the chief causes of deforestation are commercial logging, livestock ranching, and shifting cultivation. These activities can lead to either outright deforestation, or to severe depletion of the ecosystem and loss of habitat for plants and animals. Myers (1993) convincingly argues that efforts to prevent deforestation must be directed at what he calls the "main deforestation fronts." He identifies 14 of these areas in the tropics (six in the Americas; two in Africa, Madagascar being one;

and six in South-east Asia). All of the deforestation fronts are areas of high palm diversity.

The palm genus *Chamaedorea* serves as a case in point. According to Henderson *et al.* (1995), there are 77 species of this genus, extending from Mexico to Brazil and Bolivia. Hodel (1992) recognizes 96 species, and four more species have been found since then. All of the species occur in the understory of moist, wet, or mixed forests of the lowlands and mountain slopes, coinciding closely with the deforestation fronts. Hodel (1992) has provided nearly complete *in situ* information. Three-fourths of all species are threatened, i.e. have a world conservation classification of Endangered, Vulnerable, Rare or Indeterminate. It is clear that the conservation of palm biodiversity and the protection of tropical forests are strictly linked.

Besides deforestation, which may affect 90% of all palms, direct exploitation is a major threat to many useful palms. Rapidly increasing population pressure and commercial demands have led to an alarming depletion of natural palm stands in many regions (e.g. Somalia, Haiti, India).

Structure of the Action Plan

This Action Plan begins with five chapters devoted to different aspects of palm conservation and utilization on a global scale. Emphasis is placed on the most highly threatened species, as well as those having an Unknown (?) world conservation status. The next six chapters present regional views, with a general focus on tropical forest and island species. Each of these chapters is intended to be used in concert with the information provided in the initial five chapters.

The regional chapters have been authored by palm specialists knowledgeable of the respective regions, although the general level of detail varies reflecting differences in knowledge. Recommendations given are followed by the name of the contributor ('Contact'), either at the end of a recommendation or at the end of the recommendation section. All authors, research institutions, and other specialists cited may be contacted for further conservation action.

Because palm expertise is not evenly spread across the tropical world, major information gaps exist, most notably in the island of New Guinea. A major reason for compiling an Action Plan is to point out such deficiencies.

The final chapter is an attempt to draw together the different conservation and utilization themes introduced, and to forge a framework for activities that can serve palm conservation, initially for a three-year period, and on into the next century. Most chapters contain boxes that focus on topics selected to exemplify various conservation issues.

Chapter 2

In situ Conservation Status of Palms and Related Issues

The purpose of this chapter is to present an overview of the *in situ* conservation status of the Palmae, especially those species under the greatest threat of extinction. An earlier effort along these lines focused only on the Americas, and provided information on all taxa (Dransfield *et al.* 1988). Monotypic and endemic palms of unknown conservation status, as well as palm Floras, are included in the discussion because of their importance to the subject.

One of the major data generation exercises of this Action Plan was to compile a world listing of the most highly threatened palm taxa, i.e. those with an *in situ* conservation status of Extinct, Extinct/Endangered, or Endangered. Because the *in situ* status of all validly described and published palm taxa is not yet known, and several major systematic palm studies are in process which will lead to name changes, this assessment must be viewed as provisional.

The second of the major data generation activities undertaken was to identify those palms in the WCMC database categorized as having an Unknown *in situ* world conservation status.

The most highly threatened palms of the world

A total of 230 palms are considered to be highly threatened (see Appendix 2). According to their conservation category, two are Extinct, 21 probably Extinct, and 207 Endangered. As far as can be determined, only two species are confirmed to be Extinct. *Corypha taliera* is Extinct in the Wild, but persists in cultivation and therefore could be reintroduced to its native habitat in India. *Paschalococos disperta*, given a name for ease of reference, is an Extinct Easter Island palm known only from subfossil endocarps (Zizka 1991).

Sixty-nine palm genera contain highly threatened species (about 36% of all palm genera), of which 16 are monotypic. Palms endemic to one country or part of a country are also identified and number 212 (93% of all highly threatened taxa). Therefore a strong correlation exists between endemism and degree of threat. From the standpoint of palm biodiversity at the generic level, the presence of 16 monotypic species on the list is cause for alarm, especially as they represent about 8% of all palm genera.

Figure 2.1 provides an overview of the conservation status of palms by region. Regions dominated by islands clearly have the highest proportion of Endangered and otherwise threatened palms, the worst situation being on the Indian ocean and South-west Pacific islands. The Caribbean, Meso-American, and continental Asian (including Peninsular Malaysia) regions also have a high number of Endangered species. In South America the many not yet threatened palms of the Amazon region obscure the high proportion of threatened palms in the Andes and the Atlantic forest of Brazil. The situation in vast regions of Asia cannot be properly analysed due to the many species with Unknown conservation status.

Figure 2.2 depicts the distribution of highly threatened palms by country. Again, the prominence of Madagascar, Colombia, and Peninsular Malaysia clearly shows that palm conservation is a global issue, and is not restricted to just one region of the world.

Hyophorbe lagenicaulis, Round Island Bottle Palm, Mauritius. Endangered in the wild, but widely cultivated.

Wendy Strahm

From a taxonomic point of view, nearly all tribes and subfamilies contain Endangered palms (see Table 1.1). However, the genera with the most Endangered species (four or more) are either island genera (*Dypsis* and *Ravenea* from Madagascar, *Hyophorbe* and *Dictyosperma* from the Mascarene Islands, *Pritchardia* from Hawaii, *Coccothrinax* from Cuba), or very large genera (*Areca, Attalea, Calamus, Chamaedorea, Licuala, Pinanga*).

Monotypic palms

Because the potential extinction of a monotypic palm represents such a significant loss of biodiversity, all monotypic genera, regardless of their conservation status, are presented in Table 2.1 by geographic area. As Table 2.1 demonstrates, islands stand out as major repositories of palm genetic diversity. Renowned as it is for its species diversity, Madagascar is clearly second to New Caledonia in regards to monotypic palms. Moreover, the Seychelles exceed Madagascar in terms of numbers of threatened monotypic palms.

Techtiphiala ferox, an Endangered monotypic palm from Mauritius.

Wendy Strahm

Endemic palms of Unknown conservation status

The second of the major data generation activities undertaken for this Action Plan was to identify those palms listed in the threatened plant database at WCMC categorized as having an Unknown *in situ* world conservation status. This problem of having insufficient information to assign a conservation status is enormous: more than 1300 palms are so designated in the database. To narrow the assessment to a manageable number and focus on the greater conservation need, non-endemic palms were excluded although they are certainly important to know about as well. In those cases where a taxon is believed to be endemic, but there is incomplete or uncertain information about its distribution, it is included.

Appendix 3 lists 631 endemic palm taxa of Unknown world conservation status, representing 73 genera. Analysis of the geographic data in the table revealed those areas having large numbers of palms in the Unknown category (see Figure 2.1). Six countries, all but one in Asia, account for the highest numbers: Indonesia 158, Papua New Guinea 105, Brazil 40, China and the Philippines 38 each, and Malaysia 23. In addition, if political boundaries are ignored, it is noteworthy that the island of New Guinea (Papua New Guinea and the Indonesian state of Irian Jaya) has 178 palm species which lack conservation status information. If the island of Madagascar is the 'hot spot' of threatened palm species, the island of New Guinea is undeniably the 'blank spot' in regards to knowledge about *in situ* palm conservation status. The conservation status of African palms is equally poorly known, but far fewer species are involved.

Inclusion of such a long list as in Appendix 3 in this Action Plan is justified because it provides a checklist to alert botanists, conservationists, and others of the pressing data needs of these particular taxa, as well as highlighting the major geographic gaps that exist.

A slightly different approach to this subject is taken in Table 2.2. Data on 51 genera are presented showing the total number of described species, the number of endemic and non-endemic palms having an Unknown status in the wild, and the percentage the latter figures represent of all species. The cut-off point of 50% was arbitrary. Table 2.2 demonstrates two key points. First, 30 relatively small genera (i.e. containing nine or fewer taxa) have 50% or more of their taxa in the Unknown category. Second, five genera (*Calamus, Licuala, Pinanga, Daemonorops,* and *Geonoma*) together represent about 60% of the table's total number of taxa with an Unknown conservation status. Four of these five genera are Asian and two are rattan palms.

Table 2.1 Monotypic palms by geographic area and their world conservation status[*]

Distribution Species	World conservation status	Distribution Species	World conservation status
AMERICAS		**ASIA**	
Caribbean Region		**Asia (widespread)**	
Gastrococos crispa	nt	Nannorrhops ritchiana	?
Rhapidophyllum hystrix	R	Nypa fruticans	nt
Serenoa repens		**Sri Lanka**	
	nt	Loxococcus rupicola	E
Zombia antillarum	nt	**Thailand**	
Central American region		Kerriodoxa elegans	R
Acoelorraphe wrightii	nt	**Borneo**	
Neonicholsonia watsonii	R	Retispatha dumetosa	?
Schippia concolor	E	**Peninsular Malaysia**	
Central and South America		Calospatha scortechinii	E/V
Iriartea deltoidea	nt	**South-east Asia**	
Manicaria saccifera	?	Eleiodoxa conferta	nt
Amazon Region		Pigafetta filaris	nt
Aphandra natalia	?	**Ryukyu Islands**	
Barcella odora	?	Satakentia liukiuensis	E/V
Itaya amicorum	E		
Lepidocaryum tenue	nt	**AUSTRALASIA and OCEANIA**	
Wendlandiella gracilis	?	**Australia**	
Brazil, Atlantic Coast		Carpentaria acuminata	V
Polyandrococcos caudescens	?	Laccospadix australasica	R
Chile		Normanbya normanbyi	R
Juania australis	R	Oraniopsis appendiculata	R
Jubaea chilensis	V	Wodyetia bifurcata	R
		Lord Howe Island	
EUROPE		Hedyscepe canterburyana	V
Chamaerops humilis	nt	Lepidorrhachis mooreana	R
		New Caledonia	
AFRICA		Alloschmidia glabrata	R
West Africa		Campecarpus fulcitus	R
Podococcus barteri	?	Clinosperma bracteale	R
Sclerosperma mannii	?	Cyphokentia macrostachya	R
South Africa		Kentiopsis oliviformis	E
Jubaeopsis caffra	R	Lavoixia macrocarpa	E
		Mackeea magnifica	R
INDIAN OCEAN ISLANDS		Moratia cerifera	R
Seychelles		Pritchardiopsis jeanneneyi	E
Deckenia nobilis	V	Veillonia alba	R
Lodoicea maldivica	V	**Fiji**	
Nephrosperma vanhoutteanum	V	Alsmithia longipes	V
Phoenicophorium borsigianum	V	Goniocladus petiolatus	?
Roscheria melanochaetes	V	Neoveitchia storckii	E
Verschaffeltia splendida	V	**Vanuatu**	
Madagascar		Carpoxylon macrospermum	E
Beccariophoenix madagascariensis	E	Pelagodoxa henryana	E
Lemurophoenix halleuxii	E	**Easter Island**	
Satranala decussilvae	E	Paschalococos disperta	Ex
Voanioala gerardii	E		
Mascarenes Islands		**PACIFIC**	
Acanthophoenix rubra	V	Cocos nucifera	nt
Dictyosperma album	E		
Tectiphiala ferox	E		

Summary of conservation status: **Ex** 1; **E** 15; **E/V** 2; **V** 12; **R** 17; **I** 1; **?** 7; **nt** 11; **Total** 66
[*] Based on data from the threatened plant database maintained at the WCMC, as of October 1995.

Table 2.2 Palm genera with 50% or more of lower taxa having Unknown world conservation status[*]

Genus	No. of species Total	No. of species Unknown	Percentage Unknown	Genus	No. of species Total	No. of species Unknown	Percentage Unknown
Actinorhytis	2	2	100	Hyphaene	17	12	71
Ammandra	2	2	100	Daemonorops	95	67	71
Barcella	1	1	100	Licuala	111	74	67
Brassiophoenix	2	2	100	Phytelephas	6	4	67
Calyptrocalyx	29	29	100	Plectocomiopsis	6	4	67
Goniocladus	1	1	100	Pogonotium	3	2	67
Guihaia	2	2	100	Trithrinax	3	2	67
Nannorrhops	1	1	100	Wallichia	6	4	67
Neonicholsonia	1	1	100	Calamus	360	236	66
Oncocalamus	2	2	100	Ceroxylon	11	7	64
Oraniopsis	1	1	100	Rhopaloblaste	8	5	63
Podococcus	1	1	100	Pholidocarpus	5	3	60
Retispatha	1	1	100	Areca	53	29	55
Sclerosperma	1	1	100	Drymophloeus	11	6	55
Siphokentia	2	2	100	Pinanga	108	55	51
Sommieria	3	3	100	Acrocomia	2	1	50
Synechanthus	2	2	100	Borassodendron	2	1	50
Wendlandiella	1	1	100	Caryota	10	5	50
Gronophyllum	25	24	96	Chelyocarpus	4	2	50
Raphia	19	18	95	Clinostigma	12	6	50
Heterospathe	36	33	92	Colpothrinax	2	1	50
Rhapis	11	10	91	Eremospatha	4	2	50
Hydriastele	9	8	89	Eugeissona	6	3	50
Ptychococcus	8	7	88	Hyospathe	2	1	50
Cyrtostachys	10	8	80	Linospadix	10	5	50
Ptychosperma	32	25	78	Lytocaryum	2	1	50
Orania	18	14	78	Plectocomia	16	8	50
Calyptrogyne	8	6	75	Reinhardtia	6	3	50
Laccosperma	8	6	75	Trachycarpus	4	2	50
Korthalsia	26	19	73	Washingtonia	2	1	50

[*] Included are both endemic and non-endemic species. In some instances of non-endemic species, a conservation status has been assigned for a particular geographic unit, but the world status remains Unknown. Based on data from the threatened plants database maintained at the WCMC, as of October 1995.

Palm Floras

To a considerable degree, knowledge of palm diversity within a particular geographic area is linked to subregional or regional Floras. Figure 2.3 illustrates the status of floras and includes other palm treatments. Supporting information for the maps is included in Appendix 4.

Flora projects in only a few countries provide vital data for palm conservation. Several countries have older palm Floras, which are useful but usually out of date. Flora projects are very ambitious and sometimes cease without achieving their full objectives, or require decades to complete. For example, the Flora of Trinidad and Tobago was initiated in 1928, but to date only two volumes have been published. Only three countries were identified as having no plans for a national flora: Congo, Myanmar, and Vanuatu. However, many comprehensive palm treatments have recently been published in addition to traditional flora projects.

The Americas are fairly well covered in terms of palm treatments, and taxonomic data on palms of the region are among the best in the world. Africa has a number of projects, but whether they will all produce palm treatments is uncertain. Regional palm Floras have been published for West and East Africa. However, a number of national Flora projects are inactive, such as those in Angola, Guinea-Bissau, São Tomé and Principe, and Mozambique. The recently published *Palms of Africa* (Tuley 1995) gives an account of the actual status of palm knowledge in Africa, as well as useful keys and other specific information. Asia and Oceania exhibit good coverage of the palm flora. Publication in 1991 of the Palmae section of the *Flora Reipublicae* (sic) *Popularis Sinicae* has provided much-needed data on Chinese palms. Several active projects such as the regional *Flora Malesiana* project, and national efforts in Thailand, the Philippines, and Australia, will make major contributions. However India, Indochina, and the Pacific islands are badly in need of modern treatments.

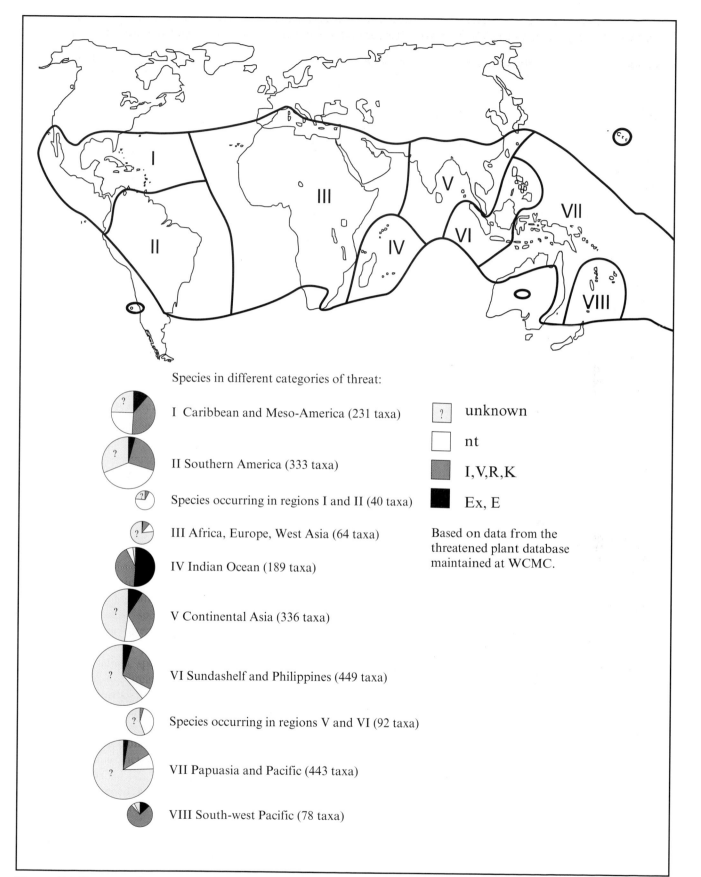

Species in different categories of threat:

I Caribbean and Meso-America (231 taxa)

II Southern America (333 taxa)

Species occurring in regions I and II (40 taxa)

III Africa, Europe, West Asia (64 taxa)

IV Indian Ocean (189 taxa)

V Continental Asia (336 taxa)

VI Sundashelf and Philippines (449 taxa)

Species occurring in regions V and VI (92 taxa)

VII Papuasia and Pacific (443 taxa)

VIII South-west Pacific (78 taxa)

?	unknown
	nt
	I,V,R,K
	Ex, E

Based on data from the threatened plant database maintained at WCMC.

Figure 2.1 Conservation status of palms in regions of the world

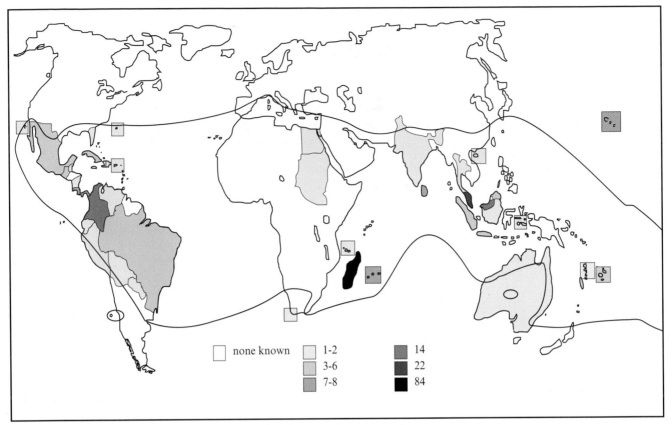

Figure 2.2 Numbers of globally Endangered palm species per region

none known   1-2   14
3-6   22
7-8   84

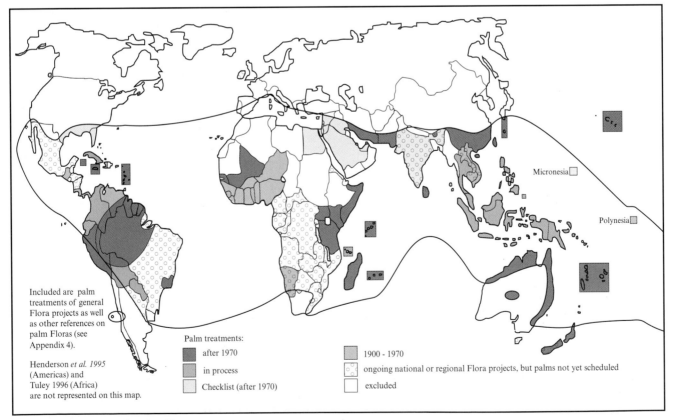

Included are palm treatments of general Flora projects as well as other references on palm Floras (see Appendix 4).

Henderson *et al. 1995* (Americas) and Tuley 1996 (Africa) are not represented on this map.

Micronesia

Polynesia

Palm treatments:

after 1970

in process

Checklist (after 1970)

1900 - 1970

ongoing national or regional Flora projects, but palms not yet scheduled

excluded

Figure 2.3 Status of palm Floras

Chapter 3

Protected Areas

Because protected areas represent the best potential for *in situ* conservation, attention in this chapter is directed toward two major issues. First, information is needed on which palm species occur within the boundaries of (or sometimes adjacent to) existing protected areas (giving priority to protected areas in palm-rich localities and to those palms that are highly threatened). Second, new candidate protected areas need to be identified that would contribute significantly to preserving palm biodiversity.

Palms in existing protected areas

WCMC conducted a study of plant and animal inventories in protected areas in the tropics (Murray *et al.* 1992). The study scanned information held at WCMC on 8715 protected areas and found 1078 species inventories. However, the number of inventories involving plants was only 2.4% and those providing data on palms was even less. Murray *et al.* (1992) used Indonesia as a case study, and recorded plant taxa listed in 18 protected areas. Results for the Palmae revealed that only one of the highly threatened species from Table 2.1, *Ceratolobus glaucescens*, is known to occur in a protected area, Ujung Kulon National Park in Java.

Clearly, the extent to which protected area status actually conserves plant biodiversity is very poorly known at the global level. WCMC, as part of its long-range planning, intends to add information to its various databases as to whether a threatened species is known to occur within a protected area. This would be invaluable information for setting species conservation priorities.

For the purposes of this Action Plan, two palm-rich geographic areas, Sarawak (East Malaysia) and Colombia, are used as examples to further assess the role of existing protected areas for conservation.

Sarawak, East Malaysia

Reliable data on the diversity of palms in Sarawak were established in the course of WWF project 3325 (Johnson 1991a). Pearce (1991) found c. 213 species, belonging to 25 genera, in Sarawak. Rattans (*Calamus* spp. and *Daemonorops* spp.) account for half of the species. The endemism rate of all palms is 26%. A particularly high proportion of endemic species are found in the *Iguanura*, *Areca*, and *Salacca* genera. As indicated on Figure 2.2, there are 14 species currently classified as Endangered in

Sarawak. Accurate data on palms within protected areas in Sarawak are more comprehensive than in most other tropical areas, due to studies carried out in the Kubah and Gunung Mulu National Parks.

Kubah National Park. Pearce (1994) carried out a research project to study the palms of Kubah National Park. The Park is located 22 km south-west of Kuching and comprises 2230 ha of undisturbed forest with varied terrain having an altitudinal range of some 760 m. The area of Kubah National Park is known to be floristically rich and to have a high number of endemic palm species. In demarcating the study area, both the Park and its environs were included. Results of the survey showed that 95 palm taxa were found within the study area, 86 within the Park boundaries. Because of the richness of the palm flora which currently extends beyond the original proposed protected area boundaries, one recommendation of the study was to expand the Park boundaries to include adjoining areas.

Despite the richness of the area of Kubah National Park, a comparison of the native palms on the species list with the list of the 14 highly threatened species in Sarawak (see Appendix 2) only reveals three matches: *Areca subacaulis*, *Calamus conjugatus*, and *Licuala orbicularis*.

Gunung Mulu National Park. A comprehensive inventory of palms was made by Dransfield (1984b). A total of 111 palm taxa were found to occur within the Park boundaries. Gunung Mulu is by far the biggest national park in Sarawak (52,865 ha), but again only three highly threatened species were found: *Areca abdulrahmanii*, *A. dayung*, and *Licuala* cf. *orbicularis*.

In summary, five of the 14 highly threatened species (36%) are under protection in the two national parks. However, no data on palms of the additional seven national parks of Sarawak (covering an area of 58,000 ha) are available.

Colombia

Of the countries of Latin America and the Caribbean, Colombia stands out in terms of the high level of knowledge of palm systematics (see Galeano and Bernal 1987; Galeano 1991) and of *in situ* palm conservation (see Bernal 1989). National maps of the vegetation types and protected areas of Colombia, produced by the Protected Areas Data Unit of WCMC in 1992, were obtained to serve as a geographic framework.

From this data it was possible to determine which of the 15 highly threatened palms in Colombia (see Appendix 2) are known or suspected to occur within demarcated protected areas (Table 3.1). However only three species (as well as two others, now being reduced to synonyms by Henderson *et al.* (1995) were found to occur in protected areas.

Table 3.1 Endangered palms in protected areas in Colombia

Species	National Park
Wettinia microcarpa	Tamá
Crysophila kalbreyeri	Los Katios [*]
	Paramillo [*]
Reinhardtia koschnyana	Los Katios [*]

[*] suspected to occur

Ceroxylon mooreanum (a synonym of *C. parvifrons*) occurs in Tamá, Farallones de Cali, and is suspected to occur in Cordillera de Los Picachos, El Cocuy, Las Hermosas, Los Nevados, Munchique, Paramillo, Puracé, and Sumapaz.

Prestoea simplicifrons (a synonym of *P. carderi*) is suspected to occur in Tinigua.

Discussion and recommendations

1) Identify palm hotspots which should be included in protected areas, containing either:

- **high palm diversity or**
- **threatened palm species.**

The examples from Sarawak and Colombia demonstrate that protected areas, established for more general purposes, also contribute to palm conservation. The *in situ* status will become clearer when additional palm checklists are completed for protected areas known to have a diverse palm flora. A major effort to identify which palms already occur within existing protected areas, as well as to identify additional areas of high palm biodiversity for creation of new protected areas, must be made.

2) Promote alternative *in situ* conservation strategies.

If the examples from Sarawak and Colombia are representative, and only a small number of the most highly threatened palms occur within existing protected areas, it is obvious that protected areas alone are not sufficient to conserve all species, although the creation of additional protected areas is very important.

Habitat preservation must be augmented with other strategies, including sustainable use projects, that will assure the survival of palm species within their natural geographic range. It is recommended that this approach be explored.

Box 3.1 The desert fan palm (*Washingtonia filifera*), a flourishing Rare species

The desert or California fan palm is one of the most common ornamental palms throughout the subtropics. In the wild this palm grows only in oases in the Sonoran Desert of the south-western United States and north-western Mexico, although it is occasionally cultivated within its native range. Its world conservation status is Rare because it occurs in disjunct, mostly small populations in areas very sensitive to habitat change. Some palm oases may have originated from seed dispersal by native coyotes which eat the ripe fruits, or from seed planted by Indians in new sites during pre-Columbian times. Studies of the 151 known palm oases indicate that *Washingtonia* populations have increased in past decades, and today the current total number of individuals in the wild may approach 25,000 trees.

A leading threat to some of the wild palm oases is competing land use for irrigated agriculture and urban development of popular resorts like Palm Springs. Fortunately, a high proportion of the oases are in remote locations of rough terrain. Perhaps the greatest threat to palm oases is changes to the aquifers that sustain the water table. Without the streams, springs, and groundwater, the palms and associated vegetation would perish within months.

Protected areas contribute significantly to the *in situ* conservation of this palm. Three of the four largest desert palm oases (Palm, Andreas, and Murray canyons) are found near the city of Palm Springs on traditional lands of the Agua Caliente Band of Cahuilla Indians, formally deeded to them in 1876. These extraordinarily scenic places — one of the rarest vegetation types in the United States — are preserved as natural areas open to the public, and supported through an entrance fee and revenue from a Trading Post. A few other palm canyons farther south are protected within the Anza-Borrego Desert State Park. The success story represented by these desert oases — and their keystone palm species — shows the significance of local involvement by an Indian group, in this case, and the state park agency to achieve a conservation goal.

Chapter 4

Economic and Ornamental Palms

Strong arguments for palm conservation concern economic and ornamental species which are currently cultivated (e.g. date palm), managed (e.g. palmyra palm), semi-wild (e.g. subspontaneous African oil palm) or wild (e.g. most rattans). Economic palms are defined here as those providing commercial and subsistence products, and ornamental palms are those deriving commercial value solely from the nursery trade. The conservation of ornamental palms is of concern because a significant number of palms in the nursery trade continue to originate from the collection of wild seed or seedlings, in some instances putting wild populations at risk. This chapter concentrates on conservation issues especially relevant to economic and ornamental palms by reviewing their world conservation status, and drawing attention to the value of genetic resources in wild relatives.

Major economic palms

The literature on the antiquity and economic uses of a wide variety of palm products is abundant (see Johnson 1988). A listing of 83 major economic species, representing 43 genera, is given in Table 4.1. Although this listing is not complete, it does contain a majority of the economically important palms, which can then be analysed according to their conservation status.

Not threatened species

Forty-eight (58%) of the listed economically important palms are known to be not threatened globally, and another three species, although no longer having distinctive wild populations, are fully domesticated and widespread. This favorable conservation status may be attributed to five factors:

1) Some species (e.g. *Borassus flabellifer*) have broad natural geographic distributions;
2) A number of the species (e.g. *Mauritia flexuosa*) occur in great numbers in nature;
3) Certain species (e.g. *Elaeis oleifera*) grow in both closed and open habitats and are able to tolerate forest degradation or clearing more readily than species of palms which are exclusively forest dwellers;
4) Protection of some species (e.g. *Arenga pinnata*) takes place because of the value of the trees for economic products by local people, hence they persist in areas of partial or even total forest clearance;
5) A few species are fully domesticated and have been introduced and become naturalized in most tropical regions, such as *Areca catechu*, *Cocos nucifera*, *Elaeis guineensis*, and *Phoenix dactylifera*.

Although these economic species are not immediately threatened, they are nonetheless affected by forest degradation and clearing which reduce their geographic

Palmyra palms (*Borassus flabellifer*) which have been pruned and are being tapped for their sweet sap, near Nagercoil, Tamil Nadu, India.

Dennis Johnson

ranges and the total genepool of each species. The result over time is the erosion of genetic diversity, so important for maintenance and improvement of cultivated species as well as for selection of promising new and not yet cultivated species.

Unknown or threatened species

There is insufficient information available to assign an *in situ* conservation status to 22 (27%) of the economic species, 19 of which are represented by rattans (*Calamus* and *Daemonorops* spp., *Eremospatha*, *Laccosperma*). At least four rattan species are known to be threatened: *Calamus ovideus* (Endangered); *C. manan* (Vulnerable); *C. andamanicus* (Vulnerable) and *C. merrillii* (Vulnerable). Given that commercial rattans are subject to the double threat of habitat destruction and over-exploitation of wild stocks, it is probable that most of them are under threat. Most populations of the commercially exploited rattans have decreased dramatically, and the supply for furniture makers is diminishing at an alarming rate (see Chapter 7). *Euterpe edulis* (Vulnerable), *Corypha umbraculifera* (Rare) and *Elaeis oleifera* (Indeterminate) are also known to be globally under threat.

Many more species are suffering from over-exploitation, and although not threatened globally, are threatened in significant parts of their range. *Thrinax radiata* in Mexico; *Euterpe precatoria* in Bolivia and Venezuela; *Syagrus coronata* in Brazil; *Borassus flabellifer* and *Caryota urens* in India; *Cyrtostachys renda* in Thailand, Indonesia and Penisular Malaysia; *Nypa fruticans* in Sri Lanka, China, and other densely populated areas such as the Philippines; and *Livistona rotundifolia* and *Licuala spinosa* in the Philippines are all examples of economically important palms with threatened populations.

Major ornamental palms

Palms have a long history of ornamental use, but thus far only a modest amount of published research has been directed toward nursery production and related issues. The international horticultural community has made a major contribution towards improving the situation by holding the First International Symposium on Ornamental Palms in Jaboticabal, São Paulo, Brazil, in January 1993. This five-day meeting covered a wide range of subjects including domestication, propagation, nursery management, floral biology, tissue culture, landscape design, and conservation (for the latter see Johnson 1994). Proceedings of the symposium are published (Demattê 1994).

The volume of trade in ornamental palms is notable. For example, in 1992 alone Holland imported 120,000 kg seeds of *Dypsis* (=*Chrysalidocarpus*) *lutescens*, one of the most commonly traded ornamental palms. Three-quarters of this seed was produced in Brazilian nurseries (van der Ven 1994). Madagascar, Costa Rica, Guatemala, and Australia are other major producers of palm seeds for international trade. Although mass production of exotic palms for indoor and outdoor planting is not always directly linked to palm conservation, it can relieve pressure on wild populations, as well as provide educational opportunities. Ideally trade in threatened species should be based on a combination of sustainable management of

Products made from palmyra leaf fiber in India.

Dennis Johnson

wild stands and cultivation of these same species in their native areas so that local people will gain a direct benefit from conserving and growing local palm species. In addition, educational programs stressing the importance of protecting palms in the wild to conserve genetic resources needed for continued utilization must be established.

Planting of native ornamental palms in avenues, public gardens, etc. may also help give native palms and genetic resources in general a higher profile. Lists of native palms with high potential for cultivation as ornamentals are given for Brazil by Matthes (1994) and Lima (1994), and Madulid (1991) for the Philippines.

Table 4.2 presents a list of 86 major ornamental palms, representing 43 genera. Determining which species should be included in such a list is a difficult task. Hundreds of species of palms are grown in botanic as well as private gardens, and it would be unwieldy to list them all. Moreover, some palms are grown for several reasons, both for their economic products as well as for landscape purposes, making it very hard to establish which use predominates. For these lists, in cases where a species is grown for both economic and ornamental purposes, it has been included only in the economic list.

Table 4.2 is derived from a recent book on ornamental palms by Meerow (1992), the most comprehensive published thus far. Because the book was published in the United States in southern Florida, it includes the most common ornamental palms of that area and does not necessarily offer a world perspective. However, Matthes (1994) presents a very similar list of palms widely cultivated in Brazil (only four species were added from this source). Table 4.2 includes all palms which are widely cultivated in Sarawak and the Philippines according to Pearce (1991) and Madulid (1991), respectively. However, it is clear that many more palm species are cultivated locally, differing from region to region. Despite these limitations, Table 4.2 provides a basis to analyse conservation issues of palms used as ornamentals.

Verschaffeltia splendida, 'Latanier latte', regenerating in the wild, Vallée du Mai, Seychelles.

Not threatened species

According to current classifications, 31 (36%) of the 86 ornamental species in Table 4.2 are not threatened in the wild. In general these are either adapted to open habitats (e.g. *Bismarckia nobilis*, the most common palm in Madagascar), or they possess a wide geographic range (e.g. *Caryota rumphiana*, which occurs in three countries in South-east Asia as well as in Australia).

Unknown or threatened species

Thirty-nine (45%) of the species in Table 4.2 are known to be threatened, i.e. Endangered, Vulnerable, Rare, or Indeterminate. It would therefore seem that palms used strictly as ornamentals are more threatened than those

with economic uses, possibly because most of the threatened ornamental species have a relatively limited geographic distribution in nature, such as *Veitchia montgomeryana*, which is endemic to the island of Efate in Vanuatu, South Pacific, and all species of *Latania* in the Mascarene Islands. These species are very sensitive to over-exploitation, habitat change, and introduction of seed predators.

Another reason may be the collecting of seed and young plants from the wild for the nursery trade such as is known to occur with *Dypsis* (=*Neodypsis*) *decaryi* in Madagascar. In addition many species of *Chamaedorea* are severely threatened due to over-collecting of seeds, leaves, or whole plants for ornamental use. Adult individuals of the buccaneer palm, *Pseudophoenix sargentii*, are collected as ornamentals in Mexico, resulting in depletion of wild populations. Many stands of the sealing wax palm, *Cyrtostachys renda*, are also disappearing in many areas for the same reason.

On the other hand, controlled collection of seeds for cultivation or for *ex situ* breeding programs can be a valuable source of income to local people, giving them a reason to take care of the wild stands and thus improving conservation *in situ*. Promising examples are *Attalea crassispatha* on Haiti (see Box 6.1) and *Carpoxylon macrospermum* on Vanuatu. The same approach is recommended for species on Papua New Guinea, *Johannesteijsmannia* spp. in Malaysia, and *Chamaedorea* spp. in Mexico (see examples in the respective regional chapters).

Among the 13 ornamental species in Table 4.2 classified as Unknown are the very commonly cultivated palms *Livistona chinensis*, *Rhapis excelsa*, and *Washingtonia robusta*. These serve as an excellent reminder of the lack of general knowledge available on even the most commonly cultivated ornamentals in the wild.

Chamaedoreas

Chamaedoreas are the most widely traded ornamental palms in the world. They are sold in great numbers in the temperate zones for house plants and indoor landscaping, and as outdoor plants in warmer regions. Originating from lowland rain forests and cloud forests in Meso-America, *Chamaedorea* species are typical understory palms. About 80 species are recognized, of which three quarters are threatened, mainly by habitat destruction, but also by over-collection. The following economic analysis is taken mainly from Hodel (1992).

Two species, *Chamaedorea elegans* and *C. seifrizii*, dominate the market. In Florida and California alone about 10 million plants were grown on a commercial basis in 1987–1988, the wholesale value being estimated at US$1 million in California. Figures are unavailable for other major producing countries in Europe, Australia, or elsewhere. While a considerable amount of *C. seifrizii* seeds are produced in nurseries in Florida, nearly all seeds of *C. elegans* and other species originate from Mexico. Seventy-five percent of these are collected from wild plants, purchased from local collectors, which is much less expensive than producing seeds in a plantation. About 500 million seeds were exported from Mexico in 1988, one kilo (about 4000 seeds) being sold at US$6–20 (*C. elegans*) or at US$30–60 for seeds of other species. Seeds are now expected to become more scarce due to habitat destruction, over-collection, and future governmental regulations restricting their export for conservation reasons. Seed production of *C. elegans* is difficult as the palm does not seed readily outside its native habitat without artificial pollination, and since inexpensive seeds have been readily available from Mexico, there has been no economic incentive to produce seeds of this species in cultivation.

Several other species collected in the wild, or grown by hobbyists and collectors and sold to other collectors, are not handled by large commercial growers. Since many of these are known from only a few small populations, trade in even small numbers can endanger these species.

Unscrupulous collectors have been known to devastate entire local populations of some of these highly ornamental species (Hodel 1988). The most threatened species concerned are described below.

Another important use of Chamaedoreas is the cut leaf industry. Cut leaves are widely used as decoration in flower arrangements or other displays. Most leaves are cut from wild plants and originate from Mexico and other Central American countries, generating a market value exceeding US$30 million a year and providing a source of employment for over 10,000 persons in Mexico. In 1986, the United States imported 350 million stems of several species. Collection of leaves requires a paid permit from the Secretaría de Agricultura y Recursos Hidraulicos (SARH) in Mexico. Experienced collectors follow a defined technique for foliage collection and damage to the palm is minimal. However, too often inexperienced children are employed who do not follow this standard, and it is not known if this activity is sustainable on a large scale at present.

Finally, various *Chamaedorea* species are employed by local inhabitants throughout its range for many other uses, the most important being the consumption of male inflorescences (pacaya). Pacaya is a popular and important vegetable, eaten raw or cooked, and sold in the markets. It is mostly harvested from plants of *C. tepejilote*, which has been cultivated for centuries, especially in Guatemala.

The following overview shows the Endangered species of *Chamaedorea* which are threatened both by over-collecting and habitat destruction, ranging from Mexico to Colombia:

- *Chamaedorea amabilis* (Costa Rica, Panama, Colombia) – Grows at middle elevations, and is highly sought by collectors, who sometimes strip entire populations from the forest.

- *C. klotzschiana* (Mexico) – Endemic to a small area of Veracruz. It is widely cultivated and highly sought by collectors. Foliage is collected for local markets.

- *C. metallica* (Mexico) – Restricted to a small area of about 3 km² in Veracruz and Oaxaca, where it is very abundant. Vovides and Bielma (1994) estimated about 50,000 adults occurring in the area. Both seeds and foliage are collected. However, the main threats are expanding coffee plantations and possibly increasing quarrying and wood cutting activities. It is recommended to establish a protected area at the site.

- *C. pumila* (Costa Rica) – Scattered at middle elevations of the Atlantic slopes of Costa Rica. In several localities whole populations of this species have been dug up by collectors, threatening the species with extinction. *C. minima*, known only from cultivated plants, is considered as a synonym of *C. pumila*.

- *C. sullivaniorum* (Costa Rica, Panama, Colombia) – Grows in dense wet forest and is highly sought by collectors. The population at El Valle (Panama), where the species formerly dominated the understory, is now severely decimated.

- *C. tuerckheimii* (Guatemala, Mexico) – This is the smallest and probably one of the most threatened *Chamaedorea* palms. Sold for many years in local markets near Cobán (Verapaz, Guatemala), the species is becoming very rare in the wild, and probably only survives in inaccessible sites. The Mexican population of the palm (in Veracruz) has also declined due to deforestation and over-collecting. At present a single population of about ten adult plants is known, found between slash-and-burn agricultural fields, and threatened by expanding pastures and habitat modification.

Recommendations

1) Increase the cultivation and production of seeds and plants of *Chamaedorea* species in nurseries in order to reduce the collecting pressure on wild populations.

2) Discourage the trade of wild collected individuals and seeds of threatened species through education in both producer as well as consumer countries.

3) Consider proposing species threatened by international trade for Appendix II of CITES.

General recommendations

Regardless of their *in situ* conservation status, economic palms as a group warrant specific measures to protect wild genepools. This is essential, given the severe limitations on the potential role of *ex situ* palm conservation, a subject discussed in Chapter 5. The following recommendations pertain to both economic and ornamental species. More specific recommendations are given in the regional chapters.

1) **Ensure that the threatened plant database at WCMC includes updated coding for species with economic and/or ornamental use or potential.**

This would permit the production of special reports on the status of economic and ornamental palms, and highlight the gaps in conservation data at the global and local geographic area levels.

2) **Increase linkages between the Palm Specialist Group and the major institutions involved in research on cultivated palms.**

Collaborate to assemble complete data on the geographic distributions of wild, naturalized, and cultivated populations. The latter to include data on major plantation areas (and their respective cultivars), seed banks, field genebanks, and botanic gardens.

3) **Promote floristic inventories of rattans in the following priority areas: Myanmar, Vietnam, Laos, Kampuchea, Indonesia (Sulawesi, Moluccas, Irian Jaya), and Papua New Guinea (Williams 1991).**

See Chapter 7 for more information on rattans.

4) **Encourage new systematic treatments of key economic genera (e.g. *Attalea*).**

5) **Develop new techniques for management of wild palm stands for either economic or ornamental purposes through extractive reserves, buffer zones, or other strategies.**

6) **Increase botanical and ethnobotanical research on palms with lesser-known indigenous groups.**

Research is necessary to discover new palm products, to improve techniques for exploitation of existing products, to assess indigenous palm resource management practices, and to determine how local people can derive greater benefits from all forms of palm utilization.

Box 4.1 Protecting wild species through artificial propagation: a pilot *in situ* nursery for cycads and *Chamaedorea* species in Veracruz, Mexico

A cycad nursery has been created at Monte Oscuro, Ejido El Palmar, Chavarillo, Veracruz, under a project of the Institute of Ecology in Xalapa, and with the collaboration of local subsistence farmers. The project began in 1991 and has as its objective to produce, on a sustainable basis, seedlings of the cycad *Dioon edule* which grows in the local tropical thorn forests. This cycad has a conservation status of Vulnerable in Mexico and is illegally collected by non-locals. In 1995, *Chamaedorea klotzschiana*, an endemic and Endangered palm which is sympatric with *Dioon edule* was also taken into cultivation. Funded by GTZ from Germany, this project includes the establishment of other campesino-run nurseries, an environmental impact study, and reintroductions of seedlings into the wild (Vovides, *in litt*.).

It is hoped that the plants produced by the nursery will relieve collecting pressure from the habitat, and at the same time serve as an incentive to the local farmers to conserve the natural habitat through benefits from sales.

Table 4.1 Major economic palms*

Species	Common name	Use	Status
Acrocomia aculeata (Jacq.) Lodd. ex Mart.	macaúba palm	oil, wine	nt
Aiphanes aculeata Willd. (incl. *A. caryotifolia*)	corozo	fruit, seeds	nt
Areca catechu L.	betel palm	betelnut, masticatory	**
Arenga pinnata (Wurmb) Merr.	sugar palm	sap, fiber, fruits	nt
Astrocaryum jauari Mart.	jauari palm	basketry, baits	nt
A. murumuru Mart.	murumuru palm	fruits, construction	nt
A. vulgare Mart.	tucuma palm	fruits	nt
Attalea butyracea (Mutis ex L.f.) Wess. Boer	corozo palm	multipurpose	nt
A. funifera Mart. ex Sprengel	piassava palm	fiber	nt
A. colenda (A. Cook) Balslev and Henderson	palma real	oil	I
A. (=*Maximiliana*) maripa (Correa) Drude	maripa palm	thatch, multipurpose	?
A. speciosa Sprengl (incl. *Orbignya phalerata*)	babassu palm	oil, multipurpose	nt
Bactris gasipaes Kunth	pejibaye	fruits, palm heart	**
Borassus aethiopum Mart.	ron palm	multipurpose	nt
B. flabellifer L.	palmyra, lontar palm	sap, multipurpose	nt
Calamus andamanicus	mofabet	cane	V
C. caesius Blume	rotan sega	prime cane	?
C. egregius Burret	duanye sheng-teng	cane	?
C. exilis Griffith	rotan gunung	cane	nt
C. javensis Blume	rotan opot	cane	nt
C. manan Miq.	rotan manau	prime cane	V
C. merrillii Becc.	palasan	prime cane	V
C. mindorensis Becc.	tumalim	cane, fruits	?
C. optimus Becc.	rotan taman	prime cane	?
C. nambariensis Becc.	hoka bhet	cane	?
C. ornatus Blume	rotan kesup	cane, fruits	?
C. ovoideus Thwaites ex Trimen	thuda rena	cane	E
C. palustris Griffith	rotan buku hitam	cane	nt
C. pogonacanthus Becc. ex H. Winkler	wi tut	cane	?
C. pseudorivalis Becc.	safed bet	cane	V
C. scipionum Lour.	rotan semambu	cane	?
C. rotang L.	perambu	cane	nt
C. simplicifolius Wei	danye shengteng	cane	?
C. subinermis H.A. Wendl. ex Becc.	rotan batu	cane	?
C. tetradactylus Hance	baiteng	cane	K
C. trachycoleus Becc.	rotan irit	cane	nt
C. tumidus Furt.	rotan manau tikus	prime cane	?
C. wailong Pei and Chen	wailong	cane	?
C. zollingeri Becc.	rotan batang	cane	?
Caryota mitis Lour.	fishtail palm	sago, ornamental	nt
C. urens L.	fishtail palm	sap, sago, thatch	nt
Chamaedorea tepejilote Liebm. ex Mart.	pacaya	inflorescences as food	nt
Cocos nucifera L.	coconut palm	coconuts, fiber, fuel	nt
Copernicia prunifera (Miller) H. Moore	carnauba palm	wax	nt
Corypha umbraculifera L.	talipot palm	sap, sago, seeds	R
Cyrtostachys renda Blume	sealing wax palm	thatch, ornamental	nt
Daemonorops margaritae (Hance) Becc.	huangteng	cane	?
D. robusta Warb.	rotan susu	cane	?
D. sabut Becc.	jungan	cane, backpacks	?

Table 4.1 ... continued. Major economic palms[*]

Species	Common name	Use	Status
Desmoncus polyacanthos Mart.	vara casha	basketry (stems)	nt
Elaeis guineensis Jacq.	African oil palm	oil	nt
E. oleifera (Kunth) Cortes	American oil palm	oil	I
Eremospatha macrocarpa (Mann and Wendl) H.A. Wendl.	African rattan	cane-rope	?
Eugeissona utilis Becc.	bertan palm	sago, thatch, multipurpose	nt
Euterpe edulis Mart.	juçara palm	palm heart	V
E. oleracea Mart.	açaí palm	palm heart, fruit drink	nt
E. precatoria Mart.	açaí palm	palm heart, stems	nt
Hyphaene thebaica (L.) Mart.	doum palm	wine, multipurpose	nt
Iriartea deltoidea Ruiz and Pavon	pambil palm	construction	nt
Johannesteijsmannia altifrons (Reichb.f. and Zoll.) H.E. Moore	umbrella leaf palm	thatch	nt
Korthalsia echinometra Becc.	uwi hurang	durable cane, fruits	nt
K. laciniosa (Griff.) Mart.	-	cane, fodder	nt
Laccosperma secundiflorum (Beauv.) Kuntze	African rattan	cane	?
Leopoldinia piassaba Wallace	piassava palm	fiber	nt
Licuala spinosa Thunb.	balatbat palm	thatch, ornamental	nt
Livistona rotundifolia (Lamb.) Mart.	anahaw palm	construction	nt
Manicaria saccifera Gaertner	temiche palm	multipurpose	nt
Mauritia flexuosa L.f.	moriche palm	fruits, multipurpose	nt
Metroxylon sagu Rottb.	sago palm	sago, thatch	?
Nannorrhops ritchiana (Griffith) Aitch.	mazri palm	fiber	?
Nypa fruticans Wurmb	nipa palm	thatch, multipurpose	nt
Oenocarpus bacaba Mart.	bacaba palm	fruit drinks	nt
O. (=Jessenia) bataua Mart.	seje palm	oil, multipurpose	nt
Oncosperma horridum (Griffith) R. Scheffer	bayas palm	construction, cabbage	nt
O. tigillarium (Jack) Ridley	nibong palm	salt-resistant stakes	nt
Phoenix dactylifera L.	date palm	fruits	**
P. sylvestris (L.) Roxb.	wild date palm	sweet sap, basketry	nt
Phytelephas macrocarpa Ruiz & Pavon	ivory nut palm	vegetable ivory	nt
Raphia hookeri G. Mann and H.A. Wendl.	raffia palm	fiber, multipurpose	nt
Salacca zalacca (Gaertner) Voss	salak palm	fruits	nt
Syagrus coronata (Mart.) Becc.	ouricuri palm	fodder, multipurpose	nt
Thrinax radiata Lodd. ex. J.A. and J.H. Schultes	chit palm	construction, basketry	nt
Trachycarpus fortunei (Hook.) H.A. Wendl.	windmill palm	construction, fiber, medicinal, ornamental	nt

* Modified after Johnson (1988).
** Widely cultivated, but no wild populations known.

(Note that data on the distribution of genera is given in Table 1.1)

Table 4.2 Major ornamental palms[*]

Species	Common Name	Origin	Status
Acoelorrhaphe wrightii H.A. Wendl. ex Becc.	paurotis palm	Meso-America	nt
Allagoptera arenaria (Gomes) Kuntze	seashore palm	Brazil	V
Archontophoenix alexandrae H.A. Wendl. & Drude	alexandra palm	Australia	nt
A. cunninghamiana (H.A. Wendl.) H.A. Wendl. & Drude	piccabeen palm	Australia	nt
Arenga tremula (Blanco) Becc.	dwarf sugar palm	East Asia	?
Bismarckia nobilis Hildebr. and H.A. Wendl.	bismarck palm	Madagascar	nt
Brahea armata S. Watson	blue hesper palm	Mexico	K
B. edulis S. Watson	Guadeloupe palm	Guadeloupe Is.	E
Butia capitata (Mart.) Becc.	pindo palm	Brazil, Uruguay	nt
Carpentaria acuminata Becc.	carpentaria palm	Australia	V
Caryota rumphiana Mart.	giant fish-tail palm	South East Asia	nt
Chamaedorea cataractarum Mart.	cat palm	Mexico	V
C. costaricana Oersted	Costa Rican bamboo palm	Meso-America	nt
C. elegans Mart.	parlour palm	Mexico, Guatemala	V
C. metallica Cook ex H. Moore	miniature fishtail palm	Mexico	E
C. microspadix Burret	hardy bamboo palm	Mexico	V
C. radicalis Mart.	radicalis palm	Mexico	V
C. seifrizii Burret	bamboo palm	Meso-America	V
Chamaerops humilis L.	European fan palm	Mediterranean	nt
Coccothrinax barbadensis (Becc.Lodd. ex Mart.) (incl. C. alta)	silver palm	Caribbean	?
C. argentata (Jacq.f) L. Bailey	silver palm	Hispaniola	nt
C. crinita Becc.	old man palm	Cuba	E
C. miraguama (H.B.and K.) Becc.	miraguama palm	Cuba, Hispaniola	nt
Copernicia baileyana León Bailey	copernicia	Hispaniola	nt
C. hospita Mart.	hospita palm	Cuba	nt
C. macroglossa H.A. Wendl. ex Becc.	Cuban petti-coat palm	Cuba	nt
Corypha utan Lam.	gebang palm	India to Australia	nt
Dictyosperma album H.A. Wendl. & Drude ex Scheffer	hurricane palm	Mascarene Is.	E
Dypsis (=Chrysalidocarpus) cabadae (H. Moore) Beentje & J. Dransf.	cabada palm	Unknown	?
D. (=Chrysalidocarpus) lutescens (H.A. Wendl.) Beentje & J. Dransf.	areca palm	Madagascar	nt
D. (=Neodypsis) decaryi (Jum.) Beentje and J. Dransf.	triangle palm	Madagascar	V
D. (=Neodypsis) lastelliana (Baillon) Beentje and J. Dransf.	teddy bear palm	Madagascar	R
D. (=Chrysalidocarpus) madagascariensis (Becc.) Beentje and J. Dransf.	lucubensis palm	Madagascar	R
Gaussia maya (Cook) Quero and Read	maya palm	Mexico, Belize, Guat.	I
Heterospathe elata Scheffer	sagisi palm	Philippines, Moluccas	?
Howea forsteriana (C.Moore and F. Muell.) Becc.	kentia palm	Lord Howe Is.	R
Hyophorbe lagenicaulis (L. Bailey) H. Moore	bottle palm	Mascarene Is.	E
H. verschaffeltii H.A. Wendl.	spindle palm	Mascarene Is.	E
Jubaea chilensis (Molina) Baillon	Chilean wine palm	Chile	V
Latania loddigesii Mart.	blue latan palm	Mascarene Is.	E
L. lontaroides (Gaertner) H. Moore	red latan palm	Mascarene Is.	E
L. verschaffeltii Lemaire	yellow latan palm	Mascarene Is.	V

Table 4.2 ... continued. Major ornamental palms[*]

Species	Common Name	Origin	Status
Licuala grandis H.A. Wendl.	licuala palm	Solomon Is., Vanuatu	?
Livistona australis Mart.	Australian fan palm	Australia	nt
L. chinensis (Jacq.) R.Br. ex Mart.	Chinese fan palm	Taiwan, Japan	?
L. decipiens Becc.	ribbon fan palm	Australia	R
L. mariae F. Muell.	Australian fan palm	Australia	R
L. saribus (Lour.) Merr. ex A. Chev.	taraw palm	South East Asia	nt
Lytocaryum weddelianum (H. Wendl.) Tol.	icá palm	Brazil	E
Phoenix canariensis Chabaud	Canary Island palm	Canary Is.	nt
P. reclinata Jacq.	Senegal date	Africa	nt
P. roebelenii O'Brien	pygmy date	Vietnam, Laos	nt
P. rupicola T. Anders.	cliff date	India	V
Pinanga kuhlii Blume	ivory cane palm	Borneo?	?
Pritchardia pacifica Seemann ex H.A. Wendl.	Fiji fan palm	Marquesas Is., Tonga	?
P. thurstonii F. Muell. & Drude	thurston palm	Fiji	R
Pseudophoenix sargentii H.A. Wendl. ex Sarg.	buccaneer palm	Caribbean	V
Ptychosperma elegans (R.Br.) Blume	solitaire palm	Australia	nt
P. macarthurii (Veitch) H.A. Wendl. ex Hook.f.	macarthur palm	New Guinea, Australia	nt
Ravenea rivularis Jum. and Perrier (known as *R. glauca*)	majesty palm	Madagascar	V
Rhapidophyllum hystrix (Pursh) H.A. Wendl. & Drude	needle palm	southern USA.	nt
Rhapis excelsa (Thunb.) Henry	lady palm	China	?
R. humilis Blume	slender lady palm	China	?
Roystonea elata (Bartram) F. Harper	Florida royal palm	Florida	E
R. oleracea (Jacq.) O. F. Cook	cabbage palm	Caribean	nt
R. regia (Kunth) Cook	Cuban royal palm	Cuba	nt
Sabal causiarum (Cook) Becc.	hat palm	Caribbean	nt
S. minor (Jacq.f.) Pers.	dwarf palmetto	southern USA	nt
S. palmetto (Walter) Lodd. ex Schultes	cabbage palm	Caribbean	nt
Serenoa repens (Bartram) Small	saw palmetto	southern USA	nt
Syagrus comosa (Mart.) Mart.	catolé, babao	Brazil	nt
S. oleracea (Mart.) Becc.	catolé	Brazil	nt
S. romanzoffiana (Cham.) Glassman	queen palm	South America	nt
S. schizophylla (Mart.) Glassman	arikury palm	Brazil (Atlantic)	?
Thrinax morrisii H.A. Wendl.	key thatch palm	Caribbean	nt
Trithrinax brasiliensis Mart.	spiny fiber palm	Brazil	?
Veitchia arecina Becc.	arecina palm	Vanuatu	I
V. joannis H.A. Wendl.	joannis palm	Fiji	R
V. macdanielsii H. Moore	sunshine palm	Vanuatu	R
V. merrillii (Becc.) H. Moore	manila palm	Philippines	I
V. montgomeryana H. Moore	montgomery palm	Vanuatu	E
V. winin H. Moore	winin palm	Vanuatu	I
Washingtonia filifera (L. Linden) H.A. Wendl.	California fan palm	Mexico, Arizona	R
W. robusta H.A. Wendl.	Mexican fan palm	Mexico	?
Wodyetia bifurcata Irvine	foxtail palm	Australia	R
Zombia antillarum (Descourt.) L. Bailey	zombie palm	Hispaniola	nt

[*] Adapted from Meerow (1992) and Matthes (1994), with some name changes and exclusion of species already listed in Table 4.1.

Chapter 5

Ex situ Conservation

This chapter addresses the general subject of *ex situ* palm conservation and how *ex situ* work can contribute to palm conservation. Also included is a list of the highly threatened palms reported to be in cultivation in botanic gardens.

The term *ex situ* as used in this Action Plan refers to botanic gardens, arboreta, and similar institutions "containing scientifically ordered and maintained collections of plants, usually documented and labelled, and open to the public for the purposes of recreation, education and research" (BGCS 1989). Private palm collections have not been included.

A number of gardens have palm collections possessing a potential conservation role or, rarely, established programs which specialize in palm conservation. Examples include Darwin Botanic Gardens, Northern Territory, Australia (Brown 1988, 1989; Wightman 1992); Fairchild Tropical Garden in Florida (Hubbuch 1989); National Botanic Garden, Cuba (Leiva 1988); Parc de Tsimbazaza, Madagascar (Du Puy *et al.* 1992); Robert and Catherine Wilson Botanical Garden at Las Cruces, Costa Rica (Bates 1987); The Palmetum, Townsville, Australia (Tucker 1989, 1990; Dowe 1993); National Tropical Botanical Garden, Lawai (Lorence, *in litt.*); and Yucatán Regional Botanic Garden, Mexico (Orellana *et al.* 1988). An ambitious effort is also in process in Colombia to create a national palm collection at the Botanical Garden in Tuluá (Bernal and Alvarez 1991).

Despite the specialization and potential documented above, the role that *ex situ* conservation can play in the maintenance of palm biodiversity is limited, although can prove crucial in cases of critically endangered species, as well as providing an excellent resource for educational work.

Major limiting factors

The role *ex situ* conservation can play in maintaining palm biodiversity is limited by five major factors.

1) Lack of information. There is a paucity of information about the growth and reproduction requirements of a majority of the described palm species. Although precise figures do not exist, it can be estimated that 500–600 of the 2300 taxa of palms have been cultivated in botanic gardens. However, few data have been systematically gathered on the habitat, growth and reproduction requirements, or on the provenance of cultivated palms. Some species, for example, grow well under cultivation but do not produce fruit. Unfortunately, only a very small number of species have ever been studied in detail in the wild.

An important but yet untapped information resource resides with private palm growers who, through trial and error, have achieved successes on a par with botanic gardens and, in certain instances, with species not found in botanic garden collections.

2) Narrow genepool. Those few individual palm species under cultivation in botanic gardens often originate from one or a few wild collections, and hence poorly represent the genetic diversity of an individual species. A particular threatened palm species that is widely cultivated, therefore, may convey the false impression of being representative of the diversity of wild populations. It is therefore important that the exact provenance of each palm accession is recorded and studbooks established, if *ex situ* breeding programs are to be launched.

3) Artificial hybridization. Although this problem has been recognized for many years, neither methods for its prevention, nor its extent and implications, have received much attention thus far. The traditional practice of placing species of the same genus in a designated plot within a garden, although possessing aesthetic appeal, can create conditions for cross-pollination and the production of artificial hybrid seed. Genera known to readily hybridize in gardens include *Chamaedorea*, *Latania*, *Pritchardia*, *Archontophoenix*, and *Phoenix*. Natural hybrids have been reported at both the specific and generic level in the Americas, involving the genera *Bactris*, *Copernicia*, *Syagrus*, and *Attalea* (Balick 1988).

In a study of the *Syagrus* collection at Fairchild Tropical Garden, Noblick (1992) confirmed that artificial hybridization has indeed occurred and the Garden "may be distributing 'illegitimate' (hybridized) seed," of *Syagrus* and other genera. Although artificial hybrids may produce unique palms for the nursery trade, distributing hybridized seed contributes nothing to *ex situ* conservation unless it reduces pressure on wild populations.

Limiting artificial hybridization is relatively easy to implement and achieve. First and foremost, genera with potentially interfertile species should have a minimal representation of species in the collection. If more than one species of a genus is to be included in a collection, they should be planted as far apart as possible. The Townsville Botanic Gardens is using this approach in cultivating five species of *Hyphaene*. Prevention of hybridization, of course, can never be fully guaranteed if there is even the remotest chance that it may occur. To confound the problem, there has been only limited research undertaken to determine how effectively pollen is transferred between palms. Hybridization can also be prevented by other more reliable methods. In dioecious genera, staminate inflorescences of species with hybridization potential may be removed before they reach anthesis, thus denying the release of pollen. With monoecious genera, this method is inappropriate, and in practical terms impossible.

4) Vulnerability. Botanic gardens are quite vulnerable to physical and biological threats to their collections. The destruction and physical damage to the palm trees of the Fairchild Tropical Garden caused by Hurricane Andrew in August 1992 is a vivid example. Fire is also a serious threat. Less dramatic but more profound in the long run are diseases such as lethal yellowing and the *Ganoderma* soil fungus, for which there are no effective controls. These types of almost irremediable threat are grim reminders that *ex situ* conservation is a risky business.

5) Palm seed. The seed of most species of palms begin to germinate shortly after dispersion; there is no natural dormancy. As a result, seed storage under either ambient conditions or in closed chambers where temperature and humidity can be controlled is not a feasible means of preserving palm germplasm at this time. Much remains to be learned about the characteristics of palm seed (see Dickie *et al.* 1993; Johnson 1991b).

Field genebanks

Field genebanks are a specialized type of botanic garden; they represent working collections of plants maintained for breeding purposes. Only the following major cultivated palms financially support the luxury of this type of *ex situ* collection: African oil palm (*Elaeis guineensis*), coconut (*Cocos nucifera*), date palm (*Phoenix dactylifera*), pejibaye palm (*Bactris gasipaes*), and the betel nut palm (*Areca catechu*). In the search for potential new plantation oilseed crops, the Palm Oil Research Institute of Malaysia (PORIM) has collected germplasm of *Oenocarpus*, *Bactris*, and *Euterpe* spp. in South America. These palms have been established at the PORIM Research Station, Kluang, Malaysia to study their agronomic needs and yield potential, and in the process, useful new information on growing these palms is being collected (Rajanaidu *et al.* 1993). Field genebanks for several American palms exist or are planned in Brazil (Valois 1994) and do exist for rattan palms in the Luasong Forestry Centre in Sabah (Malaysia).

In contrast with botanic gardens, the requirements and provenance of the palms in field genebanks are known, and collections attempt to represent the broadest possible genepool. Cross-pollination occurs among the various land races in a field genebank if it is not artificially controlled. Field genebanks are vulnerable to the same threats as botanic gardens. However, in terms of the potential to maintain palm biodiversity, field genebanks are clearly the most valuable.

Highly threatened palms in botanic gardens

One objective of this Action Plan was to determine the *ex situ* status of the most highly threatened palms (listed in Appendix 2). Table 5.1, compiled in collaboration with Botanic Gardens Conservation International (BGCI) and several major botanic gardens, is an indicative list of which species and where, of 83 taxa representing 45 genera, are reported to be in the collections of 71 botanic gardens. However, due to the dynamic nature of living collections, this table is only meant to give an idea of Endangered palms in cultivation, and it will change over time.

The following points are relevant to understanding and evaluating the data in Table 5.1:
1) Taxa under cultivation include nursery, out-planted immature and mature palms; original seed sources are from gardens and the wild. Inclusion in Table 5.1 does not mean that all of the palms are confirmed sources of seed. Even if seed is available, it is possibly of hybrid origin.
2) The 83 taxa under cultivation account for about 37% of the total number of the 230 highly threatened taxa listed in Appendix 2, but only represent three of the 21 palms that are possibly Extinct in the Wild (Ex/E).
3) There are 31 taxa confirmed to be represented in only one of the 71 botanic gardens.
4) Fairchild Tropical Garden, Royal Botanic Gardens Kew, and Townsville Botanic Gardens contain the largest number of highly threatened taxa, with 49, 35, and 29 taxa, respectively.
5) Data from the Jardim Botanico, Rio de Janeiro and the Peradeniya Garden, Sri Lanka, both major world palm collections, are not reflected in Table 5.1 because no recent, reliable censuses of their palm collections had been completed at the time of writing.

Priority activities and recommendations

Botanic gardens have neither the physical capability nor the financial resources to play a major role in overall efforts to conserve palm biodiversity. Conservation advocates cannot expect botanic gardens to become field genebanks, assuming a role they were never envisioned to play. However, through education, breeding programs, and reintroductions, they can provide significant contributions to the conservation of some of the most threatened species.

Table 5.1 Most highly threatened palms of the world under cultivation in botanic gardens[*]

Species and world conservation status	Botanic Gardens[**]
Allagoptera arenaria (E)	20,33,50,58,66,70
Areca concinna (E)	18,50,58,60,70
A. subacaulis (E)	20
Attalea crassispatha (E)	20
A. victoriana (E)[1]	20
Beccariophoenix madagascariensis (E)	20,50,58
Borassus sambiranensis (E)	47
Brahea edulis (E)	2,8,22,24,26,27,29,34,37,50,51,52,66
Carpoxylon macrospermum (E)	18,58
Ceratolobus glaucescens (E)	64
C. pseudoconcolor (E)	50,64
Ceroxylon alpinum (E)	33
Chamaedorea amabilis (E)	70
C. brachyclada (E)	20,66
C. brachypoda (E)	20,21,44,58,66,70
C. fragrans (E)	20,33,50,66,68
C. glaucifolia (E)	10,11,18,20,21,22,24,37,42,43,50,52,58,66,68,70
C. klotzschiana (E)	18,20,21,24,33,43,50,52,58,66,70
C. metallica (E)	2,9,10,18,20,21,22,24,26,30,32,33,37,50,51,52,58,60,66
C. pumila (E)	50
C. rigida (E)	24
C. simplex (E)	65
C. stolonifera (E)	7,8,9,10,20,24,28,36,42,50,52,58,63,66
C. tenerrima (E)	58
C. tuerckheimii (E)	20,30,32,70
Chuniophoenix hainanensis (E)[2]	20,53,54,57,71
C. humilis (E)	20,50,53,54,57
Coccothrinax borhidiana (E)	15,16,20,31,66
C. crinita ssp. crinita (E)	12,18,20,24,25,32,66,70
Copernicia ekmanii (E)	20,35
Corypha taliera (Ex)	20,25
Cryosophila kalbreyeri (E)	20
Cyphophoenix nucele (E)	20,50,68
Dictyosperma album var. album (E)	1,15,16,18,19,20,21,25,33,36,43,45,47,50,52,56,58,59,65,68,70
D. album var. aureum (E)	20,50,68
D. album var. conjugatum (E)	58
Dypsis (=Chrysalidocarpus) arenarum (E)	20
D. (=Neodypsis) ceraceus (Ex/E)	20
D. (=Vonitra) crinita (E)	50
D. (=Chrysalidocarpus) decipiens (E)	20,47,50,66
D. (=Neodypsis) lucens (Ex/E)	50
Gaussia attenuata (E)	20,31,35,43,50,66
Hyophorbe lagenicaulis (E)	2,14,15,16,18,20,21,33,36,38,45,50,58,68
H. vaughanii (E)	3,68
H. verschaffeltii (E)	2,3,4,13,14,16,17,18,20,34,36,38,40,41,43,45,48,50,52,56,58,61,65
Itaya amicorum (E)	58
Johannesteijsmannia lanceolata (E)	58
J. magnifica (E)	18,50,55,58
Kentiopsis oliviformis (E)	20,58,68,70
Latania loddigesii (E)	4,10,15,16,17,18,20,33,36,46,48,50,52,58,65,68,69
L. lontaroides (E)	1,10,14,15,16,18,20,21,33,43,45,62,68
Lemurophoenix halleuxii (E)	20,47
Licuala orbicularis (E)	5,58
Loxococcus rupicola (E)	50
Lytocaryum weddelianum (E)	20,58

26

Table 5.1 ... continued. Most highly threatened palms of the world under cultivation in botanic gardens[*]

Species and world conservation status	Botanic Gardens[**]
Marojejya darianii (E)	18,20,47,50,58
Nenga gajah (E)	50
Neoveitchia storckii (E)	18,20,21,50,58,68
Orania(=Halmoorea) trispatha (E)	20,50,58
Parajubaea torallyi (E)	2,50,66
Pelagodoxa henryana (E)	18,20,50,58
Pinanga javana (E)	11,12,58,64,68
Pritchardia affinis (E)	20,39,45, 66,67,68
P. aylmer-robinsonii (E)	20,23,45, 68
P. kaalae (E)	45
P. lanaiensis (E)	45, 50
P. munroi (E)	20,39,45, 67,68
P. napaliensis (E)	45, 68
P. remota (E)	45, 68
P. schattaueri (E)	20,45, 50,58, 68
P. viscosa (E)	45, 68
Pritchardiopsis jeanneneyi (E)	15
Pseudophoenix ekmanii (E)	20
Ravenea louvelii (Ex/E) (=Louvelia madagascariensis)	50
Sabal bermudana (E)	1,20,49,50,66,68
S. miamiensis (Ex/E)	20
Syagrus macrocarpa (E)	20,58
S. pseudococos (E)	20
Tectiphiala ferox (E)	14
Thrinax ekmaniana (E)	66
Veitchia montgomeryana (E)	20,58
Voanioala gerardii (E)	50

[1] Now included in *Attalea amygdalina* (E, status of *ex situ* conservation not known).
[2] Now included in *Chuniophoenix nana* (I, *ex situ* and *in situ* conservation status insufficiently known).

[*] Based on species listed in Appendix 2 and on data from Botanic Gardens Conservation International; Fairchild Tropical Garden; Royal Botanic Gardens, Kew; National Tropical Botanical Garden, Lawai; Townsville Botanic Gardens; and Waimea Arboretum, Waimea.

[**] Key to the names of botanic gardens:
1. Aburi Botanic Gardens, Aburi, Ghana; **2.** Adelaide Botanic Garden, Adelaide, Australia; **3.** Botanic Garden Komarov Botanical Institute, St. Petersburg, Russia; **4.** Botanical Gardens, Wageningen, Netherlands; **5.** Botanical Research Centre, Kuching, Sarawak; **6.** Botanischer Garten der Philipps-Universitat, Marburg, Germany; **7.** Botanischer Garten der Universitat Bonn, Bonn, Germany; **8.** Botanischer Garten der Universitat Osnabruck, Osnabruck, Germany; **9.** Botanischer Garten Munchen-Nymphenburg, Munich, Germany; **10.** Botanischer Garten und Botanisches Museum Berlin-Dahlem, Germany; **11.** Cabang Balai Kebun Raya Cibodas, Cibodas, Indonesia; **12.** Cabang Balai Kebun Raya Eka Karya Bali, Bali, Indonesia; **13.** Conservatoire Botanique National du Brest, Brest, France; **14.** Conservatoire et Jardin Botanique de Mascarin, Saint Leu, Réunion; **15.** Conservatoire et Jardin Botanique de Nancy, Nancy, France; **16.** Conservatoire et Jardin Botaniques, Geneva, Switzerland; **17.** Cultuurtuin voor Technisch Gewassen, Delft, Netherlands; **18.** Darwin Botanic Gardens, Darwin, Australia; **19.** Dyffryn Gardens, Cardiff, U.K.; **20.** Fairchild Tropical Garden, Miami, U.S.; **21.** Flecker Botanic Garden, Cairns, Australia; **22.** Fullerton Arboretum, Fullerton, U.S.; **23.** Ho'omaluhia, Honolulu, U.S.; **24.** Huntington Botanical Gardens, San Marino, U.S.; **25.** Indian Botanic Garden, Calcutta, India; **26.** Institut National de la Recherche Agronomique, Antibes, France; **27.** Isole di Brissago Botanic Garden, Brissago, Switzerland; **28.** Istituto de Orto Botanico dell'Universita di Pavia, Pavia, Italy; **29.** Istituto Ed Orto Botanico Della Universita, Pisa, Italy; **30.** Jardin Botanico del Instituto de Biologia, Mexico City, Mexico; **31.** Jardin Botanico Nacional de Cuba, Havana, Cuba; **32.** Jardin Botanico Fco J. Clavijero, Xalapa, Mexico; **33.** Jardin Botanique National de Belgique, Meise, Belgium; **34.** Jardin Botanique de la Ville de Nice, Nice, France; **35.** Jardin Botanico, Sancti Spiritus, Cuba; **36.** Jardin Botanique de Montreal, Montreal, Canada; **37.** Jardin de Aclimatacion de la Orotava, Tenerife, Spain; **38.** Lalbagh Botanical Garden, Bangalore, India; **39.** Lyon Arboretum, Honolulu, USA.; **40.** Missouri Botanical Garden, St. Louis, USA.; **41.** Mitchell Park Conservatory, Milwaukee, USA.; **42.** Mt. Coot - The Botanic Gardens, Toowong, Australia; **43.** Museum National d'Histoire Naturelle, Paris, France; **44.** National Botanic Gardens, Glasnevin, Ireland; **45.** National Tropical Botanical Garden, Lawai, USA.; **46.** Palmgarten der Stadt Frankfurt, Frankfurt, Germany; **47.** Parc Botanique et Zoologique de Tsimbazaza, Antananarivo, Madagascar; **48.** Pretoria National Botanical Garden, Pretoria, South Africa; **49.** Royal Botanic Garden, Edinburgh, U.K.; **50.** Royal Botanic Gardens, Kew, U.K.; **51.** San Diego Wild Animal Park, Escondito, USA.; **52.** San Diego Zoological Gardens, San Diego, USA.; **53.** Shanghai Botanic Garden, Shanghai, China; **54.** Shenzhen Fairy Lake Botanical Garden, Shenzhen, China; **55.** Singapore Botanic Gardens, Singapore, Singapore; **56.** Sir Seewoosagur Ramgoolam Botanic Garden, Pamplemousses, Mauritius; **57.** South China Botanical Garden, Guangzhou, China; **58.** Townsville Botanic Gardens, Townsville, Australia; **59.** Trinity College Botanic Garden, Dublin, Ireland; **60.** Tropical Botanic Garden and Research Institute, Trivandrum, India; **61.** University of Aarhus Botanical Institute, Aarhus, Denmark; **62.** University of Helsinki Botanical Garden, Helsinki, Finland; **63.** University of Turku Botanical Garden, Turku, Finland; **64.** UPT Balai Pengembangan Kebun Raya -LIPI, Bogor, Indonesia; **65.** Utrecht University Botanical Garden, Utrecht, Netherlands; **66.** Ventura County Community College District, Ventura, USA.; **67.** Wahiawa Botanic Garden, Honolulu, USA.; **68.** Waimea Arboretum and Botanical Garden, Waimea, USA.; **69.** Warsaw University Botanic Garden, Warsaw, Poland; **70.** Wilson Botanical Garden, Las Cruces, Costa Rica; **71.** Xiashi Arboretum, Pingyang, China.

Three interrelated priority activities that botanic gardens could undertake to benefit palm conservation are as follows:

1) Establish and maintain a species database of all palms under cultivation in botanic gardens, collaborating in this respect with BGCI and WCMC.

a) Gather information on provenance, vitality, and reproductive state of cultivated palms;

b) Promote the preparation of checklists in gardens whose collections are poorly known, providing needed technical assistance;

c) Attempt to gather information on palms in private collections;

d) For critically endangered species, establish an even more detailed database for all individuals in cultivation, noting provenance, reproduction, etc., similar to studbooks maintained at zoological gardens for Endangered species.

Such a database will help to identify threatened and rare palms which are poorly represented in cultivation, and serve as a basis for establishing *ex situ* breeding programs.

2) Establish *ex situ* breeding programs and reintroductions of the most threatened palms.

Reintroductions represent one way botanic gardens can contribute to future palm conservation, although they must be carefully planned. Excellent guidelines are now available and should be consulted (BGCI 1995; IUCN 1995; see also Atkinson *et al.* 1995).

Virtually nothing has been published with regard to reintroducing palms into the wild, an exception being the project at Fairchild Tropical Garden to restore populations of *Pseudophoenix sargentii* to the Florida Keys, a part of its original range (Lippincott 1992, 1995). The remnant populations of *Hyophorbe lagenicaulis* on Round Island, Mauritius, and *Hyophorbe verschaffeltii, Dictyosperma album* var. *aureum*, and *Latania verschaffeltii* on Rodrigues have been augmented by reintroductions. In addition, *D. album* var. *conjugatum* has been either introduced or reintroduced onto Ile aux Aigrettes, an off-shore islet of Mauritius, where it may or may not once have grown (Strahm, pers. comm.). On Hawaii, plants of *Pritchardia napaliensis* have been outplanted (Lorence, *in litt.*).

An excellent opportunity exists for a pilot activity: reintroduction of *Corypha taliera* into its native habitat in Bengal State, India. This palm is in cultivation in at least two botanic gardens (Fairchild Tropical Garden and Indian Botanic Garden, Calcutta), and seedlings or seed should be available eventually.

Palm breeding programs, whether followed by reintroductions or not, should be established in countries such as Madagascar where a significant number of extinctions of palm species can be expected in the next decade, if some have not already occurred. Priority should be given to Ex, Ex/E, and E category species. Of the 21 taxa designated as Ex/E in Appendix 2, only three are in cultivation. It is essential that local botanic gardens (such as the Parc de Tsimbazaza in Madagascar) are involved in such efforts, and receive financial and technical support for this important and difficult task. Other threatened palms which should be cultivated and would benefit from reintroductions are discussed in the regional chapters.

Botanic gardens should be urged to coordinate and take the lead to carry out the activities outlined above, and to collect and distribute the relevant information and experience gained. On the basis of their collections, staff, interest, and resources, botanic gardens in wealthier countries should establish partnerships with less developed gardens and set up conservation programs.

3) Education.

Environmental education, stressing the need for plant conservation, is an essential part of a botanic garden's effort to promote plant conservation in the wild. Botanic gardens can raise awareness, develop educational material, explain the economic, cultural and historic value of threatened plants, establish links with governments, sponsors and mass media, and attract and motivate volunteers and scientists to participate in conservation projects. Beautiful palm collections as part of conservation breeding or reintroduction programs serve as positive examples, and BGCI (1994) provides guidance for developing educational activities in support of plant conservation.

Box 5.1 The Palmetum, Townsville, Australia: a specialist collection devoted to palms

The Palmetum, Townsville, a botanic garden devoted to palms and administered by Townsville City Council, was officially opened in 1988 after a six-year establishment period. The climate in Townsville, classified as sub-humid dry tropical, is ideal for growing a comprehensive botanical and ecological representation of the palm family. Species from the world's driest habitats are easily accommodated, while those from moister habitats can be grown with appropriate irrigation coordinated with discerning placement within the many microclimates within the site. The only palms which cannot be grown in The Palmetum are those from radically different climates such as moist high-altitude habitats or cold temperate regions. A reasonable estimate of the number of palm taxa which could be grown in The Palmetum, taking into account the climatic and/or biological constraints of the site, is about 1600 or about 70% of the total number of taxa in the family. The only limitations to growing this number is space and the availability of propagating materials.

The palm collection presently stands at more than 700 taxa, which includes about 300 species in 103 genera in the in-ground collection, and approximately 400 species in 40 genera in the potted collection (these figures include taxa which are now considered as synonyms by Henderson *et al.* 1995). All six subfamilies in the Palmae are represented, making the collection a tremendous scientific and educational resource.

Chapter 6

Regional Priorities in the Americas

Tropical forest palm species in the Amazon Basin in particular, and palms generally occurring on islands, represent the focus of this chapter. In the Americas, as elsewhere in the tropics, knowledge about palms in their native habitats is variable. Therefore this chapter cannot uniformly cover the subject, since in many areas (such as southern Mexico) field studies remain to be done. A related constraint is the small number of local botanists who have expertise in the Palm family.

The Amazon Basin is the largest area of tropical forest least affected by human activities, and therefore provides an excellent opportunity to study and understand the systematics and ecology of palms under natural conditions. Virtually all of the recent data reported on Amazonian palms have been generated since 1985, and demonstrate the importance of the three main needs for plant conservation: precise up-to-date systematics, accurate information on the species habitat, and knowledge about immediate and long-term threats that imperil these habitats. The two Amazonian case studies demonstrate the value to conservation of thorough herbarium and field studies for revising major genera and clarifying unknown species.

This chapter also surveys the situation with respect to the threatened island palm species of the region, and discusses the situation in several South American countries with specific recommendations.

Conservation activities in the Americas are now facilitated by two major publications. The first is an account of all the species of palms occurring naturally within the Amazon, and includes discussions of ecology, utilization, biogeography, and taxonomy (Henderson 1994). The second is a field guide to all native palms of the Americas, containing taxonomic keys for field identification, distribution maps, a complete list of synonyms, and checklists of species by country (Henderson *et al.* 1995). This represents the first comprehensive treatment of all the New World palms, and the nomenclature in this Action Plan generally follows this work. However, synonyms are included for clarity, and the nomenclature of *Astrocaryum* follows Kahn and Millán (1992). Note that the genus *Catoblastus* is now included in *Wettinia*; *Jessenia* in *Oenocarpus*; and *Maximiliana*, *Orbignya*, and *Scheelea* in *Attalea*.

Amazonian forest ecosystems and their palms

To define regional priorities for palm conservation, native palm representation in Amazonian forest ecosystems must first be considered. Ten vegetation types are recognized here, plus coastal savannas and inselbergs as parts of the Amazonian complex.

1) Terra firme forests. These unflooded forests occur on clayey, usually well-drained soils, and have the highest palm diversity. For example, in a terra firme forest near Manaus, up to 20 species were found in 0.12 ha plots, while only up to ten species were found in areas of equal size in the contiguous seasonal swamp forest (Table 6.1). In Peru, 34 species in 21 genera, and 29 species in 16 genera were counted in terra firme forests on 0.5 ha and 0.71 ha plots, respectively (Kahn and Mejía 1991).

Most palms occupy the understory of terra firme forests and the number of adult arborescent palms (i.e. with height > 10 m) is very low (Table 6.2) as only a few species reach this height (Kahn *et al.* 1988; Kahn and de Granville 1992).

Table 6.1 Palm species richness per 0.12 ha plot in relation to topography in a forest of central Amazonia, near Manaus, Brazil*

Habitat	Transect 1		Transect 2	
	Total species	Understory species	Total species	Understory species
Plateau	16	14	16	14
Crest	19	16	20	17
Slope	19	17	19	16
Transition zone	5	3	10	6
Valley bottom	7	3	6	2

* After Kahn and Castro 1985.

Table 6.2 Number of palms in two height classes surveyed in six terra firme forests*

Location	Height 10 m		Area surveyed (ha)
	<	>	
Galbao Mts, French Guiana	863	1	1.26
Lower Waki, French Guiana	373	4	0.18
Lower Tocantins, Brazil	3442	4	3.84
Lower Rio Negro, Brazil	2322	4	0.72
Lower Ucayali, Peru	6999	5	0.71
Lower Ucayali, Peru	3813	25	0.50

* After Kahn and de Granville 1992.

---

2) Dry white sands with low vegetation. These plant communities are called 'campinas' in Brazil and 'chamizal' in Peru. Both palm diversity and population size are small (Kahn and de Granville 1992). The genus *Mauritiella* (*M. aculeata*) is frequently found in this vegetation type.

3) Waterlogged white sands. These soils occur on the periphery of the previous vegetation type, where there is poor water drainage. Although these soils are never flooded, the palm community is very similar to that of seasonal swamp forests, with a higher density of tall *Oenocarpus bataua*, and usually a lower density of *Euterpe precatoria* and *Mauritia flexuosa*. Palm diversity may be higher here than in seasonal swamp forests because the sandy soils are not homogeneously waterlogged, allowing terra firme species to grow in drier places (Kahn and de Granville 1992). *Euterpe catinga*, *Oenocarpus bataua*, and *Mauritia carana* associations are frequent on these soils.

4) Seasonal swamp forests. These forests are irregularly flooded by rainfall and have a high density and medium diversity of palms (Table 6.3). This vegetation type is found at the bottom of terra firme valleys drained by small streams, and palm diversity is usually lower than in terra firme forests (Scariot *et al.* 1989; de Granville 1990; Kahn and Mejía 1990; Kahn and de Granville 1992). The density of palms is very high due to the abundance of one species in eastern Amazonia (*Euterpe oleracea*), and of three arborescent species in central and western Amazonia (*Oenocarpus bataua, Euterpe precatoria, Mauritia flexuosa*). *Socratea exorrhiza* also occurs in seasonal swamp forests throughout Amazonia. In the understory are found *Elaeis*

oleifera with large leaves and a creeping trunk, plus several small species, such as *Bactris maraja* (including *B. monticola*), *Geonoma macrostachys* (including *G. acaulis*), *Hyospathe elegans*, and the very infrequent *Asterogyne guianensis* which is known in a single locality in French Guiana (de Granville 1992).

5) Permanently flooded swamp forests. These areas are usually composed of very dense populations of *Mauritia flexuosa* throughout the Amazon Basin and of *Euterpe oleracea* in its eastern part. Palm diversity is rather low (Table 6.3). *Euterpe precatoria*, *Geonoma macrostachys*, *Oenocarpus mapora*, and *Socratea exorrhiza* also occur in these swamps.

6) Forests on alluvial soils periodically flooded by blackwater. These areas are referred to as 'restinga forest' in Peru and 'várzea forest' in Brazil. The palm community under 10 m in height is very dense, with small palms such as *Geonoma macrostachys* and *Bactris bifida*. Medium-sized palms are represented by *Phytelephas macrocarpa* and *Astrocaryum* spp. (see Table 6.5). Palms represented in the canopy are *Attalea* (=*Scheelea*) *phalerata*, *Euterpe precatoria* (western and central regions), and *Euterpe oleracea* (eastern region).

7) Forests periodically flooded by blackwater. In this instance, the areas are referred to as "tahuampa forest" in Peru and "igapó-forest" in Brazil. They have a low diversity of palm species. Only a few palms occur in this ecosystem (Table 6.3) including: *Astrocaryum jauari, Bactris maraja, B. concinna*, and *B. riparia*. All of those species are riparian

Natural concentration of buriti palms (*Mauritia flexuosa*), Acre, Brazil.

WWF/Edward Parker

and are found in most inundated forest ecosystems (Kahn and de Granville 1992).

8) Swamp forests under tidal influence. *Bactris major* is a characteristic palm species of this vegetation type. *Mauritia flexuosa* forms dense stands in coastal swampy areas under tidal influence.

9) Gallery forests with low palm diversity. These are found in the northern and southern parts of the Amazon Basin. *Mauritia flexuosa* forms dense populations on waterlogged soils in the north and south and *Attalea* (=*Maximiliana*) *maripa* occupies drier soils in the north. *Acrocomia aculeatum* (including *A. totai*), *Astrocaryum gratum*, and *Syagrus sancona* are the most frequent palms in the southern region.

10) Mountain cloud forests above 1500 m. *Aiphanes* spp., *Chamaedorea* spp., *Dictyocaryum lamarckianum*, *Iriartea deltoidea*, *Prestoea* spp., and *Wettinia maynensis* are characteristic elements of the Subandean palm flora. Palm density is usually high in these forests, although it is lower than in the terra firme forests of western and central Amazonia.

11) Coastal savannas. There are few palms in this vegetation type composed mainly of grasses and occasional trees. *Mauritiella aculeata* and *Astrocaryum vulgare* occur on sandy soils in the eastern region; *Barcella odora* in northern central Amazonia; and *Astrocaryum vulgare*, *Acrocomia aculeata*, *Bactris campestris* in the coastal savannas of the Guianas (de Granville 1990).

12) Inselbergs. These are prominent steep-sided residual mountains rising abruptly from a plain. A single species, *Syagrus stratincola*, is characteristic of the inselberg flora in the Guianas (de Granville 1990, 1992).

Palm diversity and palm-rich areas in the Amazon Basin

Terra firme forests have a wide range of palm diversity which is clearly poorer in the eastern than in the central and western regions (see Table 6.4). The palm flora of Araracuara region of the Caqueta River (a tributary of the Amazon) in Colombia further demonstrates the very high diversity of palm species in the terra firme forests of western Amazonia, where Galeano (1991) identified 26 genera and 64 species of palms.

As for flooded ecosystems, no striking difference in palm diversity is found in different geographic regions because the palm flora is more homogeneous and less diverse compared to the terra firme forests of central and western Amazonia. This uniformity may be due in part to dispersal patterns in flooded areas (Gottsberger 1978; Goulding 1980), as well as to the spatial continuity within and between these ecosystems.

The diversity of palm species is clearly higher in terra firme forests of central and western Amazonia due to the great number of understory species. Generic diversity in central and eastern forests is not significantly different.

The western forests are clearly richer in genera because of the superimposition of Amazonian and Subandean floras (Kahn and Mejía 1991). Of the 34 Amazonian native genera, 28 occur in the Peruvian Amazon (Kahn

Table 6.3 Species richness of palms in flooded forests of Amazonia*

Habitat	Species	Genera	Area Surveyed (ha)
Seasonal swamp forests:			
French Guiana	11	6	0.24
Lower Tocantins, Brazil	6	6	0.12
Lower Tocantins, Brazil	6	6	0.12
Serra dos Carajas, Brazil	8	8	1
Lower Rio Negro, Brazil	6-7	6-7	0.12
Lower Ucayali, Peru	18	11	1
Upper Huallaga, Peru	15	12	0.8
Upper Huallaga, Peru	15	12	0.8
Permanently flooded swamp forests:			
Lower Ucayali, Peru	11	9	1
Forests on periodically flooded alluvial soils:			
Lower Ucayali, Peru	11	9	0.4
Upper Huallaga, Peru	15	13	0.4
Forests periodically flooded by blackwater:			
Lower Ucayali, Peru	2-5	2	1

* After Kahn and de Granville 1992.

Table 6.4 Number of palms in terra firme forests on clayey soils*									
	Locality and area surveyed (ha)								
	LU (0.71)	LU (0.5)	LRN (0.72)	LT (3.84)	GM (1.26)	LW (0.18)	P1 (0.5)	P2 (0.25)	S (1.5)
Aiphanes	0	1	0	0	0	0	0	0	0
Astrocaryum	1	2	2	1	1	1	2	2	2
Attalea	2	3	1	1	0	0	2	1	1
Bactris	10	4	11	4	3	4	6	5	2
Chamaedorea	0	2	0	0	0	0	0	0	0
Chelyocarpus	1	1	0	0	0	0	0	0	0
Desmoncus	1	1	0	0	0	0	0	0	0
Euterpe	1	1	1	1	0	1	1	1	1
Geonoma	5	8	6	2	3	0	0	2	1
Hyospathe	1	1	0	0	1	0	0	0	0
Iriartea	0	1	0	0	0	0	0	0	0
Iriartella	1	1	1	0	0	0	0	0	0
Lepidocaryum	1	1	0	0	0	0	0	0	0
Oenocarpus	2	2	2	1	1	1	2	2	1
Pholidostachys	1	1	0	0	0	0	0	0	0
Phytelephas	0	1	0	0	0	0	0	0	0
Socratea	1	2	1	1	1	1	1	0	1
Syagrus	0	0	1	1	0	1	0	0	0
Wettinia	1	1	0	0	0	0	0	0	0
Total: Species	29	34	26	12	10	9	14	13	9
Genera	14	18	9	8	6	6	6	6	7

*After Kahn and de Granville 1992.

LU=Western Amazonia, lower Ucayali River valley, near Jenaro Herrera, Peru; **LRN**=Central Amazonia, lower Rio Negro valley, near Manaus, Brazil; **LT**=Eastern Amazonia, lower Tocantins River valley, near Tucuruí, Brazil; **GM**=Galbao mountains, French Guiana; **LW**=Lower Waki River valley, French Guiana; **P1** and **P2**=Piste de Saint Elie, French Guiana; **S**=Surinam

and de Granville 1992). Eleven of these genera are only found in the western part of the basin: *Aiphanes*, *Ammandra*, *Aphandra*, *Chamaedorea*, *Chelyocarpus*, *Dictyocaryum*, *Iriartea*, *Itaya*, *Phytelephas*, *Wendlandiella*, and *Wettinia*. *Iriartella* and *Lepidocaryum* reach the central part, whereas *Barcella* and *Leopoldinia* are only known from the northern central region. The distribution of two other genera, *Asterogyne* and *Raphia*, is restricted to eastern Amazonia.

Palm frequency, density, and response to deforestation

When conserving palms *in situ*, it is very important to know both the frequency and the density of species within an ecosystem, and their response to deforestation. Usually forest species which can grow in open areas will survive massive deforestation, as these species can invade clearings, secondary vegetation and pastures. Tall palms which grow in canopy gaps in terra firme forests, as well as most tall swamp species, can occur in deforested areas. This is also the case for a limited number of understory species, essentially medium-sized palms and palms with a subterranean trunk and large leaves. However most palm species occur in terra firme forests, and many are unable to survive in deforested areas, making deforestation the major threat to palm biodiversity.

Four patterns of spatial occupation can be defined here as the result of frequency and density:

1) **Species which are frequent throughout Amazonia or within an Amazonian region, forming dense stands.**

This includes species where several dozen individuals (including seedlings and juveniles), may be found in 0.25 ha plots. Species in this category include: *Astrocaryum* spp. (*A. jauari*, *A. gynacanthum*, *A. paramaca*, *A. sciophilum*, *A. urostachys*), *Bactris* spp. (*B. concinna*, *B. constanciae*, *B. elegans*, *B. acanthocarpa* including *B. humilis*, *B. maraja*, *B. tomentosa* var. *sphaerocarpa*), *Geonoma* spp. (*G. deversa*, *G. leptospadix*, *G. macrostachys* incl. *G. acaulis*, *G. maxima* incl. *G. spixiana*, *G. poepiggiana*, *G. stricta* incl. *G. pycnostachys*, and *G. piscicauda*), *Wettinia drudei*, *Hyospathe elegans*, *Iriartella setigera*, *I. stenocarpa*, *Pholidostachys synanthera*, and *Syagrus inaja*. Tall species include *Astrocaryum chambira*, *A. jauari*, *Attalea maripa*, *Mauritia flexuosa*, *Oenocarpus bacaba*, *O. bataua* and *Socratea exorrhiza*. However, despite being frequent and forming dense populations, many of the small, understory species are unable to survive in open habitats.

2) **Species which are frequent in Amazonia, but which do not form dense stands.**

Examples are several small species of *Bactris* (*B. acanthocarpoides*, *B. hirta*, *B. killipii*) and *Geonoma*

(*G. oligoclona*, *G. tamandua*, the latter being included in *G. macrostachys* by some authors).

3) Species which are infrequent in Amazonia, but which can form dense stands.

Several understory palms which form dense populations are able to grow in open areas, e.g. *Aphandra natalia*, *Astrocaryum carnosum*, *A. ulei*, *A. huicungo*, and *Elaeis oleifera*. *Astrocaryum huicungo* is only known from the type locality, north of Moyobamba, Peru, a region that is almost completely deforested. However, this palm is surviving well by invading pastures and secondary forests. *Elaeis oleifera* is a dominant species in open areas on waterlogged soils along the Manaus-Caracaraí road, Brazil (between km 330 and 500), as well as eastward along the road to the Jatapu River (Kahn, pers. obs., August 1993); this was certainly not the case twelve years ago when populations of this species were small and scarce according to E. Lleras (pers. comm.), who carried out genetic prospecting of *E. oleifera* along the same roads in 1981.

Unfortunately, adaptability to deforestation is not the case with *Bactris* spp., *Chelyocarpus repens*, *C. ulei*, and *Geonoma* spp., which disappear along with the forest.

4) Species which are infrequent and also occur at low density. Case Study I provides a discussion of species of this type.

Most species for which ecological information is lacking are likely to be those which are infrequent (patterns 3 and 4). Many of the recently described species fall into the third pattern (*Aphandra natalia*, *Asterogyne guianensis*, *Astrocaryum carnosum*, *A. ferrugineum*, *A. scopatum*, *Chelyocarpus repens*). An exception is *Oenocarpus balickii* which presents the second pattern. The fact that none of these new species present the fourth pattern may be due to the very low probability of finding a new species in flower and fruit when their frequency and density is low. However, it is more likely that a dense stand of an infrequent species will be found in flower and fruit, allowing proper description.

Palms as keystone species

A general point is that many palms play key roles in forest ecosystem functioning through leaf and fruit productivity, animal relationships, and providing special components in the forest structure. Therefore, *in situ* conservation must take into account both the plants and their ecosystems. Conserving palms contributes generally to conserving tropical forests and their biodiversity. Because palms are one of the major components of forest ecosystems in Amazonia, palm and forest conservation are inextricably linked.

Palm species which play a key role in forest ecosystem functions usually form dense stands. For example, tall *Mauritia flexuosa* palms form such dense populations that they maintain the organic soils of the swamps by producing a large quantity of organic matter (15 tons/ha/yr, according to Kahn and de Granville 1992). Another tall palm, *Oenocarpus bataua*, occurs on waterlogged sandy soils in dense stands of more than 100 adult palms per ha, plus numerous juveniles and seedlings. Medium-sized palms, such as *Phytelephas macrocarpa* or several species of *Astrocaryum* provide shelter for a highly diversified fauna (Couturier and Kahn 1992; Kahn and de Granville 1992). Although not threatened, these species play a major role in maintaining high diversity in the forest ecosystem. Therefore, species that are not necessarily threatened, but which play a key role in the ecosystem, must be treated with the same level of concern as the threatened species. In Amazonia, as well as elsewhere, palm conservation naturally grades into general forest and biodiversity conservation.

Case study I:
palms of the Peruvian Amazon

A database containing some 3000 herbarium specimens of palms collected in Peru was analyzed to provide information on species identification rates in each genus, species distribution patterns, and palm collecting intensity throughout Peru (Kahn *et al.* 1992). All specimens of Subandean and Amazonian species were listed according to the main river valley where they were collected. The result was a clear identification of those geographic areas where palms had never been collected, or were poorly collected (Moussa *et al.* 1992).

Kahn and Moussa (1994a) analyzed a list of indigenous Peruvian palm species using data on their distribution patterns, ecology, frequency in the country, density in the ecosystems, and conservation status. The list of taxa used in the analysis followed the checklist of Peruvian palms in Brako and Zarucchi (1993). Three conclusions were reached:

1) A total of 100 Amazonian species occur in Peru: 78 are strictly Amazonian palms, 20 extend westward to the Andean piedmont, and two are also frequent in the southern savannas of Bolivia. Ten species occur with very low frequency, i.e. they are known from one or a few populations; whereas 21 are found with low frequency. Of these 31 scarce species, 19 are in low density in the ecosystems. Seven species (7%) are considered threatened. No information is available for nine species. The conservation status and habitat where each Peruvian palm is found, is provided by Kahn and Moussa (1994b).

2) A total of 19 palms are strictly subandean species, and three are strictly Andean-subandean species. Of these 22 species, 12 occur at very low and low frequency. Eight of these 12 species are also found at low densities. The authors considered that five species were threatened

33

(26%), whereas the status of five other species was Unknown. As Henderson *et al.* (1995) consider most of the species in the unknown categories as synonyms of other species, no species lists are given here.

3) Seventy (57%) of the Amazonian and subandean species grow in terra firme forests. Most are understory species which will become threatened as deforestation increases.

The current *in situ* status of Amazonian palms in Peru is not yet alarming because of the lack of roads to provide access to remote areas, and the consequent low human population density. However, under the Amazon Pact, several major highways are being planned to link Brazil, Peru, Venezuela, and Colombia. When these roads are built and colonization, timber harvest, and other activities begin, both the tropical forest and its palms will be under threat.

Case study II: the genus *Astrocaryum* in Amazonia

With 24 described species, *Astrocaryum* is the third most diverse palm genus in Amazonia, after *Geonoma* and *Bactris*. Prior to a revision of the genus for the region by Kahn and Millán (1992), ten species were poorly known. The revision confirmed the identity of those ten species, and described six new species. However Henderson *et al.* (1995) recognize only two of the 16 species of the section *Ayri*, and divided one of them into eight varieties (see Table 6.5 for synonyms). However, following Kahn and Millán (1992), of the 24 species, 21 have now been studied in the field, and inventories made. Two species, *A. ciliatum* and *A. ulei* (Table 6.5), were known *in situ* by other botanists under other names. Only one species, *A. farinosum*, required more information. A single herbarium specimen and photographs corresponding to this species were found, which was only known from the type description by Barbosa Rodrigues who failed to designate

Table 6.5 Case study II: *Astrocaryum* in Amazonia[*]

Taxon	Ecosystems[1]	Frequency[2]	Density[2]	Region
Subgenus Pleiogynanthus				
Astrocaryum acaule	SSW	M	H	Central
A. aculeatum	TF/O	M	H[3].L	Central[3]-East
A. chambira	TF/PFAS/O	M	H	West
A. jauari	R	H	H	throughout
A. vulgare	SS/SAV/O	H	M-H	East
Subgenus *Monogynanthus*				
Section *Munbaca*				
Astrocaryum gynacanthum	TF	H	H	East-Central
A. paramaca	TF	H	H	East
A. rodriguesii	TF	L	M	East
Section *Ayri*				
Astrocaryum sciophilum	TF	H	H	East
A. farinosum	TF	L	H	East
A. sociale	TF	M	H	Central
A. murumuru	SSF	M	H	East
A. chonta	PFAS	M	H	West-Central
A. gratum	PFAS/GF	M	H	West
A. ulei	O	L	M	West
A. ciliatum	TF	L	H	West
A. ferrugineum	TF	L	M	Central
A. huicungo	SSF/O	vL	H	West[4]
A. carnosum	PFAS	vL	H	West[4]
A. scopatum	PFAS	L	H	West
A. javarense	TF	M	H	West
A. macrocalyx	TF	L	H	West
A. perangustatum	TF	vL	H	West[4]
A. urostachys	SSF	H	H	West

[*] After Kahn and Millán 1992; Kahn and Moussa (1994b). Henderson (1995) includes *A. rodriguesii* in *A. paramaca* and recognizes only two species in the section *Ayri*:
  a) *Astrocaryum sciophilum* (including *A. farinosum* and *A. sociale*), and
  b) *Astrocaryum murumuru* (with var. *ciliatum*, var. *ferrugineum*, var. *huicungo* [including *A. carnosum* and *A. scopatum*], var. *javarense*, var. *macrocalyx*, var. *murumuru* [including *A. chonta*, *A. gratum* and *A. ulei*], var. *perangustatum*, and var. *urostachys*.

[1] Ecosystems:
  GF Gallery forests; **PFAS** Periodically flooded forests on alluvial soils (várzea); **R** Riparian forests including forests periodically flooded by blackwater (igapó); **O** Open areas, secondary vegetation, pastures; **SAV** savannas; **SS** sandy soils; **SSF** seasonal swamp forests; **TF** terra firme forests.
[2] Frequency in Amazonia; density in the ecosystems: vL = very low; L = low; M = medium; H = high.
[3] Species probably introduced in central Amazonia, cultivated in Manaus.
[4] Subandean species.

the type specimen. And, because his collections have been lost, the matter could not be resolved without field work. The species was collected in 1993 by Kahn and Moussa in its type locality, and data on its ecology are now known.

This case study demonstrates the need to intensify field research to fully understand the complexities of individual palm genera. Required are not only expeditions to type localities, but also long-term field studies in collaboration with national research centers.

This statement is reinforced by Case Study I, as most of the unknown species in the palm flora of Amazonian and subandean Peru belong to genera which need reassessment (*Bactris*, *Wettinia*, and *Geonoma*).

Discussion

Case Study I on Peruvian palms revealed that 43 of the 122 native Amazonian and subandean species occur with low frequency, and of those, 27 also occur at low density. Twenty of the 43 species grow in terra firme forests, meaning that about 16% of the palm species in the Peruvian Amazon will not survive major deforestation.

Since the forests of Peru contain 32 of the 38 Amazonian genera, and about 68% of all Amazonian palm species (a total of about 180 species for the Amazon basin and Guianas, according to Kahn and de Granville 1992), the results of this case study are very likely representative of the entire Amazonian palm flora.

Palm-rich areas are located in the central and western regions of the Amazon basin. The rate of deforestation in these regions is still very low, except in the Andean piedmont due to coca (*Erythroxylon coca*) cultivation.

One obvious conclusion is that palm conservation in Amazonia must be integrated into broader efforts of tropical forest conservation. The high diversity of Amazonian palms in general is mainly the result of the high diversity of understory palms in terra firme forests, and most of these species will be destroyed with forest clearing.

The *Astrocaryum* case study shows that revisions of genera tend to significantly reduce the number of species classified as Unknown. Such research must be based, however, on a blend of taxonomy and ecology, i.e. on herbarium as well as on field work, including quantitative studies of population structures and analyses of species variability within and between populations. This approach has not yet been widely adopted for tropical plant conservation. More researchers must become involved in long-term field studies on palm biogeography and ecology.

Island species

When compared to the islands of the Indian Ocean, Southeast Asia, or the Pacific Ocean, the islands of the Americas do not exhibit great palm diversity. Nevertheless, it is worthwhile to include a brief treatment of the American palms to achieve a global view of island species, as well as to document conservation measures which are being taken in the region.

Island species are defined here as those occurring exclusively on islands, large or small; those found also in mainland areas are excluded. The discussion is also limited to species known to be globally threatened.

Threatened island species

Table 6.6 lists 23 taxa of threatened island species. *Coccothrinax* and *Copernicia* represent the largest number of taxa; both are large genera with Cuba as a center of species diversity. Many threatened species occurring in restricted areas in Cuba are now considered as synonyms of common species (Henderson *et al.* 1995), but further studies are needed. All other genera, with the exception of *Juania*, have other species in mainland areas. The large Caribbean islands of Cuba, Hispaniola, and Puerto Rico account for 80% of the taxa in Table 6.6. Cuba alone has 11 taxa.

Threatened endemic species confined to one small island are *Brahea edulis* on Guadalupe Island off the Mexican west coast; *Juania australis* in the Juan Fernández Islands west of Chile; and *Sabal bermudana* on Bermuda. Threatened populations of *Aiphanes* on Barbados, Grenada, St. Vincent are now all considered to be conspecific with *Aiphanes minima*.

Discussion

Cuban palms and their *in situ* conservation status are quite well known as a result of studies by Muñiz and Borhidi (1982) and Borhidi and Muñiz (1983). However information is lacking with respect to specific conservation actions that have been taken, apart from the establishment of a national botanic garden reported to include about 40 taxa of native palms (Leiva 1988).

Of all the island areas, Haiti stands out because of the extreme human population pressures on its natural resource base, which is already badly degraded and getting worse. Henderson *et al.* (1990) studied the conservation status of Haitian palms. All but three of the 21–24 species are under some degree of threat in Haiti because of land clearance for agriculture, and cutting of fuelwood. A special conservation effort to prevent *in situ* extinction of *Attalea crassispatha* was undertaken by Henderson and Aubry (1989; see Box 6.1).

As for palms on other small islands, *Brahea edulis* is the only palm found on Guadalupe Island, a designated Special Biosphere Reserve. Aging stands of the palm still exist on this uninhabited island, but no natural regeneration is taking place due to feral goats, which eat all seeds or seedlings. Although critically Endangered in the wild, *B. edulis* is a popular ornamental palm in the south-western United States and in Mexico, and widely cultivated.

Table 6.6 Threatened island palm species of the Americas*

Species	Conservation status	Distribution
Attalea crassispatha	E	Haiti
Brahea edulis	E	Mexico (Guadalupe Island)
Calyptronoma rivalis	V	Dominican Republic, Haiti, Puerto Rico
Coccothrinax borhidiana	E	Cuba
C. crinita ssp. brevicrinis	R	Cuba
C. crinita ssp. crinita	E	Cuba
C. inaguensis (incl. C. victorini)	R	Bahamas, Turks and Caicos, Cuba
C. pauciramosa (incl. C. nipensis)	I	Cuba
Colpothrinax wrightii	V	Cuba
Copernicia berteroana	I	Dominican Republic, Haiti
C. brittonorum	R	Cuba
C. ekmanii	E	Haiti
Gaussia attenuata	E	Puerto Rico
Juania australis	V	Chile (Juan Fernández Is.)
Pseudophoenix ekmanii	E	Dominican Republic
P. lediniana	V	Haiti
P. sargentii	R	Dominican Republic
ssp. saonae var. saonae		Puerto Rico
Roystonea stellata	Ex/E	Cuba
R. violacea	R	Cuba
Sabal bermudana	E	Bermuda
Thrinax rivularis var. rivularis	V	Cuba
T. rivularis var. savannarum	V	Cuba

* Based on data from the threatened plant database, maintained at WCMC.

◄ Royal palms (*Roystonea* sp), Cuba. Two Cuban endemics of this genus are threatened.

Juania australis, a species classified as Vulnerable, resembles palms of other Pacific Ocean Islands in that it is a monotypic and endemic. However, its affinities are with South America, as it is closely related to *Ceroxylon*. This palm occurs only on Más á Tierra of the Juan Fernández Islands. One of the major conservation problems here is the presence of free-ranging cattle and introduced rabbits. The island group has been designated a national park, and the future prognosis for this endemic palm appears favorable. The Chilean Forest Service has a nursery program on Juan Fernández, in collaboration with the Park Service, to propagate all endemic species (see Stuessy *et al.* 1983). However, management to protect this species from introduced animals is still needed.

The island of Bermuda has an endemic and Endangered palm, *Sabal bermudana*, which represents the most remote extent of the natural range of the genus *Sabal*. With stable land use and a strong conservation ethic, the remaining areas of natural vegetation where this palm is found are being protected.

Conservation action

Tropical forests

Palms may represent but a small percentage of the phytomass in the average tropical forest (0.2% of the total, or 0.65 tons/ha, according to Puig *et al.* 1990), but they are key species in terms of ecosystem function. According to the habitat characterization of native Peruvian palms by Kahn and Moussa (1994b), 90% of the species occur in forests. Across the continent in the Brazilian state of Espírito Santo, part of the Atlantic Forest, Fernandes (1993) did a similar study and found that 27 of the 30 native palms (90%) were also forest species. In both studies, a few of the forest species also occur in open habitats (e.g. in Peru about 5%). Nevertheless, it is obvious that tropical forest conservation represents the main solution to conserving palm biodiversity in the Americas.

Therefore, three lines of activities of equal importance are called for: field research, creation and management of protected areas, and education.

Recommendations

Palm research

1) **Study poorly known species in the following forest areas:**
*   **Amazon**
*   **Atlantic Forest of Brazil**
*   **Pacific Coast of Ecuador and Colombia**
*   **Southern Mexico and adjoining Guatemala and Belize.**

Numerous species occurring in these regions are very poorly known. Studies of these virtually unknown species must be carried out following two approaches:

a) taxonomic research to determine if the taxa are valid, by organizing expeditions to re-collect these species and to ascertain their frequency in the region as well as their density within ecosystems;

b) ecological research to provide data on regeneration rates, phenology, reproductive biology, dispersal, and probable response to deforestation.

2) **Promote modern revisions of the poorly understood genera *Attalea, Bactris, Desmoncus,* and *Geonoma.***

A large number of species belonging to these genera have been described. Many species are very poorly known,

sometimes only from a single collection, and many are probably only variations of more common species. Most species of *Geonoma* and *Bactris* are typical understory plants, which do not survive deforestation and hence may be threatened.

Henderson *et al.* (1995) and others have identified several species complexes and tentatively lumped many species, but variability is still poorly understood, and modern revisions are needed in order to assess conservation status, and to provide a strong framework for any conservation action. Studies should include work on morphology, ecology, hybridization, and molecular genetics.

Further genera in need of a modern revision include *Brahea, Thrinax, Thrithrinax*; and, partly, *Butia, Ceroxylon, Syagrus,* and *Wettinia*.

3) **Study the vast, botanically unexplored areas of the Amazon.**

New species remain to be discovered and described. Vast areas of the Amazon have not yet been botanically explored, as shown by Moussa *et al.* (1992) for the Peruvian Amazon. Collecting expeditions must be organized that include study of the palm flora of these regions.

4) **Study sustainable management and domestication techniques of economic palms.**

The many economic palms of the Americas merit additional applied research in order to devise techniques for sustainable management of natural stands, to select superior varieties for improvement and domestication, and to develop new markets for native palm products. The extensive applied research that has been done on *Bactris gasipaes* serves as an excellent model (see Môro 1994; Bovi *et al.* 1994). Besides the utilization of the fruits of this palm (food, oil), its palm heart serves as a substitute for palm hearts of the threatened wild populations of *Euterpe* spp.

Palm hearts being unloaded, Amazonia, Belém, Brazil.

WWF/Mark Edwards

Açaí palms (*Euterpe oleracea*) and a palm thatched hut on the Amazon river, near Belém, Brazil.

Studies like these performed in the framework of the National Program of Research on Genetic Resources (PNPRG) of Brazil should be endorsed and extended. They should focus on the following native palms, which have the highest potential for domestication and economic development, and/or a high need for conservation of their genetic variability in the wild as well as in cultivation (see Valois 1994).

- macaúba (*Acrocomia aculeata*),
- tucuma (*Astrocaryum vulgare*),
- piaçava (*Attalea funifera*),
- babaçu (*Attalea speciosa*) (incl. *Orbignya phalerata*),
- pupunha (*Bactris gasipaes*),
- carnaúba (*Copernicia prunifera*),
- açai (*Euterpe oleracea, E. precatoria*),
- juçara (*Euterpe edulis*),
- patauá, bacaba, bacabi (*Oenocarpus* spp.),
- buriti (*Mauritia flexuosa*),
- licuri (*Syagrus coronata*).

Protected areas

5) Establish a list of candidate reserves with high palm diversity that need protection.

A prioritized list of candidate protected areas that contain palm-rich forests is needed. Such a list would provide guidance to individual countries in their biodiversity conservation efforts. New strategies must be adopted so that such proposals for reserves take into account the needs of local people. One reality that must be faced is that only a few of the most threatened species, or the species most responsible for the high diversity in tropical forests, are economic palms. Concerted effort must be made to convince politicians and the general public that the value of biodiversity goes beyond immediate economic gain.

6) For immediate conservation action, focus on existing reserves that are rich in palms, and on reserves where the palm flora is imperfectly known.

Some reserves in the Brazilian Amazon include forests with very high palm diversity. This is the case of the Ducke Reserve near Manaus, administered by the National Institute for Amazonian Research (INPA). This and similar institutions elsewhere in the Americas could serve as basis for studying and protecting native Amazonian palms and establish respective programs. The same approach could be developed in:

- Allpahuayo Reserve near Iquitos, Peru;
- Araracuara, Tropenbos Research Station in Colombia;
- Humboldt Research Station in Venezuela.

A large number of other protected areas could also benefit from a census and study of their palm flora.

Education

7) Produce and distribute educational materials about biodiversity and forest conservation in general, using palms as flagship species.

Forest-dwelling inhabitants of the American tropics have a strong interest in palms, because they rely on the palm family for so many products. General extension and education materials, in Spanish and Portuguese, could provide educational materials for village teachers. These would provide useful information for less-destructive utilization practices (see Kahn *et al.* 1993), as well as inform the general public about the important role palms play in the forest ecosystems and the need to protect the forest to save palms. Given their key role in Amazonian ecosystems, palms could be designated as a representative plant family for designing educational materials about biodiversity and forest conservation. The cost of such publications is modest, and they could be made available through school, extension, and non-governmental organization networks.

Islands

The situation with respect to the threatened palms on islands in the Americas differs somewhat from that of mainland tropical forest species. Obviously the need for additional field research on taxonomy and ecology exists, but the problem of large and poorly collected geographic areas is not encountered. In addition, botanists have a rough idea of which species occur on which of the islands. However, many areas in the Caribbean have not been properly explored and the conservation status of many palms is not known.

Patterns of dispersal and the geologic history of the region are complex and make biogeographic interpretations difficult. Although natural phenomena such as hurricanes, volcanic activity, and erosion have greatly altered the landscape over time, the long history of colonization and anthropogenic disturbance has had profound effects on the local environment. Many taxa have been driven to extinction in the face of deforestation, habitat conversion to sugar cane plantations and resorts, transport of non-native plants among the islands, and the introduction of a wide range of non-native animals such as rats, goats, and donkeys,. Unfortunately, the continued conversion of land for agricultural and other purposes leaves little room for recovery for many of the species that still survive. *Ex situ* conservation and intensive management must play a greater role on islands.

The current status of threatened island palm species suggests different conservation approaches on the islands in the Americas than elsewhere in the world. Under either approach, the conservation efforts in the Americas can benefit from the lessons learned and promising strategies being developed or implemented elsewhere.

Recommendations

1) A national approach is needed on Cuba with its high palm diversity and a significant number of species under threat.

A national plan for palm conservation is merited, and must be an integral part of a larger effort which embraces all the major plant groups.

2) A collaborative effort between Haiti and the Dominican Republic for the island of Hispaniola also fits this approach.

3) A species approach is probably best on small islands such as Guadeloupe, Trinidad and Tobago, or Puerto Rico.

4) Conservation biological studies are needed for the genera *Coccothrinax* and *Copernicia*.

Both genera comprise many Endangered populations on several small or large islands, of which the taxonomic identity remains unclear.

The genus *Coccothrinax* is widely distributed throughout the Greater and Lesser Antilles as well as Florida and the Yucatán Peninsula of Mexico. Estimates of the number of species in the genus range from a conservative 14 (Henderson *et al.* 1995) to a high of 49 (León, 1939; Muñiz and Borhidi, 1981). A major center of diversity is found on Cuba, where some 36 species have been described. Many taxa are restricted to very specific soil types although some species such as *C. argentata* are rather widespread.

Coccothrinax exemplifies many of the conservation problems for Caribbean plants. The species boundaries are not well defined and there is no modern monograph or phylogenetic study for the genus. The fragmented political and botanical history of the region has resulted in the description of many 'pseudo-endemic' species although the variety of soil and substrate types has undoubtedly generated many truly endemic taxa.

In an effort to address this situation and to examine Caribbean plant conservation in a holistic perspective, we propose a multi-disciplinary analysis to include monographic, systematic, phylogenetic, population genetic, ecological, biogeographic, and ethnobotanic studies of *Coccothrinax*:

a) Extensive field and herbarium work is required to properly understand the taxonomy of the genus and to establish a baseline of information for subsequent studies.

b) Biosystematic and ecological studies will follow in which the individual species and their biologies will be better characterized.

c) Molecular phylogenetic and population genetic studies will allow a better characterization of diversity within and among the species and will permit relatively independent and robust assessment of historical relationships within the genus.

d) A biogeographic study of the genus based on the phylogenetic, biosystematic, and ecological results will form a basis for a more general understanding of Caribbean plant diversification.

e) Finally, ethnobotanic studies will provide insight into the nature of human-induced changes in the biology and distribution of *Coccothrinax* and will help in the development of realistic conservation strategies for the various species.

(Contact: William Hahn)

> **Box 6.1 Haiti's endemic and Endangered carossier palm (*Attalea crassispatha*): a case study of species conservation**
>
> *Attalea crassispatha* is a large, attractive pinnate palm, known only in Haiti's south-western peninsula. It somewhat resembles the African oil palm, and is often confused with it by local people. The palm is of particular interest to botanists due to its unique flower structure and distribution, as all other species of *Attalea* are confined to Central and South America.
>
> A conservation project in the mid-1980s, undertaken to assess the *in situ* status of palms of the Americas, identified *Attalea crassispatha* as one of the rarest palms of the region, and on the brink of extinction in the wild. It was also learned that the species was only in cultivation at Fairchild Tropical Garden, Florida, the result of field collections in Haiti in the early 1940s. Although the trees in Florida have grown to adult size, for some reason flowering has never occurred.
>
> Field excursions in Haiti from the late 1980s located 25 scattered adult and juvenile individuals of this species, and naturally regenerated seedlings at several sites (Timyan and Reep 1994). The palms occur in degraded, hilly areas, most of them near Fond-des-Nègres and Cavaillon.
>
> Three equally important habitats in which this palm grows have been identified: fields, courtyard gardens, and shrub forest. The farmer's field usually consists of mixed annual crops which is converted to pasture after some years. The survival chance of *Attalea crassispatha* is the lowest in this habitat, as pressure is too high for natural regeneration. Secondary shrub forest may provide a suitable habitat, but given the local land pressure, the forest is likely to be harvested for charcoal and then converted to fields. Courtyard gardens provide the best opportunity for the survival of this palm, as it coexists with perennial crops such as coffee, plantains and mangos.
>
> The nut is a rich source of fat and is highly prized as a food and cooking oil. Additionally, the longevity and architecture of any solitary palm makes it a favorite landmark and boundary marker among farmers, although the durable and insect resistant trunk is used occasionally for construction as well
>
> In 1989 and 1991, arrangements were made with landowners to protect the existing trees, and collect the seeds for sale to nurseries. About 1500 seeds were obtained each year and distributed to two nurseries in Haiti, and to various botanical gardens via Fairchild Tropical Garden. More than 100 seedlings were distributed by October 1991, and planted on private property to ensure some type of care and management for an extended period of time. This included courtyard gardens and fields in the Fond-des-Nègres area, urban residential areas, arboreta, and two hospital grounds.
>
> However, efforts must be multiplied if the Carossier palm is ever to realize its full potential as an economically useful palm, thereby ensuring its survival. Much more educational work has to be done, involving schools and non-governmental organizations. The task of coordinating seed collection, propagation, and distribution of seedlings remains the greatest challenge at this time, and efforts to transfer the responsibility to a Haitian institution need to be completed. The survival and growth of the seedlings planted has to be monitored, as has the fate of the naturally regenerated seedlings. Finally, the exploration for new individuals in the area should be continued and protection encouraged.
>
> Two other threatened endemic palms of Haiti, *Copernicia ekmanii* (Endangered), prized for a superior quality of thatch, and *Pseudophoenix lediniana* (Vulnerable), a beautiful palm with tremendous potential as an ornamental, offer similar opportunities of propagation for their economic value.

Specific recommendations for palm conservation in South American countries

The following sections do not represent a complete assessment of the conservation needs of palms for the country, but merely highlight important steps that need to be taken. Also please note that the recommendations outlined above in most instances apply to all countries and have not been repeated in the subsequent sections.

Argentina

Plains with millions of native plants of *Copernicia alba* are a striking feature of the seasonally inundated savannas of the northern provinces. The queen palm, *Syagrus* (=*Arecastrum*) *romanzoffianum*, is one of the most southern palms of the Americas and is common on river banks, but many stands have been destroyed including the most southern stands in Buenos Aires Province where it no longer occurs.

About ten palm species occur in Argentina; one species is endemic to Argentina (*Butia poni* from the Misiones Province, though its taxonomic status is uncertain). Many of the others are widespread and common in adjacent countries. However, *Butia paraguayensis*, a trunkless palm occurring in the Ituzaingó region of the Corrientes Province, *Trithrinax brasiliensis*, *T. schizophylla*, and distinct populations of *Acrocomia* (probably belonging to *A. aculeata*) are considered as Endangered in Argentina (Pingitore 1982).

Recommendation

A new assessment of the conservation status of Argentinian palms is needed and appropriate conservation measures should be developed where necessary.

Bolivia

Native palms in Bolivia include 86 taxa (75 species). Two are endemic: *Syagrus cardenasii* (widespread), and *Parajubaea torallyi*, which forms dense stands where regeneration is ensured by local people. The other species are usually common in Peru as well (Henderson *et al.* 1995). The Bolivian palms extend in range from

40

140–3400 m altitude, and are found in four biogeographic regions (Amazonia, Andes, Cerrado, and Gran Chaco).

Many regions are poorly known botanically, and accurate information on palm biology and utilization is scarce, although at least 35 palm species are used for one or more purposes (construction, food, medicines, oils, etc.). Some species are being damaged from selective harvesting, as people fell palms for timber and palm hearts. Other human activities such as road construction, new settlements, deforestation, and shifting cultivation have a substantial negative impact on the Bolivian palms (Moraes, *in litt.*).

Recommendations

1) Conservation and sustainable use of *Euterpe precatoria* (asaí palm) in north-east Bolivia.

Euterpe precatoria is being depleted due to unsustainable harvesting practices of palm heart in Bolivia, and the situation in parts of Peru and Brazil is even worse. This species is a single-stemmed forest palm; the extraction of palm heart results in the death of the individual. In several forests, most adult plants have been removed, and even juveniles and other lower quality plants are being destroyed for their palm heart. The government is aware of the problem and has funded an Action Plan for Sustainable Use of Bolivian Palms, of which *Euterpe precatoria* is one of the eight species under study (Moraes, in prep.). However, no measures are currently being taken in order to protect this species, and there is still no official government action to stop its destruction.

Recommended actions:
a) Establish a ban on harvest of this species for a trial period of five years in north-north-east Bolivia.
b) Study population dynamics, harvesting, and management techniques which will enable this species to be used sustainably.
c) An agreement with consumer European countries must be made in order to reduce the demand in this Endangered species. France, Germany, and Spain are the main consumers, as the palm heart of this species is considered of the best quality. These consumer countries must be informed of the problem and appropriate measures taken.

Both the Bolivian government and scientific centers (e.g. the National Herbarium of Bolivia) should be responsible for the implementation of these conservation actions.

2) Inventory and assessment of the Yungas forests of Bolivia, an area of high palm diversity in the eastern slopes of the Andes, at an altitude of 250–3000 m.

This area contains some of the highest plant diversity in the Andes. Large areas of montane rain forests are still well preserved in Bolivia, while in other countries they are being destroyed. Few studies have been carried out in this large area, and most of them have been focused on vegetation descriptions as well as on scattered permanent plots. While most of these studies have considered palms as keystone species, what is now needed is a more detailed inventory of palm populations in this area (c. 400 km²). Threats, types of harvest which imperil several palm species, and conservation solutions need to be determined.

This inventory will strengthen the management program for one existing protected area, and will serve as basis for establishing another protected area in the region.

Recommended actions:
a) Study the diversity and ecology of palms in the Yungas mountain rain forests of Bolivia (inventories, stratification, distribution, life forms, relevance as keystone species, etc.),
b) Assess the conservation status of each palm species.

This work will gather valuable information for future assessment in the management and sustainable use of these biogeographically interesting neotropical forests. A team of Bolivian palm specialists that is being formed by the National Herbarium of Bolivia in La Paz, as well as by other research centers such as the Herbarium of Santa Cruz and the Universities of Beni and La Paz, should take part in this major project.

(Contact: M. Moraes)

Brazil

The palm flora of Brazil is very rich, with estimates of the number of species and varieties ranging from 221 (Henderson *et al.* 1995) to 387 (Glassman 1972), represented in 39 genera. Most of the species occur in forests, and only one quarter of the genera contain species which might occur in other vegetation types. While the palm flora of the Amazon has already been described, it is clear that many important studies remain to be done in Brazil as well as in other South American countries.

A major issue which must be underlined again is the sustainable management of economic palms, in order to maintain the diversity of genetic resources and to develop their immense economic value.

In addition to the Amazon, many regions in Brazil suffer from habitat destruction and human pressure. This includes semi-arid caatinga vegetation, which covers most of the north-eastern part of Brazil. A few palm species of the genus *Syagrus* grow under these conditions. *Syagrus coronata* is widespread, but increasingly threatened and suffering severe genetic erosion.

The forests of the Atlantic coast (restinga, rain forests, seasonal forests) are among the most severely affected habitats in the world. Due to habitat destruction over a long period only small remnants are left. Many understory palms have therefore only small and extremely vulnerable populations which deserve protection. Even if the Atlantic forest is in general poorly known in respect to palms, and no published number is available, up to 100 species are thought to occur in this region (Fernandes 1994). More research about the palm flora and the specific threats to the palms is needed in order to design and implement urgently needed management plans.

In addition to these general recommendations, two projects from the North-east of Brazil are recommended here.

Recommendations

1) *Ex situ* conservation and reintroduction of threatened understory palms of the Atlantic forest.

According to Medeiros-Costa (*in litt.*), the following palms in Pernambuco have very small and susceptible populations: *Bactris dardanoi* Medeiros-costa sp. nov. ined.; *Bactris hirta*, *Euterpe* aff. *catinga* (possibly a new species); *Geonoma pauciflora* (all occurring in Saltinho, Rio Formoso); and *Geonoma blanchetiana* (possibly a subspecies of *G. pohliana*), which occurs in Brejo dos Cavalos, Caruaru, and Brejo da Madre de Deus. Artificial propagation and reintroductions are recommended to reinforce the natural populations.

Research:
a) Check the present status of the population of each species;
b) study flowering and fruiting phenology and seed production;
c) study natural regeneration.

Ex situ conservation:
d) Propagate plants for reintroduction and distribution as ornamentals;
e) introduce these palms in the Botanical Garden of Recife.

The studies required could be conducted at the biological reserve station of IBAMA in Saltinho and at the ecological station of municipal prefecture of Caruara-PMC for the populations in Brejo dos Cavalos.

2) A major project on *Syagrus coronata*, including ecological and biological studies to allow sustainable management of this species in the cattle-breeding areas is needed.

This palm is extremely useful, mainly as a source of food for both human and animal populations. During droughts "this palm has saved the lives of many caatinga inhabitants" (Noblick 1991). The young plants germinating during the rainy season are excellent food for animals and this species is now heavily overgrazed; in the extensive cattle-breeding

Dennis Johnson

Syagrus pseudococos, an endemic palm of the Atlantic Forest, in habitat, Espíritu Santo state, Brazil. Endangered.

areas, *S. coronata* populations have become senescent, lacking any replacement by young plants.

(Contact: J. T. Medeiros-Costa)

Colombia

The native palm flora of Colombia consists of at least 227 palm taxa, and is one of the richest in the Americas. Twenty-seven species are endemic, many of them belonging to the Andean genera *Aiphanes*, *Wettinia*, and *Ceroxylon*, of which five are localized and Endangered.

Many species occur over a wide range in undisturbed areas (Pacific lowlands, Llanos, Amazon) or regenerate in open areas and are therefore not threatened. However, Colombia has the highest concentration of Endangered species in the Americas, and deserves special attention. Table 6.7 shows the 15 globally Endangered species that occur in Colombia. These data are based on Bernal (1989) and Henderson *et al.* (1995).

Seven of the Endangered species are endemic to a small area at the northern end of the Central Cordillera in Antioquia and the adjacent parts of the Río

Magdalena and Río Cauca valleys, where forest has mostly been or is currently being destroyed. The construction of a highway between Bogotá and Medellín has led to further deforestation in this area (affecting the population of *Geonoma chlamydostachys*). The region is far away from any National Park and there seems to be no protection for any of the palms concerned. The understory species of *Wettinia*, *Geonoma*, and *Aiphanes* are unable to regenerate in open areas, and the two endemic species of *Aiphanes* in particular may become Extinct very soon.

The Pacific lowlands of Colombia constitute another area which is very rich in palm species. Here many Central American species and genera reach the southern limit of their range, and due to high rainfall, several Andean species also occur. Twelve palms are endemic to the lowland forests. Two species, *Attalea colenda* and *Phytelephas tumacana*, are Endangered in the Departamento de Nariño, near the Ecuadorean border, as oil palm plantations increasingly replace their habitat. However, *Attalea colenda* is itself a valuable oil palm, and *Phytelephas tumacana* was formerly exploited as a source of vegetable ivory. Both palms deserve special attention as natural resources.

The lowland forests of the northern plains are also rapidly being destroyed as the area is a center of agricultural development. Four understory species are Endangered, all occurring in Panama or even further north, but they are Endangered throughout their range.

Table 6.7 Globally Endangered palms occurring in Colombia

Name	Distribution	Comments	R[1]	P[2]
Lowland palms				
Attalea colenda	Nariño; Ecuador	replaced by oil palm plantations	y	n
Chamaedorea amabilis	Chocó; Costa Rica	very few localities, highly sought by collectors	n	?
C. sullivaniorum	Chocó, Antioquia; Costa Rica, Panama	only two collections in Colombia	n	?
Cryosophila kalbreyeri	Northern plains; Panama	widespread, but most known localities deforested now	n	?
Phytelephas tumacana	Nariño		y	n
Reinhardtia koschnyana	Urabá (Antioquia); Costa Rica, Panama, Nicaragua	severe deforestation	n	?
Andean palms				
Aiphanes leiostachys	Central Cordillera (Antioquia)	very restricted, severe deforestation	n	n
A. parvifolia	Central Cordillera (Antioquia)	known from two collections, severe deforestation		
Attalea amygdalina (incl. *A. victoriana*)	Río Cauca basin (Antioquia, Valle)	very scarce, severe deforestation and agricultural development, cultivated in gardens	y	n
Ceroxylon alpinum ssp. *alpinum*	upper Río Cauco and Magdalena valleys, Venezuela	most surviving populations in coffee plantations	y	y
C. sasaimae	Eastern Cordillera (Cundinamarca)	a single population known growing in a coffee plantation	y	n
Geonoma chlamydostachys	middle Río Magdalena valley (Antioquia)	restricted, severe deforestation	n	n
Phytelephas schottii	Río Magdalena and Catatumbo valleys	has disappeared from most of its former range	y	?
Wettinia fascicularis	Central Cordillera (Antioquia)	few localities, in remnant forest patches, and semi-open land, although not regenerating there	n	n
W. microcarpa	Eastern Cordillera (Norte de Santander)	two localities, in remnant forest patches	n	y

[1] R - regenerating in open areas (y: yes, n: no)
[2] P - protected in National Parks or other protected areas (y: yes, n: no, ?: uncertain)

Remaining wax palms (*Ceroxylon quindiense*), on pastures in Alto Quindio Valley, Colombia. Vulnerable.

Finally, the Amazon region of Colombia is also very rich, with over 60 species found along the Río Caquetá in the Araracuara region (Galeano 1991) and three endemic species found further north (Henderson *et al.* 1995).

Recommendations

1) The forests of the Pacific coast are poorly known and are in need of further research.

2) Conservation measures for the many Endangered palms are crucial and should be developed in combination with other conservation and sustainable use projects.

3) Efforts to build up a national palm collection at the Botanical Garden in Tuluá for *ex situ* conservation and research should be supported.

(Contact: G. Galeano)

Ecuador

About 126 palms are known from Ecuador. Seven of the nine endemic species are Andean palms with restricted distribution, but locally common. They belong to genera which are particularly diverse in Ecuador and Colombia (*Aiphanes, Ceroxylon, Geonoma, Wettinia*). However, the stilt root palm, *Wettinia minima*, from the eastern slopes, and *Aiphanes verrucosa* from very high elevations in the south, are known only from a few localities. *Geonoma tenuissima*, a small understory plant of lowland forests of the Pacific coast is very scarce and probably Endangered. The 'palma real', *Attalea colenda*, which also occurs in Colombia, is commercially exploited as an oil palm. It now persists only in disturbed and cleared areas of former coastal lowland forests in Ecuador and southern Colombia. Much more information on conservation of Ecuadorian palms will soon be available after the completion of the palm treatment for the Flora of Ecuador (Barfod, pers. comm).

Recommendation

Protect palms known to be under threat and eventually assess the status of the remainder of Ecuador's palm flora.

French Guiana, Guyana, Surinam

About 60 to 70 native palms are known in each of the Guianas, with a considerable shift of species composition from east to west (de Granville, in press). Compared to other tropical countries, primary forest ecosystems are fairly intact in the region, although the deforestation rate is increasing rapidly. Palm utilization is only of local importance, and no species is known to be threatened by over-exploitation. In particular there is no palm heart industry in French Guiana, although *Euterpe oleracea* is exploited occasionally.

Some palms are very rare and endemic to French Guiana, but not threatened at present: *Asterogyne guianensis, Geonoma oldemannii, G. umbraculiformis, Syagrus stratincola* from inselbergs, and two species of *Scheelea*, as yet unpublished (*S. guianensis, S. maripensis*). However, there are species at risk.

Recommendations

1) **Assess the conservation status and cultivate the following Endangered palms:**

a) *Bactris nancibensis* sp. nov. ined. is only known from two individuals, one of which has been transplanted in the ORSTOM botanic garden, and another growing near the road near Cayenne.

b) *Bactris schaefferiana* sp. nov. ined. is known from an inhabited area near Petit Saut dam, where a few individuals have been counted growing along a small stream.

2) **Assess the conservation status of possibly threatened species.**

Scheelea degranvillei sp. nov. ined. (two collections near Cayenne) and *Bactris* sp. (cf. *capinensis*, growing on the

WWF/Luc Deslarzes

highway project Regina – St. Georges) need further research.

3) Conduct taxonomic and ecological studies of uncertain species:

a) Populations of the Oil palm *Elaeis oleifera* are found at the lower Mana River and near Kourou. As the palms in French Guiana differ from those growing in the Amazon basin, they are of special interest for any breeding programs of this economically very important oil palm.

b) *Bactris* cf. *penicillata* from marsh forest at the base of Kaw mountain, *Geonoma fusca* from "Montagne des trois Pitons" (which might be conspecific with *G. aspidiifolia*), and two species of *Geonoma* (still undescribed), one found in lower Oyapock basin and on St. Elie track, another growing on hill tops in the Tumuc-Humac range, require further study.

(Contact: J.-J. de Granville)

Meso-America

Meso-America here comprises Belize, Guatemala, Honduras, El Salvador, Nicaragua, Costa Rica, and Panama; Mexico is listed separately. This region has a rich and distinctive palm flora, which is in need of further study. Two-thirds of the 130 palms endemic to this region are considered to be threatened. *Reinhardtia koschnyana*, one of the smallest American palms and unable to regenerate in disturbed forest, is Endangered throughout its range. Most species of *Cryosophila* are very restricted, and two are considered Endangered. Many species of *Chamaedorea* are known to be Endangered; they are restricted to very small areas under threat, and/or are highly sought by palm collectors (see Chapter 4).

Other species are threatened due to the alarming rate of deforestation and habitat destruction, perhaps greater than in any other region in the world. Most of the forests of the Pacific coast as well as those on accessible mountain slopes in Meso-America have been converted to agriculture. Some large blocks of lowland forest still remain on the wetter Atlantic coast (in Belize, Honduras, Nicaragua, and Panama), but in general these lowland forests are very fragmented (Henderson *et al.* 1995).

Mexico

About 86 palms in 21 genera are known from Mexico, and 33% are endemic. Ten species are globally Endangered. *Chamaedorea* is by far the largest genus of the country, containing 41 species, of which nine are Endangered due to over-collecting and deforestation of cloud forests. *Brahea*

is another typical Mexican genus, which includes fan palms of dryer areas. The Endangered *B. edulis* is restricted to the island of Guadeloupe, where regeneration has stopped due to introduced goats. Other palms are severely threatened by over-exploitation (see recommendations below).

Recommendations

1) Design projects for a sustainable management of ornamental *Chamaedorea* palms, encouraging local cottage industry nurseries.

Effort should be concentrated on the more endangered species such as *C. tuerckheimii*, *C. metallica*, *C. klotzschiana*, and *Reinhardtia gracilis* (see Box 4.1, and Vovides and Bielma 1994).

2) Study poorly known and threatened forests.

All cloud and rain forests of southern Mexico should be inventoried, especially the Soconusco range, Triunfo, Montes Azules reserves and Lacandona forest of Chiapas, the Sierra del Madrigal and adjacent areas of Tabasco, and the Los Tuxtla range of Veracruz.

To maintain the biodiversity of these forests, protected areas need to be established, and forested land purchased for conservation. Collecting germplasm for *ex situ* conservation and propagation in botanic gardens and nurseries is also needed.

Participating bodies should include the Instituto de Ecologia, Universidad Veracruzana (Instituto de Investigaciones Biologicas) in Veracruz, and the Centro de Investigaciones del Sureste (CIES, now called Colegio de la Frontera Sur), and the Instituto de Historia Natural in Tuxtla Gutierrez in Chiapas.

3) Promote sustainable utilization of *Pseudophoenix sargentii*, *Coccothrinax argentata*, and *Thrinax radiata*.

Adult individuals of *Pseudophoenix sargentii* are increasingly collected as ornamentals, as horticulturists do not propagate this palm due to its slow growth. The natural populations (in Mexico restricted to a few coastal areas of the Yucatán Peninsula) are becoming more and more depleted (Quero 1992; Durán 1995).

Populations of *Coccothrinax argentata* and *Thrinax radiata* are decreasing due to direct exploitation and habitat destruction. The trunks are used for building rustic houses, fences and lobster traps, plus much of their natural habitat (coastal forests of the Yucatán Peninsula) has been cleared in order to open new lands for tourist development. These palms are widespread in the Caribbean, but the situation in other countries is probably similar (Quero 1992).

(Contact: A. Vovides)

45

Paraguay

About 20 palms are native to Paraguay (Hahn 1990). Many of them are widespread and common, and seem to hold up to disturbance reasonably well. However, two of the three endemic palms are threatened, and *Euterpe edulis* is threatened by palm heart extraction. Overall generic monographs are either available for all of these taxa or are in progress, but considerable biosystematic and phylogenetic work is still needed to gain a better understanding of the biology, relationships, and ecology of these species (Hahn, *in litt.*).

Recommendations

1) Conduct a survey to rediscover *Butia* (=*Syagrus*) *campicola*.

Butia campicola is a conspicuous endemic palm of the grasslands of Alto Parana which has not been collected since the beginning of the century.

2) Cultivate the rare endemic palms *Attalea guaranitica* and *Syagrus campylospatha* and protect them, if possible, in the wild.

Attalea guarantica is known from very few locations, and is one of the rarest palms of Paraguay, although Henderson *et al.* (1995) believe this palm may be an isolated population of *A. geraensis* which is more widespread in Brazil. However, whatever its taxonomic status, this palm requires conservation measures.

Syagrus campylospatha is not protected at all, although it survives fire and grazing fairly well.

3) Develop specific plans for protection of *Euterpe edulis*, which is heavily exploited for palm hearts and is sensitive to disturbance.

4) Cultivate the following palms and monitor their status in protected areas more closely:

None of the following palms are common, but all cover a reasonably wide range, and occur in one or more protected areas: *Trithrinax schizophylla*, *Bactris glaucescens*, *Syagrus petraea*, *Acrocomia hassleri*, and *Geonoma brevispatha*.

5) Survey the northern regions of the country (especially Alto Paraguay) for other species.

(Contact: W. Hahn)

Peru

About 140 palms representing 34 genera occur in Peru (Kahn and Moussa 1994a), or 128 taxa according to Henderson *et al.* (1995). Human pressure is very high in the Andean and Subandean areas. Social disorder in the highlands has caused people to migrate to the eastern Andes, and montane cloud forests have been intensively cut as a result. Many people also have been attracted by coca cultivation on the piedmont, where many areas have been deforested. Sixteen of the 20 Andean species (occurring above 1500 m) are threatened, the most threatened populations belonging to the genus *Ceroxylon*. Most of the 100 or so Subandean/Amazonian species are not threatened, but many occur at low frequency (see also Case Study I above). Threats will increase rapidly as new roads are built, in the Amazon as well as in the Andean region.

Venezuela

Approximately 106 palms are known to occur naturally in Venezuela, occupying a wide range of habitats (Henderson *et al.* 1995). The conservation status of most of them is unknown. A recent reassessment has shown that some species now have a higher degree of threat than recorded by Dransfield *et al.* (1988) (Stauffer and Garcia, *in litt.*).

Recommendations

1) Set up an urgent conservation plan and taxonomic-ecological studies for the following palms which will be threatened by human exploitation or environment changes caused by deforestation in the next 2 years:

Asterogyne yaracuyense, *Ceroxylon alpinum* ssp. *alpinum*, *Euterpe oleracea*, *Syagrus sancona*, *Aiphanes orinocensis* (possibly to be included in *A. aculeata*), *Bactris bergantina* (incl. in *B. setulosa*), *B. venezuelensis* (incl. in *B. corosilla*), and *Euterpe karsteniana* (incl. in *E. precatoria* var. *longevaginata*).

Asterogyne yaracuyense, recently described by Steyermark and Henderson, has a very restricted range and seeds should be collected and brought into cultivation (Nehlin, *in litt.*).

Euterpe karsteniana from the island of Margarita (considered as a synonym of *E. precatoria* var. *longevaginata* by Henderson *et al.* 1995) is severely exploited for the palm heart business, and even the stands in the Parque Nacional de El Copey are exploited, as palm hearts of this species can be sold for a better price than these of cultivated plants.

2) The following palms need an intensive taxonomic-ecological survey in their native zones. Many of them will probably suffer massive damage by forest fires or felling in less than 10 years:

Asterogyne spicata, *A. ramosa*, *Attalea butyracea*, *Bactris ptariana*, *Ceroxylon ceriferum*, *C. interruptum*, *Desmoncus polyacanthos*, *Geonoma appuniana*, *G. densa*, *G. paraguanensis*, *Mauritia carana*, *Oenocarpus bataua*, *Prestoea acuminata*, *P. pubigera*, *P. tenuiramosa*, and *Bactris granatensis*. Other populations are facing the same fate, but are presently considered to be synonyms of more widespread species (*Attalea macrocarpa, Bactris piritu, Euterpe aurantiaca, E. erubescens, E. montis-duida, E. ptariana, Prestoea steyermarkii,* and *Hyospathe pittieri*).

3) **The following areas should receive special attention in research projects.**

Even though many of these areas are within National Parks, conservation studies are not guaranteed. Up to date, ecological studies are needed for Venezuelan protected as well as for non-protected areas. The following regions are under major threat and need study:

a) *Venezuelan Andes:* the 'sub-paramos' and cloud forests of the Merida, Tachira, and Trujillo States are the native locations of the poorly studied genus *Ceroxylon*, 1–2 species of *Wettinia* (incl. *Catoblastus*), and at least 10–15 species of Geonomeae, of which the taxonomy is unclear. Highland crops and cattle are displacing the natural Andean forest.

b) *Coastal range:* the deciduous and semideciduous forests are rapidly being cut and burned. Several palms growing here are very poorly known, including *Bactris* and *Desmoncus*. In the cloud forest several species of *Asterogyne* and *Geonoma* have not been observed for 80 years.

c) *Venezuelan lowlands:* 2–3 species of the *Mauritia -Mauritiella* complex, and a few species of *Bactris*, need urgent taxonomic and conservation research.

d) *Orinoco Delta:* the *Euterpe-Prestoea* complex is strongly threatened by the palm heart business, and no Venezuelan research institutions have undertaken ecological studies on these species: *Prestoea pubigera* and *Euterpe precatoria* in particular need an urgent field inventory. Large populations of *Manicaria* also need to be studied.

4) **Produce a complete guide to the palms of Venezuela, incorporating studies on taxonomy, ecology, and conservation status.**

The Fundación Instituto Botanico de Venezuela, and the Centro Nacional de Conservación de Recursos Fitogeneticos, both part of the Venezuelan Ministry of the Environment, could carry out this important work. However, additional funding is needed.

(Contact: M. L. Garcia, F. W. Stauffer, S. Nehlin)

Chapter 7

Regional Priorities in Asia

A considerable amount of study has already been done on palm conservation and utilization in Asia during the WWF Project 3325, 1987–1990 (see Johnson 1991a). This project focused on four countries: India, Indonesia, Malaysia, and the Philippines, with direct participation of local palm specialists. The sections dealing with these countries in the present Action Plan are mainly based on this project, and many of its recommendations are repeated here. However, for more detailed information and background, especially about the wide range of palm utilization and its implication for conservation as well as for local economies, the reader should refer to Johnson (1991a).

Palms in Asia

As in other regions of the world, palms occur in all habitats, but the majority are confined to undisturbed forests. For palms, Asia may be divided into three major biogeographical regions: Continental Asia, the Sundashelf, and Australasia.

Continental Asia. The arid zones of Arabia and West Asia support only a few species, which all belong to the coryphoid subfamily (*Phoenix, Hyphaene*) and are mostly widespread. *Nannorrhops* is a monotypic genus endemic to this area; the palm is widely used and in some regions threatened by over-exploitation. However, the conservation status of all West Asian palms is virtually unknown.

The palm flora of South Asia is much more diverse. *Loxococcus* and *Bentinckia* are endemic to Sri Lanka and India respectively, and threatened. *Maxburretia, Guihaia,* and *Rhapis* are coryphoid genera confined to limestone outcrops in Indochina and China, *Kerriodoxa* is only known from two localities in Thailand, and *Chuniophoenix* is another coryphoid genus with two Endangered species from Hainan island (China), one endemic and another also occurring in Vietnam. Most of the other threatened species, however, belong to more widespread tropical Asian genera. Continental Asia as defined here also covers the Andaman and Nicobar islands, and the islands in the East China sea.

Sundashelf and the Philippines. Many palm genera have their center of diversity in the perhumid forests of the Sundashelf (Peninsular Malaysia, Borneo, Java, and Sumatra), including many rattans. The species diversity in general is very rich, with a high level of endemism on every island. For a significant part of this diversity to be maintained, large forested areas need to be conserved on every large island throughout the region.

Australasia. Australasia (Sulawesi, Moluccas, New Guinea, Australia, and Pacific islands) has a palm flora very different to the rest of Asia. While the palms of Australia and the South-West Pacific islands are well studied (see Chapter 11), knowledge of taxonomic species limitations, distribution, and conservation status is extremely poor in the western part of this region, and not even the rattans most commonly in trade are known by their scientific name.

A group of larger genera like *Areca, Arenga, Calamus, Caryota, Cyrtostachys, Licuala, Livistona, Oncosperma, Orania, Pinanga,* and *Sommieria*, as well as some useful and very widespread species like *Cocos nucifera, Nypa fruticans, Metroxylon sagu,* and *Borassus flabellifer,* occur throughout Asia.

Rattans

Rattans are by far the most economically important native palms; conservative estimates of the total value of world trade being as high as US$ 2.5 billion per year (Dransfield *et al.* 1989). Rattans are also very diverse, with more than 500 species described, although only a minor number are commercially important at present. In most regions rattans account for about one half of the palm species. Many populations of the most useful rattan species are now severely depleted due to over-exploitation; therefore, the management of rattans is one of the major tasks for palm conservation and utilization in Asia.

An impressive number of major publications on rattan have appeared recently. For example, a general guide to rattan cultivation has been published (Wan Razali *et al.* 1992), as has a summary of information on the most important Old World rattan species (Dransfield and Manokaran 1993). Rattan management and utilization was the subject of a conference and proceedings (Chand Basha and Bhat 1993). Country-level publications consist of a study of the rattan cottage industry in Sri Lanka and rattan in general (de Zoysa and Vivekanandan 1988,1991,1994), and an assessment of prospects for rattan cultivation in the South Pacific (Tan 1992). Systematic treatments have appeared on Bangladesh (Alam 1990), India (Basu 1992), the Western Ghats of India (Renuka 1992) and Sarawak (Dransfield 1992). Earlier works cover Peninsular Malaysia (Dransfield

1979) and Sabah (Dransfield 1984a). The *Flora of China* volume on palms also makes a major contribution to rattan systematics (Pei *et al.* 1991).

As the successor to the more informal IDRC (International Development Research Centre), the International Network for Bamboo and Rattan (INBAR) represents a new international effort to promote and coordinate development of bamboos and rattan. With headquarters in New Delhi, INBAR is initiating and developing targeted research on bamboo and rattan production and utilization. INBAR is a significant initiative that will benefit utilization and conservation of commercial rattan species.

Many other institutions in virtually all countries conduct important research on rattan (e.g. the Forest Research Institute of Malaysia, FRIM).

Four strategies for rattan conservation should be taken (Dransfield 1995):

1) Develop sustainable harvesting of wild rattan stands.

Nearly all rattan canes are collected from the wild at present. However, most populations are heavily over-exploited and cannot supply the markets to a sufficient extent. Due to the high demand, rattan are increasingly being collected even in protected areas. Millions of people benefit from collection of wild rattan and from the first steps of cane processing. If large scale cultivation is to become more important, these people must be involved (see Box 7.1). Inventories and studies of population structure, growth rates and regeneration are needed to estimate the

Domingo Madulid

Rattan collectors with small-diameter canes from the forest in the Philippines.

Box 7.1 Rattan collecting and Orang Asli

In Peninsular Malaysia rattan is collected almost entirely from the wild by Orang Asli (aboriginal people). As natural stocks of rattan are being depleted, silviculture of rotan manau (*Calamus manan*) and rotan sega (*C. caesius*), both elite commercial species, is being given increasing emphasis to ensure a continued supply.

One disadvantage of supplying rattan from cultivated sources is that it does not benefit the majority of Orang Asli who do not own land on which to plant rattan. Orang Asli in general, provided they have permanent access to adjacent forest, could be encouraged to plant rattan. One suggestion would be to plant rattans in water catchment areas as an environmentally-preferable alternative to logging. This would enable forests in catchment areas to yield economic returns, and at the same time to provide employment opportunities for Orang Asli. An Orang Asli group in Johore already harvests rotan sega on a sustained basis from the forest, taking only a few mature stems from each plant at regular intervals. Regular harvesting of this type encourages growth of the less mature stems.

Malaysia has been farsighted in setting up a multi-agency research program which covers most of the production and marketing aspects of the rattan business. The major aspect that is not receiving adequate attention is the long-term role of Orang Asli. The development of rattan plantations, the rattan processing business, and the expanding export furniture trade does not include a niche for them. Unless they can continue in their traditional and pivotal role as rattan collectors, their standard of living may suffer. The situation could be improved if Orang Asli could be encouraged to venture into the value-added side of the business by curing rattans and making rattan articles so that they receive a better price for the rattan they collect. In some areas, Orang Asli are contracted on a limited and irregular basis to make baskets for various purposes. They could also easily venture into making mats from whole pieces of rotan sega, for which there is local and overseas demand. At present demand exceeds supply for indigenous artifacts, such as fish traps and woven items, but this does not produce a regular income because of marketing problems. It would not be difficult to expand the existing system of marketing of craft items to include those made by Orang Asli.

In conclusion, a combination of silvicultural plantings sustainably managed by Orang Asli, increased value added to raw canes by curing, and more reliable markets for rattan artifacts would benefit the Orang Asli, the commercial rattan market, and the conservation of wild species.

available harvestable rattan crop in a given area of forest, and to set up sustainable management plans for harvesting.

2) Develop profitable schemes of cultivation by smallholders.

Rattan can be grown under existing plantations of tree crops, as demonstrated in villages in Kalimantan for the past 100 years. Low development costs, flexibility, lower susceptibility of the landowners to fluctuations in rattan trade (as other crops are being produced), and benefit to many rural people are obvious advantages of this approach. Today most large scale silvicultural plantation experiments are based on the experience and knowledge of traditional smallholder cultivators.

3) Develop large scale rattan plantations under native forest.

Rattan cultivation and harvesting can be carried out with minimum disturbance to forest cover, and the presence of planted rattan within native forest provides a strong disincentive for forest clearance. Even if the preparation of planting lines causes some local damage, by maintaining tree cover, rattan plantations can harbor a remarkable diversity of native plants and animals.

4) Explore and maintain the diversity of rattan.

The maintenance of the diversity of rattan is of crucial significance to the further development of rattan as a plantation crop. Surveys of the exact distribution of all species and of their commercial importance and potential for further economic development should be carried out, with the main aim to broaden the base of species in cultivation at present. Indochina, the eastern parts of Indonesia, and Papua New Guinea are especially in need of surveys.

Asian palms with economic development potential

Apart from rattans, *Areca catechu* (betel palm), *Arenga pinnata* (sugar palm), *Borassus flabellifer* (lontar palm),

Nipa palms (*Nypa fruticans*) on banks of a swampy river, Asmat, Irian Jaya, Indonesia.

WWF/Ron Petocz

Dennis Johnson

Fruits of the salak palm (*Salacca zalacca*) being sold in Bogor, Indonesia. World conservation status of Not threatened.

Caryota spp. (fishtail palms), *Corypha* spp. (talipot palms), *Eleiodoxa conferta* and *Salacca* spp. (salak palms), *Metroxylon sagu* (sago palm), *Nypa fruticans* (nipa palm), *Oncosperma* spp. (nibong palms), and *Phoenix sylvestris* (Sugar date palm) are currently important economic palms with potential for further development.

Research is continuing on individual palms in this group: a small book was produced in Indonesian on the 18 so-called varieties of *Salacca zalacca* (Tim Penulis 1992); proceedings of the fourth international sago symposium were published (Ng *et al.* 1991); a fifth sago symposium was held in January 1994 in Thailand and proceedings published (Subhadrabandhu and Sdodee 1995); and a revision of the genus *Arenga* has been completed by Johanis Mogea of Indonesia.

The socioeconomic potential of these native palms should be brought to the attention of international and bilateral development agencies. An applied research project to further the management and/or cultivation of economic palm species in Asia should also be promoted.

The parallel developments in many countries strengthen justification for a regional research project on Asian economic palms other than rattans. CIFOR (Center for International Forestry Research), the new international research center founded in 1992 (headquarters in Bogor, Indonesia) is a good candidate agency to undertake such an effort, since palms are appropriate to two of their four research programs: Management and Conservation of Natural Forests, and Reforestation of Degraded Lands.

In situ palm conservation

The conservation status of the threatened palms, recommended for conservation action as a result of WWF Project 3325, has scarcely improved in the past years, and the same threats continue to impact palm populations. Over 50 species are classified as Endangered in the four countries studied.

However, local spin-off publications from Project 3325 have publicized the need for palm conservation. An entire issue of the *Malayan Naturalist* (1989, Vol. 43, Nos.1–2), for example, was devoted to conservation and utilization of Malaysian palms. It was based on data from Project 3325. In addition, a beautifully-illustrated, full-color booklet for school children on palms, written in Bahasa Malaysia and English editions, has been published by the Malayan Nature Society (Kiew 1993). Two Endangered palms of Malaysia, *Johannesteijsmannia lanceolata* and *Pinanga acaulis*, have recently been refound and their populations are now being monitored.

Much more information about the extremely precarious status of the most threatened palms and their habitats should be brought to the attention of politicians, governments, research institutions, aid and development agencies, as well as to the general public.

Additional data on *in situ* status of palms need to be collected as part of any field research project. Conservation projects should urgently be developed, where possible in cooperation with other projects, and the involvement of local people is essential.

Research

Table 7.1 shows the conservation status of palms in Asia. Note that the knowledge of palms is very unevenly distributed. For example in Laos and Kampuchea not even basic species lists are available, and virtually nothing is known about the conservation status of palms in countries like Myanmar, China, large areas of Indonesia, and Papua New Guinea.

The upcoming taxonomic treatments of palms for the *Flora of Thailand*, the *Flora of Ceylon*, and especially

Table 7.1 Conservation status of palms in Asian regions*

Region	Total no. of species	World Conservation Status[1] E	E/V	V	I	R	K	?	Nt	References
Continental Asia										
Yemen	7	1	.	.	.	.	.	6	.	
Iran	2	.	.	.	.	.	.	2	.	
Afghanistan	1	.	.	.	.	.	.	1	.	
Pakistan	3	.	.	.	1	.	.	2	.	
India	92	1	.	12	.	11	.	68	.	Basu (1991)
Sri Lanka	17	8	.	3	.	.	.	.	6	Johnson (1992)
Bangladesh	18	.	.	2	7	.	.	9	.	Alam (1990), MansurAzim (1989)
Bhutan	20	.	.	4	.	1	.	14	1	
Nepal	11	.	.	.	.	.	.	11	.	
China	82	2	.	11	.	.	.	69	.	Wang and Yang (in prep.)
Taiwan	6	.	.	.	.	1	.	3	2	
Japan	8	.	1	.	.	2	.	3	2	
Myanmar	62	.	.	.	.	.	.	38	24	
Vietnam	69	.	.	6	3	22	12	19	7	Loc (1992), Thin (1991)
Laos	10	.	.	.	1	3	.	6	.	
Kampuchea	12	.	.	.	.	4	.	8	.	
Thailand	98	2	3	.	2	3	.	79	9	Anon. (1991), Thin (1991)
Peninsular Malaysia	211	26	49	90	1	17	.	17	11	Kiew (1991)
Sundashelf										
Sabah	163	5	.	3	1	7	.	134	13	Dransfield and Johnson (1991)
Sarawak	250	27	.	60	3	34	72	36	18	Pearce (1991)
Brunei	119	.	.	1	.	1	.	116	1	
Kalimantan	121	.	.	1	2	16	.	94	8	Mogea (1991)
Sumatra	153	3	1	6	2	18	.	100	23	"
Java	47	5	.	8	2	4	.	17	11	"
Lesser Sunda Islands	4	.	.	.	.	.	.	3	1	"
East Timor	1	.	.	.	.	.	.	1	.	"
Philippines	172	.	.	.	4	63	3	.	102	
Australasia (part)										
Sulawesi	48	1	.	1	.	7	.	32	7	
Moluccas	45	1	.	2	.	1	.	37	4	
Irian Jaya	126	.	.	.	.	1	.	121	4	
Papua New Guinea	193	.	.	.	2	3	.	176	12	
South Solomon Island	44	.	.	1	1	18	2	15	7	Johnson (1992)

* Based on data from the Threatened Plant Database, maintained at the World Conservation Monitoring Centre, as of October 1995.
[1] See Appendix 1 for World Conservation Status definitions.

for the *Flora Malesiana* will significantly improve the situation. A new study of palms under cultivation in India has also been published (Basu and Chakraverty 1995).

Specific recommendations for Asian countries

Pakistan

Only three palms are native to Pakistan and all are of some economic importance (*Phoenix loureirii, P. sylvestris,* and *Nannorhops ritchiana*). *Nannorhops ritchiana,* the Mazari palm, is heavily over-exploited, as the leaves are used for producing ropes and basketry. Harvesting is strictly prohibited during the growing season, and it is also prohibited to remove the young lead shoot (Kohat Mazri Control Act from 1953, see Mughal 1992). However, Gibbons and Spanner (1995) reported that in many regions entire populations have been wiped out. Most plants are reduced to just one or two leaves by repeated and indiscriminate cutting. As a result, they never set seed and the vitality of the plants is reduced.

India

Although the palm flora of India is not very rich in comparison to South-east Asian countries (92 species representing 21 genera), the traditional utilization of palms is diverse, ancient, and well documented in early writings. At least half of the species are utilized to various degrees (Basu 1991). Some palms are over-exploited, and others are threatened by deforestation and fragmentation of their natural habitat. Twenty of the 30 endemic species are threatened. Again rattans are of particular conservation concern, and several other specific conservation measures are needed for different regions.

Recommendations

1) **Rattans: promote the domestication and cultivation of the most promising large-diameter canes.**

About eight large-diameter rattan species are under intense pressure in the wild, largely due to commercial over-exploitation. The Indian Forest Department has imposed some restrictions on exploiting wild rattans, and has lengthened the legal harvesting cycle to allow better natural regeneration. However, these efforts will not produce long-term results because the demand for raw rattan encourages unscrupulous forest contractors to exploit immature plants, thus degrading or destroying the resource base.

Research and field trials are called for in several ecological regions to develop species suitable for cultivation in different locations.

Peninsular India

The coconut (*Cocos nucifera*) and the arecanut (*Areca catechu*) are cultivated as commercial crops. The sugar date (*Phoenix sylvestris*) and the palmyra (*Borassus flabellifer*) are semi-domesticated palms. Their main product is sweet sap, which is very important for local economies. Many other parts of the palms are widely used. Several populations of palmyra are being depleted at an alarming rate due to over-collecting of foliage or stems for timber and fuel. Wild palms are especially diverse in the forests of the western Ghats.

Recommendations

2) **Monitor threatened palms occurring in the wet forests of the western Ghats.**

Bentinckia condapanna is a relict and very restricted in its range (see Matthew 1991). This palm is endangered by deforestation and by elephants feeding on its young leaves.

Pinanga dicksonii is suffering from deforestation. Populations of *Arenga wightii, Caryota urens,* and several rattans (*Calamus* spp.) are decreasing due to over-exploitation.

3) **Monitor *Hyphaene dichotoma* and undertake measures to facilitate natural regeneration.**

This palm occurs on the west coast of India, where the natural habitat is under intense human pressure.

Eastern and north-eastern India

The evergreen submontane, semi-evergreen, and moist deciduous forests harbor a wide variety of palms as well as many orchids, ferns, aroids, and bamboo. Several palms are utilized, including the now Vulnerable rattan *Calamus inermis.*

Recommendations

4) **Reintroduce *Corypha taliera*, Extinct in the Wild.**

Corypha taliera is a giant hapaxanthic palm (dying after flowering once). It is the most endangered palm of India and formerly occurred in West Bengal (Birbhum district). The last known wild individual was felled in the 1980s by villagers in the mistaken belief that it was an abnormal palmyra palm (*Borassus flabellifer*), and hence demonic. The species is now probably Extinct in the Wild. A reintroduction effort combined with an education and awareness program on conservation is recommended so that villagers appreciate (and protect) such rarities.

5) **Monitor threatened and rare palms.**

Five of six species of *Pinanga* are endemic to India. They grow exclusively in the understory of moist forests, and all are therefore threatened to a varying degree. *Phoenix rupicola* is restricted to a small range and its natural habitat is highly disturbed.

6) Cultivate and study *Trachycarpus takil* and *Wallichia* spp.

Trachycarpus takil, a cooler-climate palm of the Himalayas, is rare and should be brought into cultivation and promoted as an ornamental palm. *Wallichia* spp. are monocarpic palms, growing in the forest; they are sensitive to exposure and need protection by the forest canopy. Their conservation status is not known. None of the four species is cultivated, and one is endemic to India (*W. triandra*).

Nicobar and Andaman islands

Wild palms are one of the most important components of the luxuriant and species rich tropical rain forest of the Andaman and Nicobar Islands. Twelve of the 26 palms are endemic. Although all of them are listed only as Rare or Vulnerable in Basu (1991); Mathew and Abraham (1994) consider most of them more threatened, but did not employ IUCN conservation categories. A high rate of deforestation on many islands and catastrophic events such as storms or volcanic eruptions are threats to these palms, which often have a very restricted distribution.

Recommendation

7) **Check the conservation status of the following Rare and Endangered palms:**

a) *Bentinckia nicobarica* is not known from recent collections and is on the verge of extinction.

b) *Calamus dilaceratus* and *Corypha macropoda*, both from the Andaman Islands, are known from their type collection only.

c) *Korthalsia rogersii* and *Pinanga andamanensis* are known from one location only.

d) *Calamus pseudo-rivalis*, *C. unifarius* var. *pentong*, *Daemonorops kurzianus*, *D. manii*, and *Pinanga manii*, known from both the Andaman and Nicobar islands, have recently only been collected on the South Andaman Islands.

e) *Rophaloblaste augusta*, the single species of a monotypic genus, is Rare and endemic to the Nicobar Islands.

(Contact: S. Abraham, S. K. Basu, S. P. Mathew)

Sri Lanka

Sri Lanka presents a promising example of how to deal with deforestation and human population pressures, dilemmas typical of island species conservation. An island with an area of 65,610 km², linked to the Indian mainland by a chain of shoals and small islands, Sri Lanka has a small but rich flora with a high proportion of endemic species. According to a recent review of natural resources of the country, natural forest cover is estimated at 27% of the land area with an annual rate of loss of 40,000 ha (Baldwin 1991). Sri Lanka has a human population of 17.8 million which is increasing at an annual rate of 2.1%. Nevertheless, the country is one of the few in the world with over 10% of its land under strict protection.

About 2900 species of flowering plants occur in Sri Lanka, and 830 (29%) are endemic (Gunatilleke and Gunatilleke 1990). Over a century ago Trimen (1885) recognized the high endemism of the Sri Lankan flora and its concentration in the wet south-western part of the country. The high species richness and endemicity is attributed to the dissected topography and high rainfall that prevail in the south-west, combined with geographical isolation.

Palms in Sri Lanka

The native palm flora of Sri Lanka comprises seven genera and 17 species (see Table 7.2). One genus (*Loxococcus*) and 11 species are found only on the island, giving an endemism rate of 65%. Note the field study recently completed for the revision of the palm family for the *Flora of Ceylon* (Read 1969; de Zoysa, in prep.). In addition, at least four widely cultivated or naturalized species such as coconut (*Cocos nucifera*), arecanut (*Areca catechu*), palmyra (*Borassus flabellifer*), and talipot (*Corypha umbraculifera*) are significant locally in rural areas and in the country's economy. Several other species such as the African oil palm (*Elaeis guineensis*) and date palm (*Phoenix dactylifera*) have been introduced during the last century. The country's major botanic gardens in Peradeniya, established in 1822, houses one of the world's finest palm collections.

Habitats. Most Sri Lankan palms belong broadly to either open or forest habitats. The first type includes communities dominated by palms in open swamp forest (*Areca concinna*, *Calamus rotang*, and *C. rivalis*), estuaries (*Nypa fruticans*), and exposed rocky ridge tops (*Oncosperma fasciculatum*). The second type are found in the forest understory and in association with gaps and disturbance (*Caryota urens*, *Calamus zeylanicus*, *C. ovoideus*, *C. digitatus*, *C. radiatus*, *C. pseudotenuis and C. thwaitesii*). Except for *Nypa fruticans*, which has very specialized habitat requirements, most other palm species have overlapping ranges.

Little quantitative information is available on palms in studies of woody species, mainly because surveys usually measure individual trees over 30 cm girth at breast height (gbh). *Caryota urens* is the only Sri Lankan palm which falls into this category. Unpublished information cited in Ratnayake *et al.* (1991) found that only two individual *Caryota* palms above 30 cm gbh were among 29,500 individuals in 44 ha at seven separate sites studied by Gunatilleke and Gunatilleke (1991).

A comparative study of natural forest and areas disturbed by mechanized logging and shifting cultivation was done by de Zoysa *et al.* (undated, 1986, 1988, 1989). The four palm species recorded in these studies (*Calamus zeylanicus, C. ovoideus, C. digitatus,* and *Caryota urens*) were represented in the natural forest understory as juveniles, but in the logged areas, where a mosaic of large and small gaps exist, they grew into adults. However, no palms on logging trails and in shifting cultivation sites were observed. Field observations and information from villagers indicate that many of these palm species grow at the edges of larger clearings or in small gaps. Additionally, two rattan species (*Calamus ovoideus* and *C. zeylanicus*) under trial cultivation in *Pinus caribaea* plantations where diffuse light is plentiful, have shown impressive growth rates. By the sixth year the rattans had reached 6–8 m in length and had begun producing sucker shoots (de Zoysa and Vivekanandan 1994). The infrequent occurrence of many palm species in natural forest, and their abundance in disturbed sites, shows that minor disturbance favors palm growth. However, major disturbance such as logging trails and forest clearance for shifting cultivation obviously is harmful.

Conservation status. There are only a few comprehensive studies on the endangered, endemic and lesser-known palms. The present assessment, based on seven years of field observations and analysis, concludes that in Sri Lanka eight species of palm are Endangered, and that three more species are Vulnerable (Table 7.2). This is not

surprising considering: 1) palms are restricted to localized areas within an already small wet south-western zone, 2) natural areas are highly fragmented, and 3) even the non-endemic species are often restricted to South India and Sri Lanka.

Ashton and Gunatilleke (1987) list four species of palms (*Calamus delicatulus, C. digitatus, C. pachystemonus,* and *C. radiatus*) among 94 threatened plant species mostly restricted to the lowland zone of Southern Sinharaja-Hiniduma-Kanneliya. All the other threatened palms (except *Nypa fruticans*) are also found in this region and at least five species appear to be centered there.

Although the increase in the number of palm species classified as threatened in recent years is cause for concern, this may partly reflect greater knowledge regarding their distribution and ecology. Ashton and Gunatilleke (1987) point out that very few species (and no palms) have become extinct since their initial documentation by Thwaites (1864) and Moon (1824) despite massive deforestation in the south-west over the past century, although this is no cause for complacency.

Ex situ **conservation.** Endemic palm species are poorly represented in the country's botanic garden collections. The Royal Botanic Gardens in Peradeniya has a single individual of *Loxococcus rupicola* of seed-bearing maturity in cultivation, some not threatened species such as *Caryota urens* and *Calamus thwaitesii*, and recently a single individual of *Calamus ovoideus* was introduced. Peradeniya's palm collection is greatly in need of a reliable census and senile individuals, with no provenance, need to be replaced. However, the garden does contain several seed-bearing individuals of species almost Extinct in the Wild (S.K. Basu, pers. comm.) which should be used for propagation and research.

Utilization. The history of palm utilization is as ancient in Sri Lanka as in other parts of Asia. Documents such as Watt's "Dictionary of Economic Products" (1883–1889) list the multitude of ways in which palms have been utilized, although this information is limited largely to a few well-known palms such as the palmyra, talipot, coconut, areca nut, *Caryota urens*, and rattans such as *Calamus thwaitesii* and *C. rotang*. The only mention of an endemic palm in Watt's dictionary is that of *Areca concinna*. However, the utility value of Sri Lankan endemic palms is usually included in the original taxonomic descriptions by Thwaites (1864), Beccari and Hooker (1892), and Trimen (1898).

Recent developments have included more scientific approaches to the study of economically important palms. For instance, a research institution focuses exclusively on the coconut palm in Sri Lanka, and a promotional and marketing board has been established for palmyra palm products. Studies of the ecology,

Species	Distribution[1]				Status
	1	2	3	4	
Areca concinna *	.	.	x	.	E
Calamus delicatulus *	.	.	x	.	E
C. digitatus *	.	.	x	x	V
C. ovoideus *	.	.	x	x	E
C. pachystemonus *	.	.	x	.	E
C. pseudotenuis	.	.	x	x	nt
C. radiatus *	.	.	x	.	E
C. rivalis *	.	x	x	.	V
C. rotang	x	.	.	.	nt
C. thwaitesii	.	x	x	.	nt
C. zeylanicus *	.	.	x	.	E
Caryota urens	.	.	x	x	nt
Loxococcus rupicola *	.	.	x	.	E
Nypa fruticans	Estuaries				E[2]
Oncosperma fasciculatum *	.	.	x	.	V
Phoenix farinifera	x	.	.	.	nt
P. zeylanica *	Coastal				nt

Table 7.2 Conservation status of Sri Lankan palms

* Endemic to Sri Lanka.
[1] Distribution in Sri Lanka: **1** dry lowlands, **2** intermediate lowlands, **3** wet lowlands, **4** (wet) middle elevations.
[2] Sri Lanka represents the western-most extent of the natural range of *Nypa fruticans*. Its world conservation status is not threatened. For the other 16 species in this table, the world conservation status is the same as the status indicated for Sri Lanka.

cultivation, and economics of the *Caryota* palm have assessed the potential of this species for wider commercialization (de Zoysa 1992; Ratnayake *et al.* 1991; Everett, unpublished).

The ecology and cultivation of the ten native rattan species, and the socioeconomics of the associated industry, have been studied by de Zoysa and Vivekanandan (1988, 1991, 1994). An ongoing study of agroforestry systems and forest underplantings is examining several large diameter rattan species such as *Calamus ovoideus* and *C. zeylanicus* (Gamage *et. al.*, unpublished).

Conservation Actions

Sri Lanka has made considerable progress towards conserving both natural areas and species. Outlined below are accomplishments to date, and a summary of further action recommended for palm species.

Recent plant conservation measures in Sri Lanka began in earnest in the 1970s when the forests of the south-west were assessed for their timber potential for plywood. When logging began in Sinharaja, a forest of legendary importance, a public outcry pressured the government to ban timber harvesting. Since then, Sinharaja has become synonymous with evolving national conservation policies. Declared a UNESCO Man and Biosphere (MAB) reserve in 1978, new legislation (the National Heritage Wilderness Act) was formulated for strict protection of this area by the Forest Department. Sinharaja had been on the proposed World Heritage Site list since 1986, and with this national commitment it was declared a World Heritage Site in 1990.

The National Heritage Wilderness Act marked an important point in the conservation of the biologically diverse forests of the south-west and central mountains. This region has only 9% of its land under forest cover and currently 1% is under strict protection. At the present time, all logging in this wet south-western zone has been suspended, and a comprehensive conservation review is under way to identify a minimum protected area network (Green 1992). The Knuckles Forest, Peak Wilderness, and thirteen other areas have been selected for strict conservation. The first conservation management plan was drawn up for Sinharaja in 1985. At present similar plans are being finalized for Knuckles Forest, and the same process has begun for the other recently identified areas.

Ecological research studies in Sinharaja began in 1978, soon after logging was suspended, and they have spearheaded research efforts over the last decade or so (Gunatilleke *et al.* 1993). Initially these studies focused on the structure and floristics of the forest, which provided a powerful justification for strict conservation of Sinharaja itself. Subsequent research has been conducted on fauna, soil microbiology, modified forest structure and floristics, reproductive biology of economically

important plant species, silviculture, ethnobotany, and socioeconomics.

While biological research has laid a strong foundation, more recent sociological research has been oriented toward policy and management (Gunatilleke *et al.* 1993). Many of the plant research studies cited above have used permanent plots designed for long-term study and monitoring. The review to identify a minimum-sized protected area network has used rapid assessment methods suited for the survey of large areas. Many species earlier thought to be extinct have been rediscovered in the course of this survey, e.g. *Calamus pachystemonus* (Jayasuriya, pers. comm.)

What are the implications of such research activities for the conservation of threatened palm species? Clearly, effective palm conservation cannot be achieved in isolation. Rather, any strategy adopted should invest in conserving natural areas within which palm species can be studied. A broad policy and management framework has been established in Sri Lanka, and the process is ongoing. A systematic field sampling of flora and fauna to assess levels of biodiversity and conservation value is also in place. Studies focusing on palms include a taxonomic and resource survey of rattans, as well as fieldwork on the Palmae for the revised *Flora of Ceylon* (de Zoysa, forthcoming). Although these two studies provide a strong foundation, they do not provide sufficient detailed quantitative information for a complete palm conservation Action Plan, defining priorities for action.

General plant conservation recommendations

A general framework for plant conservation action in Sri Lanka, which would directly benefit palms, can be separated into *in situ* and *ex situ* activities.

In situ conservation:
a) research on biology and social sciences,
b) policy and legislation formulation,
c) management planning and implementation,
d) training and institution building.

Ex situ conservation:
a) cultivation in botanic gardens, especially Peradeniya;
b) creation of genebanks;
c) promotion of native palms as ornamentals.

Seven specific points for the study of individual threatened palm species — not all of which have been discussed — and some broader activities, are summarized as follows.

1) Conduct a survey of palm populations.

Survey and assess all native palms, with a particular focus on threatened species, using a rapid survey technique to compile a resource map and to ensure that the best representative populations have been included in the currently recommended minimum protected area network. Potential threats within each site must also be documented.

2) Study population biology.

Carry out censuses of individual palm species and record demographic details in selected populations inside and outside of protected areas.

3) Study reproductive biology.

Conduct research on reproductive biology, including phenology, pollinators, effective population size, seed and seedling physiology, storage, and germination.

4) Investigate economically important palms.

For economically important groups (such as rattans), investigate effective plantation technologies. Essential projects should include social science research to assess the importance of economic plants to forest dwelling and craft communities, and policy research to enhance the value of these undervalued forest products and provide incentives for sustainable harvesting.

5) Protect *Nypa* under coastal legislation.

For palms in specialized habitats such as *Nypa,* a framework should be sought for designating new protected areas under coastal conservation legislation.

6) Assess effectiveness of protected areas.

Assess current protected area legislation for effectiveness, noting how well it is enforced, and whether strict laws without due respect to traditional harvesting rights lead to illegal and destructive harvesting.

7) *Ex situ* conservation.

Systematically bring all native palm species into cultivation in the botanic gardens Peradeniya and Gampaha. All

---

Box 7.2 Profile of an Endangered island species: *Loxococcus rupicola* (Thwaites) Wendl. and Drude, the dotalu palm of Sri Lanka

Status: Endangered. This monotypic and endemic palm is known from a few populations in low and middle elevation (< 600 m) rain forests. The total number of populations and individuals is unknown. It is unclear if existing populations represent the total range of habitats of the species or if they are relict populations confined to inaccessible sites.

Distribution: Ratnapura and Galle Districts. It grows in the Sinharaja World Heritage Site and adjacent forests, and other small remnant forests in the south-western part of the country.

Habitat and ecology: Gregarious, found in small populations on rocky outcrops. One of the best known populations is at the summit of Sinhagala (742 m), in the Sinharaja WHS, where they usually occur on rocky ridge tops, in shady cool environments near streams. Rarely found in valleys. Usually occurs together with *Oncosperma fasciculatum* Thwaites, which occupies drier, more exposed micro-habitats in the same site. Flowers in December and fruits mature in April.

Threats: The species is at risk from alteration of microclimate, especially moisture and temperature, and because it is collected by local people for its edible palm heart. Currently seedlings raised from wild-collected seed are sold to plant collectors, which could pose a threat if not controlled.

Conservation measures: No specific conservation measures are known to have been taken. This species is cultivated as an ornamental which could be a threat as well as a conservation measure. There are indirect benefits from the recent series of conservation measures at the national level.

Vimukthi Weeratunga

Loxococcus rupicola, an endemic, monotypic palm, in habitat, Sinharaja, Sri Lanka. Endangered.

Conservation measures proposed: Reconnaissance surveys are recommended to map all the sites where the species exists, and record the number of individuals, demography, and possible threats at each site. At least the basics of reproductive ecology should be studied, to learn how best to conserve wild populations as well as to cultivate this species. New genetic material needs to be brought into botanic gardens and a program to popularize it as an ornamental should be developed with proper safeguards.

Biology and potential value: Seeds are used for masticating with betel leaves, comparable to *Areca* species. Palm hearts are eaten by local people as a delicacy. It is increasing in popularity as an ornamental, with its elegant habit, dark leaf sheath edged with pale orange and rachis of the same color, bright vermillion flowers and reddish-brown ripe fruits.

Cultivation: A single mature individual of about 80 years old is growing in the Peradeniya Botanic Gardens. There are also a few young plants, but these have not yet begun to bear seed. Although a small market exists among collectors and it is occasionally cultivated in village home gardens, there are no records of where individuals of this species have been planted and what their survival rate has been.

existing and projected collections need to be carefully documented.

(Contact: N. de Zoysa)

Bangladesh, Bhutan, Laos, Myanmar, Kampuchea, Vietnam, Thailand

Each of these countries has significant palm populations needing research. Investigations of conservation and utilization of palms in these countries should be promoted. The rattan trade is becoming increasingly important and other palms are becoming threatened by deforestation, tourist activities, and over-exploitation. Much information has been gathered during the preparation of the palm treatment of the Flora of Thailand (Barfod, pers. comm.), but is not yet published or available at the time of writing this Action Plan.

China

About 90 palm species of 16 genera are known from China. Half of the species are rattans. A comprehensive palm treatment is published as part of the *Flora of China* (Pei *et al.* 1991). Written in Chinese, it contains good line drawings, plant names, and citations in English, making it somewhat accessible to non-Chinese readers. The first volume of the Red Data Book for Chinese plants has been published in English (Fu 1992). A significantly increased Red List (Wang and Yang, in prep.) includes thirteen palms. Two of them are classified as Endangered: *Chuniophoenix hainanensis* and *C. nana*, both from Hainan island. Of the eleven Vulnerable palms, *Trachycarpus nana*, *Plectocomia himalayana*, and *Licuala dasyantha* are endemic, while most of the others are quite widespread in other tropical countries. In China, however, they are under severe threat mainly from habitat destruction, and the existing nature reserves are in need of effective management. No information is available about the status of rattan exploitation in this country.

Recommendation

Protect *Chuniophoenix* spp. on Hainan island.

Chuniophoenix hainanensis is endemic to Hainan island and highly endangered by over-exploitation; its durable stems are much sought after for the manufacture of arts and crafts. The palm occurs in a nature reserve, but control of cutting and effective management measures urgently need to be adopted in order to rescue this small and beautiful forest palm. In addition, propagation trials should be undertaken in order to expand plantations of this species.

Table 7.3 Threatened palms in the Philippines[*]

Taxon	Status	Location
a) Palms threatened by over-collection		
Areca ipot	V	Luzon
Calamus caesius	I	Palawan
C. discolor var. *discolor*	I	Luzon
C. merrillii	V	widespread
Pinanga geonomiformis	I	Quezon
Pinanga maculata	I	Palawan
b) Palms mainly threatened by deforestation		
Daemonorops curranii	I	Palawan
D. gracilis	I	Palawan
D. virescens	I	Palawan
Phoenix hanceana var. *philippensis*	V	Batanes
Salacca clemensiana	I	Davao, Zamboanga
c) Palms known from one or a few localities		
Areca costulata	I	-
Caryota rumphiana var. *oxyodonta*	I	Laguna
Heterospathe elmeri	I	Negros, Camiguin
Veitchia merrillii	I	Palawan

[*] Palms which have not been seen for 50 years (but which still may be extant) are not included in this list.

Philippines

The known Philippine palm flora presently consists of 157 species, of which 109 are endemic. Forest destruction and degradation in the Philippines is worse in comparison to other Asian countries. High population density, logging and shifting cultivation has led to the decrease in the forest cover in all regions, and only nine of the nation's 73 provinces have a forest cover of more than 40% remaining.

According to Madulid (1991), 49 of the 70 threatened palms have not been collected for 50 years. They are often known from only one or a few localities, and in some cases these areas have been logged. It is therefore quite possible that at least some of these species have already become extinct. Fifteen other species are threatened either by habitat destruction, over-collecting or because of their extreme rarity (Table 7.3).

Palm utilization, and the rattan business, is as important as in other Asian countries and faces the same threats (see below).

Recommendations

1) Produce a manual of Philippine rattans for foresters and other users.

Foreign exchange earnings of the rattan furniture industry reached US$76.2 million in 1987. Demand for rattan canes has been increasing rapidly in recent years for both domestic and international markets. However, the natural supply of rattan is being diminished due to over-collecting and forest clearing or degradation. Even rattan furniture makers supplying the domestic market are having to turn to imported raw materials from elsewhere in South-east Asia. Rattans comprise nearly half the entire known Philippine palm flora, but they have yet to be fully inventoried taxonomically. The systematic complexity of rattan creates confusion for foresters, collectors, traders, and manufacturers, and hinders regulation of rattan collecting as well as wider utilization of lesser-known species.

Recommended action: Domingo Madulid and Edwino Fernando have prepared a research proposal to complete a Manual of Philippine Rattan. Funding is urgently needed to get this project done in two to three years.

2) Study taxonomy, ecology, and biology of Philippine rattans and other palms.

While taxonomic studies on rattan palms are presently being conducted by D.A. Madulid and E.S. Fernando for the Flora of the Philippines, other groups are in urgent need of taxonomic as well as ecological study. These include Philippine *Pinanga*, *Oncosperma*, and *Arenga*.

3) Study artificial propagation of rattan and other palms.

Present projects include technology and marketing studies at the Forest Products Research and Development Institute, tissue culture at the U.P. Institute of Plant Breeding, and seed/gene banks at the University of the Philippines at Los Baños (UPLB). The genebank continues to expand with the addition of specimens from other localities.

Further action is needed in the field of propagation and cultivation of economic palms and research on application of palm products. Several genebanks/seedbanks should be established in various parts of the country.

4) Study biology, ecology, and sustainable harvest of under-utilized but economically important Philippine palms.

Buri (*Corypha elata*), kaong (*Arenga pinnata*), betel (*Arecha catechu*), sago (*Metroxylon sagu*), and nipa (*Nypa fruticans*) palms are predominantly wild sources of raw materials for economic products on domestic and international markets. Continued existence and future expansion of these palm-based industries hinge on reliable supplies of raw materials of high quality.

Government and international development agencies should provide support to encourage further studies to develop the potential of these useful palms. Of particular concern is that such development be carried out within the broader context, i.e. taking into account the potential for outright domestication, design of palm-based agroforestry systems, and management of wild stands. Given the many parallels that exist in the development of individual palm

species, it is highly desirable that research programs establish close contacts and share information on successes and failures.

5) Conduct additional fieldwork on rare and threatened Philippine palms.

More information is urgently needed on the 63 species classified as Indeterminate. Additional field work on threatened palms should be promoted and supported in order to identify the most endangered species and appropriate conservation actions.

6) Raise a public information campaign on the value of palms and their conservation.

Those who dwell in the tropics know how valuable palms are, especially to the rural poor. But because many of the palm products are not commercialized, in the strict sense, their importance is unappreciated in developing countries. As a result, the palm family has not been afforded development attention commensurate with its true potential and worth. Only a handful of people are aware of the magnitude of economic products and biological diversity which would be lost if native palm populations are reduced to scattered individuals, or if some species become extinct.

Efforts must be made to disseminate information as widely as possible on the value of palms, by means of meetings, symposia, and publication of books and articles in scientific, technical, and general periodicals. Slide shows or videos would be very useful in reaching students of various levels, as well as teachers, conservationists, politicians, and decision-makers at all levels of government.

(Contact: D. Madulid)

Malaysia

Peninsular Malaysia

The palm flora of Peninsular Malaysia is fairly well known. A wealth of detailed information on all topics can be found in Kiew (1991). The Peninsular has a very diverse palm flora and contains 194 species represented in 31 genera. Forty-two percent of the palms are endemic, including the rattan *Calospatha* (monotypic), and threatened species of *Maxburretia* which are confined to limestone outcrops. A recent revision of the conservation status (Kiew 1991) showed that 20 palms are Endangered, 53 likely to become Endangered, and 111 otherwise threatened.

Conservation. The most important protected areas for palm conservation are the Taman Negara National Park and the Endau-Rompin State Forest Park. They protect about half the palm flora (99 species), of which one is

Forest interior, Taman Negara, Malaysia with *Licuala*, *Daemonorops* and *Nenga*.

Endangered and 13 Vulnerable and likely to become Endangered. However, clear-felling of forests surrounding these protected areas will no doubt lead to increased rattan collecting within the reserves. Penang Hill and Ulu Trengganu are other areas of high palm diversity in need of protection.

Even if many Malayan palms are cultivated in botanical gardens or research stations, these include only a few of the threatened and endemic species. The genepool of commercial palms (rattans, salac) in cultivation is not yet adequate to select elite strains.

Utilization. Palm utilization comprises modern plantations of African oil palm and coconut, as well as introduced species with commercial value such as betelnut, sugar, sago, and salac palms. Indigenous commercial palms include *Cyrtostachys renda* (ornamental), *Nypa fruticans* (for thatch, cigarette papers and many other uses), *Oncosperma tigillarum* (for trunks), *Eleiodoxa conferta* and *Salacca affinis* (both for salac fruits), and commercial rattans. However, the commercial value of many palm products has decreased in the last decades. Palms used for subsistence include species of *Arenga, Eugeissonia, Johannesteijsmannia, Licuala*, and *Oncosperma* used for thatch, food wraps, fruit or palms hearts; and small-diameter rattans collected by the Orang Asli for cordage, basketry, fish traps, and a wide range of miscellaneous uses.

Rattans. Commercial rattans are the most important non-timber forest products. Even if rattan is a minor product compared with timber, harvesting and processing is labour intensive and a major source of income for thousands of local people. Raw rattan harvested in the forest is processed by curers in small-scale manufacturing. This includes cleaning, sun-drying and boiling in oil for large-diameter canes, sorting according to diameter and quality, different ways of smoothing, cleaning and bleaching, and further processing like splitting or coring. The majority of rattan furniture makers are backyard family firms and only a few larger companies exist. These are currently unable to work to capacity because of insufficient supply of rotan manau, the premium rattan species. Rattan cultivation is still experimental. At the present stage cultivation in rubber plantations or logged forests is important for selecting potential cultivars. However, rattan cultivation will not benefit the majority of the thousands of rattan collectors if these are not involved in the process.

Recommendations:

1) **Commercial rattans. In order to maintain rattan as a long-term resource and promote a sustainable rattan business, the following actions are recommended:**

a) Maintain the export tax on rotan manau;
b) Review the export tax on other rattans;
c) Adopt government policies to provide incentives to local entrepreneurs and to encourage utilization of a wider range of rattans in the furniture industry;
d) Conduct research to ascertain available rattan stocks;
e) Encourage rattan curers to also process canes, and furniture manufacturers to form co-operatives and expand markets;

59

f) Adopt government policies to acknowledge and promote the role of Orang Asli (see Box 7.1).

2) Commercial cultivation of salac palm fruits (*Eleiodoxa conferta*, *Salacca affinis*).

Conduct a survey of wild populations during the fruiting season, and collect seed of superior plants for establishment at a research facility as a permanent living germplasm collection.

3) Study the potential of collecting wild palm seeds for ornamental purposes.

Conduct field surveys to establish population levels, followed by phenological studies, to determine fruiting cycles and seed production rates. Such studies are necessary to determine if continuous seed collection is a sustainable activity, i.e. that natural populations will not be unduly affected in the long term. If populations cannot sustain continuous collection, cultural practises might be introduced to enhance natural populations and to enable the commercial exploitation of palm seeds. Projects of this

Caryota maxima, a montane forest palm, in habitat, Peninsular Malaysia. Vulnerable.

Ruth Kiew

nature can only be attempted for very few species, e.g. *Johannesteijsmannia* spp.

4) Establish a protected area for Palms on Penang Hill.

The forests of Penang Hill are important as a water catchment and recreational areas and also harbor a particularly high number of Endangered tree species. Threatened palms of this area are *Calamus viminalis*, *C. penicillatus*, and *Licuala acutifida*.

5) Protect and manage coastal palms.

Livistona saribus is restricted to a small area on the west coast. *Phoenix paludosa* populations on the east coast are under threat from land development and petroleum exploration. Stems of *Oncosperma tigillarium* are used for large estuarine fish stake traps; there is no good substitute, and supplies are becoming scarce. Land development for housing and industrial estates is reducing wild populations of the palm. Populations of these species should be surveyed, seeds collected, and appropriate conservation measures should be adopted.

6) Revise the Peninsular Malayan palms.

In order to assess the conservation status of all Peninsular Malayan palms, sound taxonomic studies must be conducted, especially for *Pinanga, Salacca*, and *Iguanura*. To produce a revision of all palms, a database should be set up.

7) Establish a living palm collection.

A suitable area in FRIM ground has already been identified. A palm collection is very important for research on palm biology and *ex situ* conservation of threatened species.

(Contact: R. Kiew, L. G. Saw)

Sarawak

Sarawak is a land of varied topography and geology, which has provided a wide variety of habitats for palms. While much of the natural vegetation of Sarawak has been considerably modified due to logging, shifting cultivation, conversion of agriculture, etc., the National Parks and Wildlife Sanctuaries enjoy protected status.

More than 214 named native palm species belonging to 25 genera have been recorded as occurring in Sarawak. However, as recently as 1990 three new palm species were collected during the study of the Palms of Kubah National Park. The rattans make up almost exactly half the Sarawak palm species with *Calamus* (56 species) and *Daemonorops* (27 species) being the largest rattan genera. Other species-rich genera are *Pinanga* (34 species) and *Licuala* (about 29 species). Endemism is relatively high (at least 26% of the species) with *Areca, Iguanura*, and *Salacca* having a particularly high proportion of endemic species.

While the great majority of palm species in Sarawak occur in lowland dipterocarp forest, some prefer swamp forest or kerangas forest on nutrient-poor white sand. Many species are not restricted to one particular habitat, but others do show habitat preferences such as the coastal fringe, hill or montane forest, or the banks of fast-flowing streams. Only three species are commonly found in secondary forest.

The rattans of Sarawak have been thoroughly studied, and their conservation and utilization documented from herbarium and literature studies. Detailed studies of the palms resulting in palm checklists have been made for two of Sarawak's National Parks (Gunung Mulu N.P. and Kubah N.P., see Chapter 3). Many more areas in both gazetted and proposed National Parks and Wildlife Sanctuaries, as well as elsewhere, still need to have their palm flora investigated.

Utilization. Sarawak is a land inhabited by a large number of different ethnic groups. As the topography and soils vary, so do the lifestyles of these groups. The permutations of different cultures, lifestyles, and surrounding vegetation has lead to the development of a wealth of ethnobotanical knowledge. In many cases, members of the more isolated ethnic groups carry with them a tradition of intimate association with the forest and its products. Palms are, in Sarawak as elsewhere, one of the chief groups of plants yielding useful products ranging from rattan cordage to *Licuala* leaves for making sunhats; from fishing rods to walking sticks; from nipah sugar to cigarette papers. As lifestyles change, it is becoming increasingly urgent to record traditional information concerning such palms before it is lost.

Many native Sarawak palms are commercially exploited. In addition to the many different species of rattan extracted for sale or used for making local handicraft items, palms are the source of temporary thatch, sugar (*Nypa*), fruits (*Eleiodoxa, Salacca*), and palm heart (*Eleiodoxa, Arenga, Eugeissona, Borassodendron, Oncosperma,* and *Plectocomiopsis*). Other species have potential as ornamentals (*Areca, Iguanura, Licuala, Pinanga*, etc.), or for their attractive and durable wood (*Oncosperma*).

Important non-indigenous species include the oil palm (*Elaeis guineensis*) which is currently the most important of Sarawak's agricultural palm crops, and the sago palm (*Metroxylon sagu*), widely planted in swampy areas.

Both the Sarawak Forestry Department and the Sarawak Agriculture Department are carrying out studies on various aspects of rattans with a view to investigating their performance as plantation species.

Recommendations

Objectives: a) identify areas of high palm biodiversity in Sarawak; b) identify specific threats to palms in Sarawak, and species most at risk (commercial collection for the rattan market and to fulfill demand by palm enthusiasts; habitat destruction); c) take steps to reduce such threats.

1) Compile a database of collection data for palms at the Sarawak Forest Department Herbarium.

A database of the data (including collection date, locality, habitat, ethnobotany or utilization, and local names and dialects) should be compiled for all palm collections in the Sarawak Forest Department Herbarium, using the existing card index system, and with the addition of information from the existing ethnobotanical collections. This would be a desk project and should take only a few person-weeks to complete.

2) Using this database, identify palm-rich locations.

Action to be taken once such palm-rich areas are identified could include:

a) Designation of specific palm-rich sites (for locations currently protected by their status as national park or wildlife sanctuary). This would be of value in the planning of further field studies, when management decisions concerning such areas need to be taken, and in the international arena of biodiversity conservation.

b) For areas currently not protected or being exploited, knowledge of palm-rich sites would be used in planning further investigation, formulating recommendations for the protection of such areas, and the collection of palm material for *ex situ* conservation and germplasm banks as appropriate.

c) Interpretation of the palm flora to the public in programs designed to raise awareness and interest in palms. Palm trails could be laid out in accessible and heavily-used National Parks (such as Kubah National Park, near Kuching, Sarawak's capital), and attractive information packages prepared for such trails. Members of local communities could be involved in providing information on local names and uses and might possibly be trained as guides taking visitors around palm trails.

3) Carry out further field investigations on Sarawak palms.

Field collection needs to be carried out in selected national parks and wildlife sanctuaries, in order to obtain new records of palms in addition to those which can be extracted from the database (see Recommendation 1). Currently there are lists of palm species for only two of Sarawak's national parks.

Field collection is also required in potentially palm-rich areas which are facing habitat degradation, with particular attention to the involvement of members of local communities in the collection of local names and ethnobotanical information for the area. The numerous ethnic groups, lifestyles, and habit types represented in Sarawak result in a plethora of plant names and ethnobotanical information, much of which has not yet been recorded.

Rare or threatened species, including those that have not been recently recollected, should be searched for in the field, both at reported sites and potential sites, to establish the current degree of threat, and to facilitate protection of localities or *ex situ* conservation measures.

4) Identify threats to particular palm species in Sarawak.

Determination of which particular species are threatened due to commercial exploitation, and the degree of threat. Two major groups of species are the rattans in demand for handicrafts and furniture, and ornamental palms in demand by palm enthusiasts.

5) Study the effectiveness of current palm protection measures.

Include studies on enforcement in protected sites, on protected species, and plant export regulations.

6) Studies on ways of reducing the threat to local palms.

a) A study of the economics of rattan collection for the commercial market.
b) A feasibility study for rattan plantations for the smallholder, covering such aspects as availability of land and suitable sites, choice of species, availability of stock and information on cultural methods, growth and yield estimates, and barriers presently preventing rattan from being seen as a worthwhile plantation crop. Such a study should complement investigations by the Sarawak Forest Department and the Sarawak Agriculture Department.
c) A pilot study on the production of material of local ornamental species for sale, including the development of a list/brochure of species currently in demand with cultural/habitat requirements, a list of species with potential as ornamentals, and methods of stock multiplication.

7) Taxonomic studies on species of *Licuala* and *Pinanga* in Sarawak.

These genera are the largest in Sarawak, after rattans, which are in need of taxonomic work, both from the point of view of biodiversity and, in the case of *Licuala*, to determine how far the site specificity found in Peninsular Malaysia occurs in the very different set of species found in Sarawak.

Implementation

The Sarawak State Government would automatically be consulted in the first instance for any project involving plants of Sarawak. If the State Government were agreeable to any (or all) of the suggested projects being carried out, various types of arrangement could be explored including involving the Sarawak Forest Department (which has, in the past, given very generous logistical help in studies on palms in Sarawak); employing independent researchers (if funding were available); and involving Malaysian universities in some of the projects, either at undergraduate (research project) or postgraduate level. University Malaysia Sarawak located near Kuching has a strong interest in the study of biodiversity in Sarawak.

(Contact: Kit Pearce)

Sabah

For its relatively small area (approximately 10% of the island of Borneo), Sabah has a rich and diverse palm flora, although the knowledge of it is poor. Present knowledge covers 131 palms, representing 25 genera and 14 endemics. The rattans have been intensively studied and account for 82 species. The conservation status of most of the palms is Unknown, and only ten can be considered as not threatened.

The endemic palms *Arenga retroflorescens* and *Salacca lophospatha* are Endangered; the latter is known from the type collection only. *Salacca clemensiana* is known from the Philippines as well, and Endangered at least in Sabah. Five other palms are known to be threatened in Sabah (see Dransfield and Johnson 1991).

Indonesia

The palm flora of Indonesia is one of the richest in the world. About 477 palm species are known to occur in Indonesia, representing 46 genera. More than 150 species were added during the research work of the WWF project no. 3325 (Mogea 1991), and 225 palms are endemic. Seventy percent of these belong to the rattans *Calamus* and *Daemonorops* (western part), the genera *Licuala* and *Pinanga* (mostly undergrowth palms), and *Gronophyllum* (eastern part). Six species are Endangered and 74 are threatened.

Palms are widely used for subsistence and commercial purposes, and up to now are known to involve about 10% of the native species. Coconut and the African oil palm are major plantation crops in Indonesia. Rattans are the most important non-timber forest product of the country.

Pinanga latisecta, a forest palm in habitat, Sumatra, Indonesia. Its world conservation status is Unknown.

Johanis P. Mogea

62

Ceratolobus glaucescens, an endemic forest Javanese palm under cultivation, Bogor Botanical Garden, Indonesia. Endangered.

Recommendations

1) Conduct detailed field studies on the *in situ* conservation status of Endangered species and bring them into cultivation.

Ceratolobus glaucescens (Java) and *C. pseudoconcolor* (Java, Sumatra) belong to a small genera of rattans confined to the Sundashelf. *Drymophloeus oliviformis* occurs on Ambon Island, which is heavily deforested. *Iguanuara leucocarpa* and *Plectocomiopsis corneri* are understory palms from Sumatra, both belonging to western Malesian genera. They should also be brought into cultivation. All of these palms are endemic and occur in areas of high population and serious deforestation.

2) Study other threatened palms.

Sixty-eight palms are classified as Vulnerable, Rare, or Indeterminate (see Mogea 1991). *In situ* conservation data on these species are inadequate. Additional field studies on this group of palms should be carried out in addition to the activities in Recommendation 1 and, whenever possible, in association with other field investigations. In addition, the conservation status of most of the remaining Indonesian palms is Unknown.

3) Conduct studies on palms in areas of timber concessions.

New forest areas are being opened up for timber concessions, and palm and other plant and animal species are adversely affected as a result of roadbuilding and logging activities. At present, no monitoring of threatened species is being done.

A mechanism needs to be established whereby a specialist can conduct studies of the palms in such areas, collecting new field data, making herbarium collections, and attempting to minimize the impact as much as possible by identifying sites of particular scientific interest. Ideally, a team of specialists should be present, covering as many plant and animal groups as possible.

4) Inventory palms in parks and protected areas.

Indonesia has an active program to establish parks and protected areas, although in many if not most cases details of the palm flora are poorly known.

Field work on palms in parks and protected areas needs to be conducted, thereby adding to the knowledge of the biological diversity within their borders, while at the same time generating *in situ* palm conservation data. Knowledge on which threatened species occur within protected areas will permit greater attention to palm species which do not enjoy such protection.

5) Promote and develop the native palm resources of Indonesia.

Fruits of the salak palms (*Salacca* spp.) are widely consumed throughout the country, and are only collected from the wild. The sugar palm (*Arenga pinnata*) is a multipurpose palm, but used primarily as a source of sap for sugarmaking, and is cultivated on an informal basis. These palms, as well as the lontar or palmyra palm (*Borassus flabellifer*), have a strong development potential in Indonesia. Research projects are called for to study selection, cultivation, harvesting, processing, and marketing of the wide range of possible products of these palms.

(Contact: J. Mogea)

Papua New Guinea

Papua New Guinea has a very rich and distinctive palm flora. About 193 described palm species are reported to occur in Papua New Guinea; many are not yet described and will have to be added as a result of future research. Knowledge of taxonomic species limits, distribution, and conservation status in general is very incomplete. However, major logging operations are increasingly threatening biodiversity throughout the country, and studies are urgently needed. Many studies are now conducted within the framework of the Flora Malesiana project. One of the richest areas in respect to palm diversity under immediate threat is the Bewani-Ituli region. This should be used as a case study for other regions in Papua New Guinea.

Rescue of the palm communities of the Bewani-Ituli region

The Bewani-Ituli Region is one of the areas with the most diverse palm flora in Papua New Guinea, as far as is presently known. Palms as a group dominate the vegetation, and sometimes form monospecific stands. About 37 species of 24 genera are known to occur in an area of less than 100 km^2, eight of them yet undescribed.

The people living in this area have a very intimate knowledge of their palm species, as shown by the distinctive name they have for each one, also taking into consideration varietal names that are recognized based on form, dimension, and application to cultivation. Indeed, specific names are given to the terrain where certain palms are found, and the palms themselves are used as 'guides' to that terrain. Palms also play an important role in local mythology and theology.

Researchers in the fields of ethnobotany, anthropology, or linguistics could find a wealth of relevant information for study in this region. Most local people would welcome interested researchers to stay with them and to learn about them and their region.

Threats

Three major logging companies are operating close to the area, and are approaching from the west (Pigi) and north (Kilifau). New roads are built and camps/villages created to support the logging operations. Emergent dissatisfaction and uncertainty from locals with the major logging operators in the area have caused interruptions in the operations, as companies must obtain permission from landholders prior to cutting. At Bewani itself major logging operations are planned. A divergence of opinion exists in the community at Bewani concerning the benefits and drawbacks of logging. Many people in Bewani are supportive of the idea of maintaining their forests in natural conditions.

Most threatened palm species

Sommieria affinis ('Man') was only discovered in Papua New Guinea in 1979, and by far the largest and most intact population is found in this region. The palm is gregarious in habit; it has absolutely no tolerance for full exposure and will die unless protected by shade by a forest canopy. Whether *Sommieria* will be able to withstand constant intrusion and disturbance of its colonies remains to be seen.

Occurring only in association with *Sommieria* colonies, albeit very sparsely, is a yet to be described and collected species of *Gronophyllum* ('Filiawoi-Yama'), a very distinct species, and one of considerable horticultural potential. Also, two undescribed species of *Licuala* ('Brubinei Broal')

Juvenile habit of *Sommieria affinis*.

Michael Ferrero

Immature infructescence of *Sommieria affinis*.

a) Long-term benefits of lifestyle and livelihood will be intact. Without native habitat, native lifestyle (e.g. food, medicine) will disappear.

b) Future generations can continue living in the area if they have ownership of the land which will hopefully remain intact.

c) Ecotourism can generate some income, although perhaps not in the quantity of royalties from logging. Tourism, however, could continue indefinitely, whereas logging will not.

d) Money can be generated by the sustainable harvest of palm seeds. Currently *Sommieria* spp. trade as ornamentals at US$2 per seed.

e) A research facility (if based in the area) can draw international visitors, scientists, etc. and can actively involve locals who will be able to draw income as guides, interpreters, and collectors.

f) Guest houses and village accommodation can be established for visitors, either by individuals using their premises or by construction of new ones. Income can thus be generated from accommodation fees.

g) Local knowledge of flora as well as customs and language can be maintained and used in education programs at school. This will allow the local people to maintain their cultural identity.

Implementation

Planning and discussion of the projects should be in close cooperation with the landholders and the local councils. It is unlikely that funding will be available from the national government. However, the Forestry Research Institute might be interested, if substantial financial benefits are expected to result from research, e.g. the sustainable use of rattans or other forest products.

If the establishment of a research base is to be considered, a circular should be sent to appropriate universities and research institutes to determine the level of interested researchers.

In support of such a research facility, Bewani has a well maintained airstrip, a road to Vanimo (dry season only), a small hospital, and a school, managed by the township of Bewani.

(Contact: Michael D. Ferrero)

and *Calyptrocalyx* ('Yamu-Tumune'), are very rare, the former only known from one other locality in Irian Jaya. These palm species are of highest conservation priority, as all the other species can be found throughout Papua New Guinea, and many are cosmopolitan.

Recommendations

1) Set up a conservation and development plan in collaboration with the landholders in the Bewani-Ituli region.

Instead of clear-felling of vast areas, alternative development plans have to be considered. Long term planning could bring many benefits to the local people.

Chapter 8

Priorities in Madagascar

A separate chapter is devoted to Madagascar because of its extraordinary palm diversity coupled with the high rate of endemism. Madagascar is the fourth largest island in the world and has been separated from adjoining continents since the break-up of Gondwana, some one hundred million years ago. The distance from mainland Africa, more than 500 km, has meant that both flora and fauna have developed in effective isolation. The island has a topography of dramatic escarpments, mountain ranges, and upland plateaus, as well as coastal plains and gently sloping foothills. This topography, in combination with a diversity of geological types, and influenced by diverse tropical climate types, has resulted in a wide range of habitats.

Palm flora

The palms of Madagascar were the subject of a systematic study at the Royal Botanic Gardens, Kew (1991–1994), which resulted in a new and hopefully more stable classification. The study has resulted in a publication (Dransfield and Beentje 1995) which details palm habitats, distribution, utilization, and conservation, as well as classification.

As a result of extensive fieldwork during this study, palm collections from Madagascar have increased almost threefold and three new genera as well as some eighty new species have been discovered. Many species have been re-collected for the first time since their description earlier this century, and critical collections are clarifying the variability of species, resulting in many species being merged. This first overall study of the island's palms since Jumelle and Perrier (1945) makes serious changes in currently accepted names, both at the specific and generic level. For example, within the subtribe *Dypsidinae* major nomenclatural changes have taken place, and the six genera previously accepted have been merged into one. The final tally for Madagascar under this revised classification ends up as 16 genera with 176 species. Before this work was completed, the Madagascar list contained 116 palm species described in 20 genera.

Aside from four palm species which are also found to occur on the African mainland, all of these species are endemic to Madagascar, resulting in an endemism rate as high as 98%. *Hyphaene coriacea* is common in the drier parts of western Madagascar, and *Elaeis guineensis*, *Raphia farinifera*, and *Phoenix reclinata* have probably been introduced, since no wild populations have been found. The coconut has also been introduced and is cultivated widely.

The absence of large grazing animals and the relatively late arrival of humans have probably contributed to the evolution of an astonishing number of extraordinarily diverse palms. Systematic problems with species delimitation and interpopulation variability indicate that in some palm groups speciation is still continuing at a rapid rate. The palms of Madagascar are most diverse in the lowland to submontane forests of the east and north-east.

Madagascar's endemic palms are under threat, as is much of the island's flora. The 86 species classified as Extinct, Critical, or Endangered (Table 2.1) represent only a portion of the bad news. Many of the remaining species are Vulnerable or Rare. The prospects for an enormous loss of palm diversity are unparalleled anywhere else in the world.

Threats

Many species have very restricted distribution areas. Species such as *Marojejya darianii*, *Ravenia louvelii* (=*Louvelia madagascariensis*), and *Voanioala gerardii* are known from single populations, encompassing less than 1 km^2 in the wild. With such species even minor local disturbances to the habitat can have critical results. But sadly, habitat disturbances occur on a much larger scale these days, and Madagascar is no exception. The demand for agricultural land to feed a growing population, coupled with outdated food production methods due to lack of expertise and funds, has resulted in a continuing medium-scale forest clearance on a national basis. Lowland forest especially has become fragmented, and specialized habitats such as white sand forest are now restricted to only a few square kilometres.

Specific threats to palms include over-harvesting for timber (such as in Lokobe Integrated Natural Reserve), cutting palm heart (probably a prime cause for the decline in numbers of such palms as *Beccariophoenix madagascariensis* and *Dypsis decipiens*), and destructive collecting by overzealous palm growers. This last factor has affected the populations of *Marojejya darianii* and *Voanioala gerardii*, where all seed is collected and so rejuvenation is arrested. Following publication of an article in a popular palm journal on the population of *Beccariophoenix madagascariensis* (Dransfield 1988), a tree of this species was cut down to obtain the seed, resulting in a 10% decline of the then known population.

Conservation needs

While habitat conservation and the more narrow species conservation approach both have a role to play in the safeguarding of Madagascar's palm diversity, the former is undoubtedly the most desirable approach. It is, however, the most difficult to achieve because of the needs of Madagascar's growing population which place much of the remaining forest under considerable pressure.

To increase food production on the current agricultural land base is an obvious but time-consuming solution. For example, employing techniques already in use in countries such as Indonesia and the Philippines, Malagasy rice production could be doubled without increasing the rice-growing area.

Timber production and firewood harvesting are factors in forest disturbance and deterioration, and the demand for these products is increasing. Small-scale plantations of fast-growing and coppicing species, especially on a village level, would do much to channel the demand for firewood (95% of cooking is done on fuel wood and charcoal) towards sustainable rather than destructive harvesting. Improvements in charcoal making techniques are being tested in small-scale trials in Antananarivo. Such mundane matters deserve much more support from the conservation world. The introduction of more fuel-efficient charcoal stoves (such as the clay-lined types) is a similar small-scale measure with enormous potential profits to the natural forests in general, and therefore for the habitat of many threatened palms.

A serious problem is the seasonal burning of vast areas of grasslands, both in the south and in large areas of the east coast. The purpose of burning is the stimulation of young grass shoots for cattle grazing, but the areas burnt seem out of proportion to the number of cattle that benefit. The poor quality of the fodder grasses that survive burning is certainly a contributing factor to the ever-increasing regularity of the burning, which nibbles away steadily at the remaining forests. Any alternative, either in fodder production or in management techniques, would contribute enormously to long-term solutions for many of the country's problems, since any regeneration of the vegetation is prevented by fire.

Protected areas are vital for *in situ* conservation, but establishing parks or reserves without involving local people is useless and even self defeating. If the needs of local people are not taken into account and reserves are seen as an alien imposition from either the capital or even from foreigners, resentment will work against long-term conservation. There are several 'paper' reserves or parks where local involvement is minimal, and the day-to-day need for food and money causes over-harvesting or even plunder of the resource. For example, in the Manombo Special Reserve, a last remnant of forest surrounded by burned grassland, the extraction of timber and clearing for agriculture presently threaten populations of several palm species, some of which are completely new to science.

Integrated conservation projects should provide alternatives for food and firewood requirements. The demarcation of a forest core and buffer zones is a well-established principle, and in the WWF project in the Manongarivo Special Reserve, the theory seems to work in practice with a large degree of success. Local people have been involved in delimiting the Reserve, and are able to continue their traditional activities in the forest buffer zones. To compensate them for loss of potential agricultural clearing areas, there are village health projects, help with village schooling projects, and improvements in rural access. The fact that the WWF base camp hut near the buffer zone was built with wood of *Ravenea robustior*, a Vulnerable palm, at first seems shocking, but the buffer zone and core zone delimitations help protect the majority of the populations which used to be over-harvested!

The species approach to palm conservation is a desperate measure, but sometimes it works. *Dypsis* (=*Neodypsis*) *decaryi*, the triangle palm, a well-known ornamental, occurs in a small area in southern Madagascar that has suffered from both burning of the habitat (dry low forest) and over-collecting of seed. Five hundred hectares, encompassing the main part of the total population (about one thousand trees) has been set aside as Parcel 3 of the Andohahela Integrated Natural Reserve. In this location, conservation

Triangle palm (*Dypsis decaryi*), a palm limited to a small area in the South of Madagascar. Vulnerable.

WWF/Olivier Langrand

goes hand in hand with education, and since the plot is adjacent to a main road, tourists also visit the palms regularly.

The awareness level of the Malagasy people of the need for palm conservation, and indeed conservation in general, is very low — most people are more concerned with having enough to eat and increasing their income above the level of less than US$1 per day. Conservation education will only work when it is accompanied by the prospect of increasing the standard of living: easier access to firewood, a better stove, increased rice harvest, cleaner drinking water, and so on. Most rural people in the forest areas realize the need to conserve forests because they provide essential medicinal plants, timber, food, and a host of secondary forest products. There remains an urgent need for investment in education and small, local improvements which will directly benefit conservation efforts.

Recommended actions

The three following recommendations are examples of the type of actions that need to be taken in Madagascar.

1) Protect *Ravenea louvelii* and other restricted and critically endangered palms.

Ravenia louvelii (formerly *Louvelia madagascariensis*) is restricted to an area of less than 1 sq km near Andasibe; specific protection measures should be relatively easy to implement, and would probably save the species from extinction. The same could be done to highly restricted-area species such as *Marojejya darianii*, *Voanioala gerardii*, and *Lemurophoenix halleuxii*.

2) Extend Manombo Forest Reserve and implement its strict protection with local involvement.

Manombo Forest Reserve is the last remnant of lowland forest in Fianarantsoa Province, and home to several strictly endemic and as yet undescribed palm species, as well as to several critically endangered palm species. It is a small reserve (5020 ha) and is being destroyed by commercial timber harvesting and the resultant agricultural clearance. The addition of another 5000 ha of unprotected forest which is adjacent to the Reserve is recommended, as well as strict protection from commercial activities and agricultural conversion. This would be an excellent subject for a pilot project with local involvement in conservation, and a showcase for community buffer zones coupled with village woodlots and charcoal improvement schemes.

3) Establish breeding programs in botanic gardens.

It is recommended that the Parc Botanique et Zoologique de Tsimbazaza receive funds to set up an *ex situ* breeding program. Staff would need to be trained and a secure area set up for species that are in danger in the wild, e.g. *Marojejya darianii*, *Beccariophoenix madagascariensis*, *Ravenia louvelii*, *Borassus madagascariensis*, *B. sambiranensis*,

Orania trispatha, *Lemurophoenix halleuxii*, *Voanioala gerardii*, and *Dypsis utilis*. The Botanic Garden at Iavalohina near Toamasina (Tamatave) would be an excellent coastal counterpart in such a program.

(Contact: H. Beentje, J. Dransfield)

Box 8.1 Public awareness of palms in Madagascar

A very effective illustrated leaflet entitled "The Palms of Madagascar" was produced in 1990 as part of a WWF-supported cultivation project at the Tsimbazaza Botanical and Zoological Park. Written by Voara Randrianasolo and John Dransfield, the leaflet was translated into French and Malagasy to broaden its audience within the country. The objective of the leaflet was to inform Park visitors of the great diversity of native palms, the inadequate field information known about many of them, and the various useful products they provide. Two sections of the leaflet are quoted as follows:

"Why should we protect palms in Madagascar?
... If present rates of forest clearance and palm exploitation go on, many palms will be threatened with extinction in the very near future. Extinction and even severe depletion of the wild palm populations will have a serious effect on the life of rural people. There is also another consideration: some of the wild palms of Madagascar may be lost before their economic potential is realized. This potential may not be directly related to everyday life in Madagascar but it could involve the commercial trade in ornamental plants, a trade of very great monetary value. There are thus very good reasons from a social and economic point of view to protect palms from extinction, but there is also an important scientific reason. The Madagascar palms present some of the most exciting, interesting and crucial evidence for understanding the evolution of the whole world's palms; in a sense they are the key to answering some of the most important questions we have. From a scientific viewpoint it would be tragic if they were allowed to disappear, even before they are properly studied, and it would be a horrible loss for Madagascar.

"What can be done to protect Madagascar palms?
The obvious way to safeguard these special plants is to protect representative areas of their habitats as nature reserves. Many species occur in reserves which are already established, but unfortunately they are still not safe even within these areas. Better control and policing is required to halt the felling of palms for palm cabbage but this alone is not enough; greater public awareness of the effects of over-exploitation is also needed. The establishment of living palm collections will also help in education and should soon begin to provide seed for the cultivation of Malagasy palms in other countries as part of a conservation programme."

Chapter 9

Regional Priorities in Africa and Indian Ocean Islands

This chapter examines the situation on the African mainland and in three Indian Ocean island groups of high palm diversity and endemism: the Mascarenes, the Comoro Islands, and Seychelles. For Madagascar see Chapter 8. Recommendations for conservation action are given after each section rather than combined at the end of the chapter.

The African mainland

Africa is defined here as consisting of the mainland and the continental islands in the Gulf of Guinea (Equatorial Guinea, São Tomé, and Principe) and the island portions of Tanzania (Zanzibar and Pemba). As delimited, Africa

The Mpapindi palm (*Dypsis* [=*Chrysalidocarpus*] *pembanus*), a small island endemic, in habitat in the Ngezi Forest Reserve, Pemba Island, Tanzania.

Dennis Johnson

has the smallest palm diversity of any tropical area in the world. Native are 16 genera, accounting for only about 50 species. The genera *Medemia, Laccosperma, Eremospatha, Oncocalamus, Podococcus, Sclerosperma* and *Jubaeopsis* are endemic to Africa; *Podococcus* and *Jubaeopsis* are monotypic. A single species of *Dypsis* (*Dypsis* =*Chrysalidocarpus pembanus*) is restricted to Pemba Island. Naturalized through introduction are the genera *Cocos, Areca,* and *Nypa,* the latter reputed to be a weedy species in West African mangroves. The largest native genus is *Raphia* with about 19 spp. A study of the palms of mainland Africa was recently completed (Tuley 1995). Despite the relative lack of palm diversity, native species occur in great numbers, and provide a conspicuous element of many landscapes.

Palms in habitat

1. Tropical rain forest, swamp, and riparian habitats. The status of these palms, taken in concert with the overall concern for the preservation of such habitats, is clearly related to the degree of forest clearing or degradation in the area concerned. This is obviously highly variable, and closely related to population pressures and the effectiveness of forest law, forest reserve ordinances, and similar measures. Growing in wet habitats are the *Raphia* species, all of the African rattans as well as the genera *Podococcus, Sclerosperma,* and *Jubaeopsis.* Widely cultivated species such as *Elaeis guineensis* present little or no problem.

Two montane species of *Raphia,* both described by Otedoh (1982), are problematic. *Raphia mambillensis* has a distribution which includes Cameroon, Central African Republic, Nigeria, and Sudan; its conservation status is Unknown in all four countries. Although its riparian habitat is under considerable pressure, the palm is widely found in cultivation. *Raphia ruwenzorica* occurs in Burundi and Zaire; its conservation status in both countries is Unknown and no recent information is available on the situation in this difficult area.

Jubaeopsis caffra has a very limited distribution in South Africa, but the river-valley sites where it occurs in Natal and Transkei appear to be well protected in recent times. Moreover, it is well established in cultivation for ornamental purposes. Its world conservation status is Rare.

2. Palms of arid areas. These palms, in the genera *Borassus, Hyphaene,* and *Phoenix,* generally are not a cause for concern, although there are reports of over-exploitation in

69

Tuareg house made of palm fibers, the living palm is nearby (*Hyphaene thebaica*). Although traditionally sustainably used, many African palms are now heavily exploited and threatened.

WWF/John Newby

some areas, e.g. *Borassus flabellifer* in Guinea-Bissau (Castel-Branco and Tordo 1956). Two other species, *Medemia argun* and *Livistona carinensis*, are Endangered.

Given the problems with warfare and difficulties of access, the rather isolated species of the Horn of Africa should receive special attention: *Livistona carinensis* is Endangered in Somalia and Djibouti (the conservation status in Yemen is not known). Its small population has decreased in the last ten years from 50 to only 11 individuals (Thulin 1995). Also many populations of *Hyphaene* (including the endemic *H. reptans*) are reported to be decreasing, and like *Livistona*, are threatened by over-exploitation for leaves and trunks.

In southern Africa, the status of *Raphia australis*, described by Obermeyer and Strey (1969) from South Africa and Mozambique, requires clarification. Currently it is classified as Vulnerable in Natal and Unknown in Mozambique.

Recommended actions

Six major issues need to be addressed which embrace both conservation and utilization.

1) Habitat protection.

Support should be given to protected area legislation, projects, and related activities where palms are a significant component of the vegetation. The activity should be coordinated with appropriate governmental agencies and non-governmental organizations working in the regions concerned.

2) African rattans.

Though rattans play a very important role in the local economies of most West and Central African countries, they have been almost completely neglected by the scientific community, forestry institutions, and official

---

Box 9.1 African oil palm (*Elaeis guineensis*): genetic resources and their value to the industry

Although Africa has minimal palm species diversity, it is the native habitat of the world's most important economic palm, *Elaeis guineensis*. The African oil palm has become, over the past three decades, a major world source of vegetable oil. At present, annual yields reach five to six tons of oil per hectare, more than any oilseed crop. This enormous global industry is founded on a very narrow genetic base derived mainly from four individual palms introduced from Africa to Asia. A major objective of the industry in recent years has been to broaden the genetic base for breeding purposes to maintain and improve production. Studies have shown the crucial value of natural (wild and sub-spontaneous) oil palm groves in Africa as a leading source of new genetic material for production traits and disease resistance. For example, some Nigerian dwarf palms have yield potential that could double current production levels as well as reduce harvesting cost because of their short stature. Studies have also been carried out on *E. oleifera*, the American oil palm, the only other species of the genus. Although its oil yields are not economic and it has an undesirable procumbent growth form, *E. oleifera* is of interest to breeders because it can readily be crossed with the African species, making feasible the transference of desirable traits such as moderate growth, disease resistance, and a higher percentage of mono-unsaturated oils.

Malaysia, the world's largest producer and exporter of palm oil, has taken the lead on genetic prospecting, through PORIM (Palm Oil Research Institute of Malaysia). Palms with desirable traits are under cultivation in a field genebank in Malaysia for study and breeding purposes. As a result of PORIM's research and that of other institutions in Asia, Africa, and Latin America, more scientific information is known about the African oil palm than for any other palm species. Within the palm family, it represents the foremost example of the value of conserving the widest possible range of wild germplasm.

Rattan palms at the Ndian river, Korup National Park, Cameroon.

legislation. An overview of the rattans of Nigeria has recently been published (Morakinyo 1995). It includes data on pan-African distribution, utilization, and ecology. However, the taxonomy of the group remains confused and little is known about their ecology and international trade (an unknown amount of furniture and raw unprocessed rattan is now being exported to Asian countries). Due to the heavy and uncontrolled exploitation, several species of rattan are suspected to be Endangered in parts of their ranges (Morakinyo 1995).

A major study of the systematics and economic botany of the African rattan species should be implemented as a matter of priority. This includes extensive studies of herbarium specimens, further collections, and field studies (especially in poorly known regions of Angola, Central Zaire, Gabon, and Congo), and the establishment of a rattan arboretum (see below).

3) Ron palm (*Borassus aethiopum*).

The ron palm plays an important role for local economy throughout Africa. All parts of the palm can be used and are sources of substantial income to the local people. However, many of the wild and semi-wild populations are severely depleted and the ongoing sustainable use projects in Niger (with participation of IUCN) should be continued and extended to other regions (Price 1995).

4) *Livistona carinensis* and *Hyphaene* spp.

Immediate conservation action should take place to rescue the last stand of *Livistona carinensis* in Somalia, where only 11 individuals are known in the area around Karin and Galgala. The palm is felled for trunks and the young leaves are grazed or used for basketry. Species of *Hyphaene* in this region are also undergoing similar pressures.

5) Pan-African palm collection.

The proposed Pan-African collection of palms, to be established at the Victoria Botanic Gardens, Limbe, in southern Cameroon, should be supported. In addition to its role in *ex situ* conservation, the collection could form the basis for economic trials, studies of palm biology, and future palm conservation activities in Africa.

(Contact: P. Tuley)

Indian Ocean Islands

The most striking aspect of the palms of the smaller Indian Ocean islands is that every species is threatened to some degree, with several species known only from a handful of individuals in the wild. The reasons for the decline in numbers of these palms are similar, and include habitat destruction, over-utilization, introduced animals which either destroy the plants or prevent regeneration, and introduced plants which are competitively superior. In addition, hybridization of closely related species or taxa and self-incompatibility provide the final blow to some already decimated populations.

Mascarene Islands

The Mascarene Islands, consisting of three major islands (Mauritius, Réunion, and Rodrigues), are located 640–800 km east of Madagascar. They are of volcanic origin; the oldest (Mauritius) is 7.8 million, the youngest (Rodrigues) only 1.5 million years old. The islands were

71

Table 9.1 Conservation status of the palms of the Mascarene islands

Distribution*	Status	Habitat, population, threats
Réunion		
Acanthophoenix rubra	V	regenerating in forests, but threatened by palm heart extraction
Dictyosperma album var. *album*	E	regenerating in forests, but threatened by palm heart extraction
Hyophorbe indica	E	lowland, persisting in low numbers only
Latania lontaroides	E	lowland, destroyed on all arable land
Mauritius		
Acanthophoenix rubra	E	upland forests, has virtually disappeared from the wild; threatened by palm heart extraction
Dictyosperma album var. *album*	E	upland forests, has virtually disappeared from the wild; threatened by palm heart extraction
D. album var. *conjugatum*	E	remaining on offshore islands; population now increasing (from 2 individuals only)
Hyophorbe amaricaulis	E	upland forests; 1 individual surviving, no regeneration
H. lagenicaulis	E	remaining on offshore islands; population now increasing (from 10 individuals only)
H. vaughanii	E	upland forests; regeneration inhibited by alien weeds and seed predation
Latania loddigesii	E	remaining on offshore islands; regenerating well
Tectiphiala ferox	E	remaining in upland forests; regeneration inhibited by alien weeds and seed predation
Rodrigues		
Dictyosperma album var. *aureum*	E	few individuals; threatened by hybridization
Hyophorbe verschaffeltii	E	less than 60 individuals; threatened by hybridization
Latania verschaffeltii	E	500 individuals, not regenerating due to overharvesting; threatened by hybridization

* All genera are endemic to the island group. Additionally, 11 of the 13 taxa are endemic to a single island, and only *Acanthophoenix rubra* and *Dictyosperma album* var. *album* occur on both Réunion and Mauritius.

uninhabited until the early 17th century when European settlers arrived, bringing with them animals and plants from home. Thereafter, the unique flora and fauna of the Mascarenes quickly disappeared or was reduced to fragmented populations. The accessible lowlands, which were once hypothesized to have been a 'palm savanna', were the first areas to be cleared. However, remnants of this savanna still exists on two outlying islets (Round Island and Gunner's Quoin), which are within 25 km of Mauritius.

Of the five palm genera native to the Mascarenes, one is endemic to Mauritius (*Tectiphiala*), whereas four are endemic to the island group: *Hyophorbe*, *Acanthophoenix*, *Dictyosperma*, and *Latania* (see Moore and Guého 1984). Currently, palms are highly Endangered in the wild on Mauritius and Rodrigues (apart from *Latania loddigesii*, which has a fairly good population on Round Island), and Endangered or Vulnerable on Réunion. Of a total of 13 taxa endemic to the Mascarenes, Mauritius has the greatest diversity, with eight taxa, probably because it is of the oldest of the island group; Réunion and Rodrigues have, respectively, four and three palm taxa (Table 9.1).

Mauritius

Massive forest clearing on the mainland for sugar cane production probably eradicated the lowland palm species *Hyophorbe lagenicaulis* and *Latania loddigesii*, whereas palms

Hyophorbe amaricaulis growing in the Curepipe Botanic Garden. ▶

Wendy Strahm

which may have grown down into lowlands (*Dictyosperma* and *Acanthophoenix*) are now only found in scattered remnant upland patches where they have virtually ceased to regenerate. Lack of regeneration is even more acute with the two upland species of *Hyophorbe* and *Tectiphiala*.

Threats. The main environmental problems are invasive introduced plant species such as strawberry guava *Psidium cattleianum* and privet *Ligustrum robustum* var. *walkeri* which grow very quickly in clearings (normally where palm species might be expected to regenerate) and outcompete the native species.

Introduced animals also are a major problem for palm regeneration. Rats (*Rattus rattus* and *R. norvegicus*) and monkeys (*Macaca fascicularis*) eat immature palm fruits (with the latter also destroying the palms themselves). Wild pigs (*Sus scrofa*) root up fruits and seedlings, and deer (*Cervus timorensis*) and giant African land snails (*Achatina* spp.) browse any palm seedlings which might manage to grow. Finally, in the exceptional cases where palms have managed to regenerate, they are often cut down for their edible heart which is much in demand on Mauritius, particularly as the tourist industry continues to boom.

Conservation measures. An existing program on Mauritius to conserve palms includes both *in situ* and *ex situ* protection. Managed areas are fenced to exclude deer and pigs (monkeys and rats are impossible to exclude) and weeded of introduced species. Palm fruits are then bagged, collected, and grown in the nursery for reintroduction in the wild. This program, in collaboration with the Mauritian Government and various NGOs, has been successful in restoring several endangered species to the wild. Plants of the highly Endangered *Hyophorbe vaughanii* and *Tectiphiala ferox* have been planted out in protected reserves from 1993, and this work is continuing.

The other Endangered species found in upland Mauritius, *Dictyosperma album* var. *album* and *Acanthophoenix rubra*, are of slightly lower conservation concern since they are widely cultivated as ornamentals as well as for their edible meristem. However, both have virtually disappeared from the wild and the few remaining wild populations are a conservation priority and may be a source for cultivation and reintroduction.

Finally, the situation of the last remaining *Hyophorbe amaricaulis* is desperate. The palm is on the brink of extinction; it regularly flowers but only produces sterile fruits, seemingly because the male flowers open before the female, precluding pollination. However, even when pollen was collected and dusted on open female flowers, viable seeds were not produced. An embryo is produced but does not develop, possibly because of the absence of a genetic enzyme. Jennet Blake at Wye University, U.K., has observed this phenomenon in certain coconuts in the Philippines and suspects that the same phenomenon may

be occurring in this last example of *H. amaricaulis*; more study is obviously needed. Although this palm does not produce viable seeds, plants have on several occasions been cloned by tissue culture of the embryo at Wye, Edinburgh, and Kew, and tissue culture of anthers was also initially a success at Paris. Unfortunately, each time the plantlets were removed from aseptic media they died. The first goal to conserve this palm is to bring it into cultivation where it can be studied; the need is urgent because the sole surviving specimen is very decrepit and could die very soon.

Lowland palms on offshore islands. Lowland palms (*Hyophorbe lagenicaulis*, *Latania loddigesii*, and the endemic *Dictyosperma album* var. *conjugatum*) are also in jeopardy since they now only exist on offshore islands. The most important of these is Round Island, although a small population of *Latania* still survives on Gunner's Quoin and a few on Flat Island.

The last remnant of palm savanna is found on Round Island, a 151 ha uninhabited island 24 km north of Mauritius and a haven for three species. Round Island is the smallest island in the world with an endemic palm taxon (although this taxon may once have grown on the

Four Endangered Mauritian palms on stamps, *Hyophorbe vaughanii*, *Tectiphiala ferox*, *H. lagenicaulis*, and *H. amaricaulis*.

mainland). Of three palms, only the *Latania* grows in any number and is now regenerating following the eradication of goats in 1979 and rabbits in 1986. The two other species had been decimated by these introduced animals, with populations reduced in 1986 to only nine adult *H. lagenicaulis* and two *D. album* var. *conjugatum*. *Hyophorbe lagenicaulis* has started to regenerate vigorously with 271 plants of all ages counted in December 1992, and over 500 to date, a large increase over the 35 of all ages which were found in 1986. Seed collected and sown elsewhere on the island from all the original nine plants are probably represented in the populations on the island today. In addition, a group of six young plants produced from seed of a different adult tree (which was dead by 1982) managed to withstand stress from rabbit browse, and three of these plants are now adult.

Therefore, although the founding population of all the *Hyophorbe* palms on the island today can be traced to just ten individuals, there seems to be no problem with regeneration. In cultivated palms derived from seed sources other than the ten individuals mentioned above, different genes probably exist and this needs to be studied. The depletion and subsequent increase of *H. lagenicaulis* on Round Island from ten individuals, coupled with the significant number of cultivated individuals around the world (see Table 5.1), could provide a very interesting study of genetic variability and reproductive success, with likely ramifications for conservation of this and other plant species.

Prospects for the endemic *Dictyosperma album* var. *conjugatum* are not as hopeful, although with a concerted effort restoration of a wild population should be possible. For over a decade the wild population has consisted of two adult individuals (one erect and one recumbent which died as this account was being prepared). No natural regeneration

Endemic leaf scale insect infestation on underside of *Dictyosperma album* var. *conjugatum* frond. Endangered.

has occurred although both individuals have occasionally produced viable seeds. Seeds from these two palms have been planted on the island and introduced to another offshore island, Ile aux Aigrettes, where a second wild population is being established. However, due to the close proximity of cultivated *D. album* var. *album* on Mauritius (Ile aux Aigrettes is less than 1 km offshore) hybridization may occur. The only safe place to maintain *D. album* var. *conjugatum* as a distinct taxon is on Round Island.

All of these species are well known in botanic gardens although the origin of most cultivated stock is unknown and the possibility of artificial hybridization having taken place in gardens (*Hyophorbe* spp. and *Dictyosperma* spp. each readily interbreed) makes most propagated stock unsuitable for reintroduction. Nevertheless, since these species are so threatened in the wild, any cultivated material needs to be carefully maintained.

Réunion

This island has similar problems to Mauritius, although its upland vegetation is more intact, and fewer animal introductions have occurred. It has fewer palm species (only four) probably because it is a more recent volcanic island. There are two endemic palms. *Latania lontaroides* has been destroyed on all arable land and is classified as Endangered. *Hyophorbe indica* is classified as Vulnerable due to its low numbers and continued destruction and degradation of the native forest.

The other two native palms, *Acanthophoenix rubra* and *Dictyosperma album* var. *album*, respectively Vulnerable and Endangered in Réunion, still regenerate in forests, and in certain areas form a noticeable component of the vegetation. The major reason that the palms are more numerous than in Mauritius is because the forests are less degraded by introduced plants, and there are no feral monkeys or pigs. Unfortunately, deer were introduced, eradicated by over-hunting, and are now being introduced yet again to the island. This will have a very adverse effect on the regeneration of all palm species and should be stopped.

Another major conservation problem on Réunion is that both *Acanthophoenix* and *Dictyosperma* are felled for their edible heart. Although the practice is illegal, it continues unabated and has severely decimated wild populations; penalties for felling palms must be enforced. Réunion has only one tiny (68 ha) nature reserve and although large tracts of land are nominally protected as forest reserves (which can still be converted into plantations), more stringent legal protection of these areas is needed.

Rodrigues

This island, the smallest and most remote of the Mascarenes, has two endemic palm species, *Hyophorbe verschaffeltii* and *Latania verschaffeltii*, as well as an endemic variety, *Dictyosperma album* var. *aureum*.

The native palms on Rodrigues are all extremely threatened (see Strahm 1989), with *Dictyosperma* only known from a few plants growing by houses. The nominate variety from Mauritius has been introduced and may already be more common than the endemic variety; hybridization between the two could result in the loss of the Rodrigues variety.

Hyophorbe verschaffeltii is the second rarest palm with probably less than 60 individuals in the wild and no regeneration. Rodrigues does not have feral pigs, monkeys, or deer; but cows, sheep and goats browse the island and prevent natural regeneration. This very ornamental species is widely cultivated elsewhere and is being increasingly propagated on Rodrigues itself. Unfortunately, its congener *H. lagenicaulis*, has been introduced and the possibility of hybridization exists. These introduced plants should be removed to protect the endemic species, but to date this has proved impossible because they are being grown in private gardens.

Latania verschaffeltii is classified as Endangered. Regeneration within the population of about 500 individuals is almost nil, and the leaves are commonly harvested for thatching. Leaf harvest is supposed to be supervised by a Forestry officer (currently there are only five for the island population of over 36,000) to ensure that three leaves are left on the tree, although this is insufficient because most trees then fail to fruit due to stress. Moreover, fruits that do form are then eaten, making it difficult to collect ripe fruits for propagation. In addition, the Mauritian species, *L. loddigesii*, has been introduced to Rodrigues and an entire valley is now populated with both species. The potential for hybridization poses a serious threat to the long-term survival of *L. verschaffeltii* as a distinct species.

Recommendations

1) Involve local people in palm conservation.

Educational programs, as well as incentives (increased revenue from ecotourism as well as income from palm plantations) and disincentives (stricter laws for cutting down palms) need to be improved. Economic palms are already widely cultivated, but income from these plantations does not filter down to local people, who continue to cut down palms in the wild. Strategies which encourage small planters to cultivate palms rather than collect them from the wild, and educational programs on why this is necessary, are urgently needed.

2) Fence and weed areas of native forests.

The only way to maintain genetically viable wild populations of palms in the Mascarenes (which can also be said for the vast majority of the native plants) is through laborious hands-on management (which could provide a source of jobs for local people). Strict nature reserves must be fenced to exclude browsing animals, and weeded of alien plants.

3) Create more protected areas on Réunion.

More protected areas on Réunion need to be created and existing laws enforced.

4) Reintroductions.

Species which have ceased regeneration naturally need to be artificially propagated, and then planted in suitable areas.

5) Protect the native palms of Rodrigues from hybridization.

Legislation banning the introduction of closely-related palm species to Rodrigues needs to be formulated in order

Palm nursery on Rodrigues growing seedlings for reintroduction.

Wendy Strahm

to protect the tiny native wild populations which remain, and introduced palm species need to be removed.

On Mauritius and Réunion, cultivation of closely-related palm species is not as dangerous provided they are grown far from nature reserves, but nevertheless should be discouraged and the cultivation of native species encouraged.

6) Stop the introduction of deer, and control illegal importation of monkeys to Réunion.

A major issue on Réunion is to stop the introduction of deer, and to eradicate those which have already been brought in. This action is technically feasible, but politically difficult.

In addition, on Réunion the importation of monkeys is legally controlled, but many primates are brought in illegally from Mauritius. Penalties for keeping monkeys must be imposed and existing animals destroyed. Both monkeys and deer have been shown to have disastrous effects on the regeneration of palms (as well as most other native plant species) in Mauritius and the same mistakes should be avoided on Réunion.

(Contact: W. Strahm)

The Comoros

The Comoros comprise four volcanic islands located off the north west coast of Madagascar. The largest of the group, Grand Comore, which has an active volcano, has tremendous human population pressures and all the lowland forest has been cleared. Forest at elevations of 600–1900 m remains, but the understory has been removed to cultivate bananas. The much smaller island of Moheli has the best remaining area of forest since it is less densely populated and the forest is protected by growing on steep slopes. The island of Anjouan is the most degraded of all due to intense cultivation and erosion. Mayotte, the only island which has remained under French rule, is also very degraded with only one forest which could be conserved if action is taken now. However, in addition to human population pressures, the flora of the Comoros is also seriously threatened by introduced plants and animals.

Four endemic palms have been described from the Comoros: *Dypsis humblotiana* and *D. lanceolatus* (formerly *Chrysalidocarpus*), both with an Indeterminate conservation status; *Ravenea hildebrandtii* (Indeterminate) has not been collected for a long time and in October 1993 only two female trees of *Ravenea moorei* (Endangered) were seen in its habitat on Grande Comore (Dransfield and Beentje 1995). Both genera have their center of diversity in Madagascar. Recent information on their current status and conservation needs is very scanty.

Recommendation

Because the flora of the Comoros is so poorly known, research is urgently needed on the taxonomy, conservation, and regeneration of all plants, including the palms.

Seychelles

This group of granitic islands is located some 1100 km north-east of Madagascar. From the standpoint of palm diversity, the Seychelles are extraordinary. Each of the six endemic palms is represented by a monotypic genus. They are: *Deckenia nobilis*, *Lodoicea maldivica*, *Nephrosperma vanhoutteanum*, *Phoenicophorium borsigianum*, *Roscheria melanochaetes*, and *Verschaffeltia splendida* (see Bailey 1942). All of these are classified as Vulnerable, and strict legislation concerning nature conservation on Seychelles exists.

Five of the species are not presently under genuine threat in the wild, but given the small area of the islands, it is prudent to maintain the Vulnerable designations. They are all well represented in national parks and nature reserves.

Lodoicea, the well known 'Coco de Mer', is a special case. About 3000 individuals of the palm occur naturally on Praslin and Curieuse, and it has been introduced to Mahé and Silhouette. The population structure is being severely affected by the gathering of fallen nuts, which are sold to tourists as souvenirs at a price of approximately US$100 each. Only older palms have grown naturally; most palms 20–50 years of age were planted. There is almost no natural regeneration taking place on forestry 'crown land' or in nature reserves although *Lodoicea* is cultivated within nature reserves which coincide with its natural range. Therefore the species as such is not threatened, although its natural population is critically Endangered. It is becoming somewhat like *Ginkgo biloba*, i.e. apparently extinct in the wild but common in cultivation.

This example raises some very interesting conservation issues, since the line between *in situ* and *ex situ* is somewhat blurred. Does assisted regeneration within a palm's native area constitute a positive or negative action? Could the *Lodoicea maldivica* example represent a new model for palm conservation in areas such as islands where pristine natural forests no longer exist, and human population pressures preclude other measures? These questions need to be further studied before definitive recommendations for the conservation of *Lodoicea* on the Seychelles can be made.

(Contact: F. Friedmann)

Chapter 10

The Mediterranean Basin

Only two native species of palms are known in this region: the Dwarf palm, *Chamaerops humilis*, and Theophrastus's date palm, *Phoenix theophrasti*. Both are threatened.

Conservation of Theophrastus's date palm, *Phoenix theophrasti*

Introduction

Theophrastus's date palm is an endemic species of the Greek and Turkish Aegean region (Eastern Mediterranean). It has been known since antiquity as Theophrastus of Erese mentions it in his "History of Plants" written in the fourth century B.C.

However, it was only considered to be an acclimatized form of the cultivated date-palm (*Phoenix dactylifera*) until its description as a distinct species (Greuter 1967; Barclay 1974). Its distribution is very sporadic in the Aegean area, and its particular ecology makes it especially vulnerable to human pressure. It is therefore essential to take practical and legal measures to ensure its conservation.

Ecology and distribution

Theophrastus's date palm is very scattered in the Aegean area, preferring to grow in sandy beds of temporary streams, but it can also be found on rocky grounds. Its presence usually indicates the proximity of underground water (Jenhani 1992). This palm never grows far from the sea, or at over 250 m altitude. It has been recorded from the numerous sites in the Aegean region, although it is nowhere extremely common (see Table 10.1).

Vulnerability, threats, and present protection measures

Different archeological signs and place names, as well as descriptions by botanists from the past centuries indicate that some populations of Theophrastus's date palm have considerably decreased (Vaï) or completely disappeared (Ierapetra or Almyros in Crete). The threats presently facing Theophrastus's date palm are essentially linked to the development of tourism and, to a lesser extent, to agriculture.

The Vaï palm grove is a victim of its own success. Several restaurants have been established close by, and a hotel complex is presently planned. Even if the core of the palm grove is relatively well protected by a fence, it is possible that the increased exploitation of underground water may directly and irremediably affect the largest date palm population existing. Such damage could occur suddenly and without warning. In addition, the present palm grove is probably only one quarter the size of that of last century, due to land clearing for cultivation. The other populations of Theophrastus's date palm also are vulnerable to human pressure, as shown by the very damaged individuals of Stalida. They are often especially vulnerable due to their small size.

The taxonomic status of the population at Gölköy near Bödrum is still not clear, and may prove to be

---

Table 10.1 Distribution of Theophrastus's date palm, *Phoenix theophrasti*, in the Aegean region

Location	Population size
Island of Crete (Greece)	
Vaï (Sitia)	a few thousand individuals
Gazi (Temenos)	5 individuals
Maridhaki (Monofatsi)	200 individuals
Preveli (Hag. Basileos)	100 individuals
Finikias (Hag. Basileos)	few individuals
Stalida (Pedias)	80 individuals (in bad condition)
Martsalos (Kainurio)	some twenty individuals
Moni Chrisoskalitsas (Kissamos)	few individuals
Turkey	
Finike (Antalya)	few individuals (?)
Marmaris-Datça Road (Mugla)	few individuals
Eksere/Datça (Mugla)	few individuals
Gölköy (Bodrum)	some hundred individuals, although this population is of unknown taxonomic status

The possible presence of *Phoenix theophrasti* on the islands of Kalimnos, Nisiros, and Simi requires confirmation (Turland *et al.* 1993).

---

distinct. Several features are shared with, or are intermediate between *P. theophrasti* and *P. dactylifera*, but future studies are needed to show if it constitutes a separate taxon, and whether hybridization may be involved. This palm grove occurs in a marshy area, and has been known for hundreds of years. Although it grows within a protected area, plans are being made to drain the area to build a golf course. Since the construction of a drainage trench, the water level and period of flooding has been reduced, and may already have reached a critical level. An additional threat to the palm grove is fire. In June 1993 a fire set to clear land for development got out of control and partly destroyed the palm grove, although fortunately the grove recovered well. The small stands of *P. theophrasti* on the Datça Peninsula and at Finike Bay mostly grow on steep calcareous cliffs or along remote, inhabited beaches, and are therefore quite safe at present. However, a growing tourist village at Finike Bay poses a threat to certain outlying parts of this population (Boydak and Barrow 1995).

Theophrastus's date palm is considered as Vulnerable on the Red List for Europe (UN Economic Commission for Europe 1991). It must be considered Endangered following the new IUCN Red List Criteria (IUCN 1994).

It is protected under the Bern Convention (Convention of September 19, 1979 relating to the preservation of the wildlife and natural environment in Europe) and by the Habitats Directive of the European Community (Directive on the Conservation of Natural Habitats and of Wild Fauna and Flora 92/43/EEC), describing it as a species of community interest, conservation of which requires the designation of special conservation areas. Moreover, the Habitat Directive gives priority to the designation of special conservation areas for *Phoenix* palm groves as natural habitats. The Vaï palm grove is also protected under Greek legislation (Montmollin and Iatroù 1995).

Recommendations

Even if Theophrastus's date palm will probably not disappear tomorrow, it is important to understand the ecological requirements of this species, and to take practical and legal measures for the conservation and strengthening of existing populations. These measures should give priority to the small isolated populations, in order to safeguard the genetic variability of the species. The following steps are proposed:

1) **Study the population structure, ecology, and conservation status of all populations.**

a) Census the existing populations, and determine the vitality and reproductive potential of each population.
b) Define the ecological requirements of Theophrastus's date palm, especially relating to water requirements (both quantitatively and qualitatively).

c) Outline the present and potential threats for each population.

2) **Design and implement a management plan, based on scientific research.**

Before taking conservation action, clear objectives of conservation need to be formulated. The management plan has to consider the following measures:
a) practical conservation measures for threatened populations (*in situ* conservation) adapted to the ecological requirements of the species;
b) increasing numbers of populations under a critical size (*ex situ* propagation and management);
c) additional legal protection of Theophrastus's date palm populations (protected areas);
d) information and encouragement of local communities to participate in the conservation process.

3) **Urgently implement practical and legal conservation measures to protect the threatened populations at Gölköy, Vaï, and Stalida.**

Conservation of the dwarf palm, *Chamaerops humilis*

The dwarf palm occurs in the western Mediterranean basin in open habitats at low elevations, usually near the coast. Its conservation status in northern Africa, Italy, and Portugal is poorly known. The populations of Spain and the Balearic islands are not considered as threatened (Threatened Plants Unit 1983), indeed it is in some places a very common plant in scrub and forest vegetation. However, the palm is now Extinct in Malta, and has been rapidly declining in France where it was even thought to be Extinct due to urbanization and collection. Very small relict populations have since been discovered, but are highly threatened (Roux 1995). The situation is probably similar in other regions.

Recommendations

1) **Check the actual range of occurrence, and record population sizes.**

2) **Monitor individual populations to assess dynamics and reproductive capability.**

3) **Conduct additional cytological studies.**

4) **Protect the most important populations.**

In France this could be either through acquisition by the "Conservatoire de l'espace littoral et des rivages lacustres" or by "Arrêté de conservation de biotope" (see the French Red List Roux 1995 for more details).

(Contact: B. de Montmollin)

Chapter 11

Regional Priorities in Australia and the Pacific Islands

This chapter deals with Australia, New Zealand, and the south-west Pacific Islands. The latter include the island groups of New Caledonia, Fiji, and Vanuatu which have high palm diversity and endemism. Additionally, a section on Hawaii and a short discussion on other Pacific Islands is included.

Australia

Australia, defined here to include the continent as well as the off-shore island territories of Lord Howe and Norfolk Islands in the Tasman Sea, and Christmas Island in the Indian Ocean, has about 63 indigenous species in 23 genera with an endemism rate of 86%.

The conservation status of Australian palms has been documented by Thomas and McDonald (1987), Briggs and Leigh (1988), Dowe (1990), Leach et al. (1992) and Leigh and Briggs (1992). Due to the continuing development of an extensive network of national parks and protected areas, all but two of Australia's 63 palm species have some form of conservation protection. The two species which presently do not receive such protection, although threatened, have been placed on nature protection lists which are being developed by various State

governments for legislative purposes (e.g. the Nature Conservation Act, Queensland 1992).

Twelve species of Australian palms with a Vulnerable or Endangered conservation classification are listed in Table 11.1. An additional 16 species are Rare, but these shall not be considered here as they grow in national parks or other protected areas, and are relatively well protected.

Status of Endangered and Vulnerable taxa

Two species of Australian palms, *Archontophoenix myolensis* and *Ptychosperma bleeseri*, are Endangered, while ten species are Vulnerable (see Table 11.1). Only one Endangered species (*A. myolensis*) and one Vulnerable species (*Livistona lanuginosa*) are not conserved in a national park or other protected area. Of the remaining ten threatened taxa, varying percentages of their populations are conserved, thus offering some protection.

Considerable action has been taken to conserve *Ptychosperma bleeseri*, which is restricted to monsoon forest patches in the Top End of the Northern Territory, Australia. The species has been the focus of an intense collaborative program jointly undertaken by the federal government's Endangered Species Program, the

---

Table 11.1 Highly threatened palms of Australia and its territories*

Species	Status[1]	Distribution[2] < 100 km² >		Prot. Area[3]
Archontophoenix myolensis Dowe	E	+		no
Arenga australasica (H.A. Wendl. & Drude) S.T. Blake	V		+	yes
Calamus warburgii Schumann	V	+		yes
Gulubia costata Becc.	V		+	yes
Hedyscepe canterburyana (C. Moore & F. Muell.) H.A. Wendl.& Drude	V	+		yes
Lepidorrhachis mooreana (F. Muell.) Cook	V	+		yes
Livistona alfredii F. Muell.	V	+		yes
L. drudei F. Muell. ex W. Watson	V		+	yes
L. lanuginosa A.N. Rodd *in edit.*	V	+		no
L. mariae F. Muell.	V	+		yes
Normanbya normanbyi (W. Hill) L. Bailey	V	+		yes
Ptychosperma bleeseri Burret	E	+		yes

* Compiled from Thomas and McDonald (1987), Leach *et al.* (1992), and the proposed list for The Nature Conservation Act, Queensland (1992) prepared by Department of Environment and Heritage in conjunction with Queensland Herbarium.

[1] Status: All conservation status is global with the exception of *Calamus warburgii* which is also found on the South Solomon Island and Papua New Guinea and has a global status of Rare; and *Gulubia costata*, which is more widespread and not threatened globally.

[2] Distribution: Species are either noted as having a geographic range of less than 100 km² or greater than 100 km² (but usually in small, disjunct populations).

[3] Protected area: This indicates whether or not the species is conserved in a protected area.

Conservation Commission of the Northern Territory, the Palm & Cycad Society of the Northern Territory, and private landholders. Studies to establish population numbers and demography have been completed (Russell-Smith and Lucas 1990), while a strategy for protecting the remaining populations has been put into place (Wightman 1992; Liddle 1993). A number of protected areas have been created explicitly to protect this species. Land has been acquired from private owners and mutual agreements with other landholders regarding access, etc., have been established. The main populations have been fenced to deter feral pigs, water buffaloes, and horticultural pilfering, the major threats to the palm. As a result of these activities, *Ptychosperma bleeseri* is now a well protected species.

The need to conserve *Archontophoenix myolensis* and *Livistona lanuginosa* has yet to be recognized; details and conservation recommendations for these species are noted below.

Recommendations for species conservation

1) *Livistona lanuginosa* — the Cape River *Livistona*

Status: Vulnerable. This Coryphoid palm is one of only two species of Australian palms not conserved in a national park or declared protected area. All known populations occur on private land in an area which is being developed for pastoral and/or agricultural activities.

Distribution: Queensland, Australia. Known from the Cape and Campaspe rivers, and middle reaches of the Burdekin River, but also suspected to occur on the Suttor, Selheim, and Belyando rivers.

Habitat: seasonally dry creek beds and banks, where underground water is available, in open *Eucalyptus* forest.

Cultivation: successfully used as a street tree in Townsville, proving tolerant of drought and exposure, though otherwise only cultivated by enthusiasts; growing in The Palmetum (12 mature plants) and Anderson Park Botanic Gardens (6 mature plants), Townsville, Australia.

Conservation problem: this species is not conserved in a national park or other declared protected area. The region in which it occurs is being developed as an agricultural and pastoral area.

Recommended action: Declare a suitable area of either the Cape or Campaspe rivers, which both contain suitable representative populations of the palm, as a national park. Sufficiently detailed demographic data on which to make such a decision are lacking. A survey to obtain these data could be achieved through the study of aerial photographs of the appropriate parts of the Burdekin River system, or by a ground survey.

2) *Archontophoenix myolensis* – the Myola *Archontophoenix*

Status: Endangered. This Arecoid palm is one of only two species of Australian palms not conserved in a national park or declared protected area. All known populations occur on private land in an area which is being developed on an urban/rural basis.

Distribution: Queensland, Australia. Known only from the Warrill Creek and Barron River area of eastern Atherton Tablelands.

Habitat: moist riverine forest, at 350–400 m elevation, high rainfall with a strong seasonal influence.

Cultivation: Anderson Park Botanic Gardens, Townsville (4 plants).

Conservation problem: this species is not conserved in a national park or other declared protected area. The entire known population, estimated at less than 100 individuals, is confined to a very small area. The surrounding area is rural/urban, with a rapidly increasing population.

Recommended Action: The entire area where this species is found should be declared a national park, although currently detailed demographic data is lacking. Therefore, a ground survey to determine exactly where this species is found urgently needs to be undertaken, and protected area status should follow.

(Contact: J. Dowe)

New Zealand

New Zealand and its off-shore islands are geographically and floristically quite isolated. Only three palm species, belonging to one endemic genus, are native to New Zealand. *Rhopalostylis sapida* has an Indeterminate (but threatened) conservation status. *Rhopalostylis baueri* var. *cheesemanii* is confined to Kermadec island and Rare (var. *baueri* being confined to Norfolk Island of Australia, and equally Rare).

South-west Pacific Islands

In the present context, the South-west Pacific comprises the island groups of Vanuatu, Fiji, and New Caledonia. The palm flora includes 76 species in 35 genera. There is considerable diversity at the generic level, with 15 monotypic genera (some of which may yet prove to be congeneric) and with five genera with only two to four species. The number of moderately large genera (i.e. more than ten species) confined or almost confined to the region is only two (*Basselinia* and *Veitchia*), both of which are a result of recent adaptive radiation, while species belonging to very large genera (*Calamus* and *Licuala*) are at the geographical limit of genera which have their centers of diversity elsewhere. The endemism rate of species within the individual island groups is very high, with many confined to single islands (Table 11.2).

The fan palm *Licuala ramsayi*, in habitat, wet coastal lowland, ▶ Queensland, Australia. Vulnerable in Australia.

Wendy Strahm

Table 11.2 Palm distribution in the South-west Pacific

Area	Genera	Species	Endemics	% Endemism
Vanuatu	7	17	12	72
Fiji	10	26	24	92
New Caledonia	18	33	32	97

Table 11.3 The most threatened palms in the South-west Pacific*

Species	Occurrence[1]	Conservation status
Alsmithia longipes H. Moore	Fiji	V
Balaka seemannii Becc.	Fiji	V
Burretiokentia hapala H. Moore	New Caledonia	V
Carpoxylon macrospermum H.A. Wendl. & Drude	Vanuatu	E
Cyphophoenix nucele H. Moore	New Caledonia	E
Cyphosperma tanga H. Moore	Fiji	V
Kentiopsis oliviformis (Brongn. & Gris) Brongn.	New Caledonia	E
Lavoixia macrocarpa H. Moore	New Caledonia	E
Neoveitchia storckii (H.A. Wendl.) Becc.	Fiji	E
Pritchardiopsis jeanneneyi Becc.	New Caledonia	V
Veitchia montgomeryana H. Moore	Vanuatu	E
V. vitiensis (H. Wendl.) H. Moore	Fiji	V

* Compiled from data from the World Conservation Monitoring Centre (April 1993). However, Lear (March 1994, *in litt.* to the WCMC) considers two additional species of *Veitchia* (*V. pedionoma* and *V. petiolata*) from Vanua Levu (Fiji) as Endangered, and a third species from the same island (*V. filifera*) as possibly Extinct. *Veitchia spiralis* from Aneityum (Vanuatu) is now also considered as Endangered.

[1] All palms are endemic.

Conservation status

According to WCMC, of the 76 palm species in the region, six are Endangered and six are Vulnerable. A regional breakdown indicates that Vanuatu has two Endangered taxa; Fiji, one Endangered and four Vulnerable; New Caledonia, three Endangered and two Vulnerable (see Table 11.3). Conservation action is already being taken or initiated with five species: *Neoveitchia storckii* in Fiji, and *Kentiopsis oliviformis*, *Lavoixia macrocarpa*, *Cyphophoenix nucele*, and *Pritchardiopsis jeanneneyi* in New Caledonia.

A priority listing of five species which are recommended as conservation subjects follows. The selection has taken two factors into consideration: the lack of conservation action, and the potential contribution which these actions would make to the maintenance of genetic diversity within the family.

Recommendations for species conservation

1) *Carpoxylon macrospermum*

Status: Endangered. A monotypic genus with affinities in the *Clinostigma* alliance (subtribe Iguanurinae); distinguished from other taxa by characters of fruit structure. Indeed, this taxon is the sole representative of a strongly divergent line of evolution within the *Clinostigma* alliance.

Distribution: Vanuatu. Rediscovered in 1987, the palm was suspected to be Extinct in the Wild until a PEP (Profitable Environmental Protection) funded project revealed that some wild palms still exist. About 150 mature individuals are known of which about 40 occur naturally in rain forest on Tanna, Futuna, and Aneityum; the remainder are cultivated in villages on several islands. The Tanna population includes virtually all of the genetic variability inherent in the remaining individuals of the species and should be the focus of any species recovery program.

Habitat: lowland rain forest; grows as an emergent.

Cultivation: Brest Conservatoire, France (2 plants); The Palmetum, Townsville (4 plants); Darwin Botanic Gardens (2 plants); University of the South Pacific Botanic Garden, Suva, Fiji (3 plants); a few private collections.

Conservation problem: this species is not conserved in a national park or other declared protected area in Vanuatu. Wild populations are extremely small and may need reinforcement. A pilot seed export business has been established in order to export and sell seeds collected from cultivated plants as a funding mechanism to support conservation activities. The first shipments could be sold for US$6 per seed, and this activity should be continued.

Recommended action:

a) Conserve the palm's genetic variability by protecting the appropriate wild stands on Tanna and elsewhere.

b) Conduct studies on ecology and population biology of the species in order to define conservation measures.

c) Establish viable *ex situ* populations throughout the range in Vanuatu, and then reinforce the wild populations if necessary.

d) Continue the seed export business as a funding mechanism for conservation activities.

(Contact: J. Dowe, S. Siwatibau)

2) *Alsmithia longipes*

Status: Vulnerable. A monotypic genus with affinity to others in the *Clinostigma* alliance, but isolated and distinct by virtue of characters of leaf, inflorescence, and fruit structure. A combination of large inflorescence and large fruit with an elaborately sculptured endocarp distinguish it from related taxa.

Distribution: Fiji. Known from a single population at moderate to high elevation on the eastern slopes of the island of Taveuni (Moore *et al.* 1982; Dowe 1989). This area has an estimated rainfall of 6000 to 10,000 mm per annum.

Habitat: moderate to high altitude rain forest, with a very high rainfall, as an understory to semi-emergent component.

Cultivation: Flecker Botanical Gardens, Cairns (8 plants); Anderson Park Botanic Gardens, Townsville (4 plants); University of the South Pacific Botanical Gardens, Suva, Fiji.

Conservation problem: this species is not conserved in a national park or other declared protected area. The area in which the remaining populations occur is being logged.

Recommended action:

a) Halt logging where the species occurs, and promote designation of a protected area;

b) arrange regular collection of fruit by the Department of Forestry for distribution to appropriate botanic institutions which will undertake *ex situ* conservation.

3) *Cyphosperma tanga*

Status: Vulnerable. A species which expresses a unique line of palm evolution in the South-west Pacific region; distinguished from other taxa in characters of leaf, inflorescence and fruit structure.

Distribution: Fiji. Endemic to the island of Viti Levu at 600–900 m elevation in the vicinity of Navai, Ndromodromo Creek and Namboutini (Moore 1979; Dowe 1989). The remaining populations are scattered, with most having only a few plants. With removal of the natural forest for the establishment of pine plantations, the colonies have become increasingly isolated from each other.

Habitat: rain forest at 600–900 m elevation, as an understory component.

Cultivation: not known to be in cultivation.

Conservation problem: this species is not conserved in a national park or other declared protected area in Fiji. The remaining populations are in forested areas which are planned to be converted to pine plantations.

Recommended action:

a) Declare a representative area in which this species occurs as a protected area;

b) arrange regular collection of fruit by Department of Forestry (Fiji) or Department of Botany, University of the South Pacific, for distribution to appropriate botanic institutions which will undertake *ex situ* conservation.

4) *Balaka seemannii*

Status: Endangered.

Distribution: Fiji. Endemic to the island of Taveuni, at 0–1000 m elevation (Dowe 1989). Extensive areas of its former range have been converted to coconut plantations, while the remaining areas are being logged. This distinct species grows in the same area as *Alsmithia longipes*, which is subject to the same threats.

Habitat: rain forest at 1–1000 m elevation, as an understory component.

Cultivation: The Palmetum, Townsville (4 plants); Mt. Coot-tha Botanic Gardens, Brisbane; Flecker Botanical Gardens, Cairns (12 plants); University of the South Pacific Botanical Gardens, Suva, Fiji; numerous specimens in other gardens in tropical areas, although identity may not be correct for some.

Conservation problem: this species is not conserved in a national park or other declared protected area in Fiji. The area in which the remaining populations occur is being logged.

Recommended action:

a) Halt logging in the area;

b) declare an adequate protected area.

5) *Veitchia montgomeryana*

Status: Endangered. This palm has congeneric species in Vanuatu, Fiji, and the Philippines. It is notable as an integral indicator in the biogeography of the genus, and palms in general, for the South-west Pacific; distinguished from other taxa in floral and fruit characteristics.

Distribution: Vanuatu. Known only from Efate where it is now confined to remnant forest patches, particularly in the southern parts of the island (Dowe 1989); it is an uncommon species in the interior forests. The population (1992) is estimated to be only a few hundred individuals.

Habitat: lowland rain forest, emergent, usually on limestone.

Cultivation: The Palmetum, Townsville (3 plants); Mt. Coot-tha Botanic Gardens, Brisbane; Flecker Botanical Gardens, Cairns; numerous specimens in other gardens in tropical areas, although identity may not be correct for some (Moore 1957).

Conservation problem: this species is being used as a source of palm heart salad in restaurants in the Port Vila area. Plants from the remnant forest patches are being taken; subsequently, the number of remaining plants is dwindling. The species is not conserved in a national park or other declared protected area in Vanuatu, though the palm is reported to be cultivated in many botanic gardens and private collections throughout the world.

Recommended action:

a) Declare an appropriate area where the palm still occurs in reasonably large numbers (such as the Telecom reserve at Snake Hill or the verges of Tagabe Airport), as a protected area;

b) ban the commercial exploitation of palm heart (and/or promote cultivation of appropriate species for that purpose);

c) arrange regular collection of fruit by Department of Livestock and Forestry (Vanuatu) or ORSTOM (Vanuatu) for distribution to appropriate botanic institutions which will undertake *ex situ* conservation.

(Contact: J. Dowe)

Hawaii

The Hawaiian Archipelago harbors about 23 species of a single palm genus, *Pritchardia*. Each species is confined to a single island. While a few species are common, others are extremely rare with only a few individuals remaining; eight are at the verge of extinction.

Field observations reveal that populations within areas free of feral pigs regenerate well, as evidenced by seedling establishment (Pu'u Kukui, Maui; Huelo Islet, Molokai; Ola'a Forest tract, small Hawai'i Volcanoes National Park, Hawai'i). In most other populations seedlings are not observed. All populations are otherwise threatened to some extent by invasive plants which outcompete the seedlings. Rats are major seed predators. Although efforts are being made to prevent such losses, a recent assessment has shown, that these are often ineffective (Gemmill *et al.* 1993).

The species federally listed as Endangered or proposed for listing (*) include:

Kaua'i:

- *Pritchardia napaliensis** (less than 90 individuals left; some young plants, propagated by the National Tropical Botanical Garden, have been outplanted);
- *P. viscosa** (only 2 mature individuals);

Hawai'i:

- *P. schattaueri** (the Giant Pritchardia, only 12 individuals left in three populations);

- *P. affinis* (about 60 individuals known in the wild);

Moloka'i:
- *P. munroi* (only one single wild individual);

Niihau:
- *P. aylmer-robinsonii*[*] (known from only two individuals in a single wild population);

Nihoa:
- *P. remota*[*] (known from two populations with about 680 individuals);

O'ahu:
- *P. kaalae*[*] (two populations).

Other rare or threatened populations include *Pritchardia glabrata* from Maui, *P. hardyi* (30 individuals) and *P. hillebrandii* from Moloka'i (with healthy populations on an off-shore island), probably one of three more (yet undescribed) species from Kaua'i, and *P. lanigera* from Hawai'i.

Recommendations

1) Add the above mentioned species to the Federal list of Endangered Species.

2) *In situ* conservation.

Preserve the intact natural populations of *Pritchardia* species. Banding of trees against rats (seed predators) is essential for many populations; intensive field studies, pig eradication programs, and/or construction of exclosures around selected populations are required as well. This involves many people, agencies, helicopter time, etc.

3) *Ex situ* conservation.

Collect seeds over time from as many wild plant individuals as possible to maximize the level of genetic diversity. The seedlings of each accession should be genetically characterized to maximize the genetic diversity that is to be re-introduced into the natural population. The National Tropical Botanical Garden is currently propagating rare and Endangered species for future augmentation of stabilized (free of feral animals) populations. Research

Pritchardia hillebrandii, Huelo Islet, north coast of Maloka'i, Hawai'i.

Pritchardia minor, Koke'e, Kaua'i, Hawai'i.

Chrissen Gemmill

Chrissen Gemmill

on conservation genetics is currently in progress (Gemmill *et al.* 1993; Gemmill, in progress; Hahn and Gemmill, in prep).

(Contact: C. Gemmill, D. Lorence)

Other Pacific Islands

The knowledge of the palm flora of the many small Pacific Islands is incomplete. Some species are widespread while others are confined to a single island, like the Rare and monotypic *Pelagodoxa henryana* from the Marquesas, or *Pritchardia* sp. from the Cook islands. According to the threatened plant database held at WCMC, Western Samoa harbors 11 endemic species, belonging to the genera *Clinostigma*, *Balaka*, and *Drymophloeus*; the Caroline islands have three palms, all endemic (*Clinostigma*, *Ptychosperma*); the Federated States of Micronesia have a single native species (the endemic and threatened *Clinostigma carolinensis*); American Guam only *Nypa fruticans*; from Palau and Tonga, only widespread species of *Heterospathe* and *Pritchardia*, respectively; and finally, *Caryota urens* from South Solomon. However, the conservation status of all these palms is insufficiently known and more field studies are needed.

Recommendation

Field surveys in Pacific Islands.

A general recommended conservation action for Oceania is to carry out field surveys of those island groups where the flora is poorly known to re-collect palm species needing further study and to assess the *in situ* conservation status of all palms.

(Contact: J. Dowe)

Chapter 12

Action Plan for Palm Conservation and Utilization

This chapter summarizes the recommendations and projects proposed in the previous chapters. While many actions are in urgent need of attention and are ready to be implemented, others need more detailed planning and a leading organization to be appointed to do so. Some, maybe of equal importance, are not even described in this Action Plan, as information for many regions is unavailable.

Priorities

The actions recommended here address a range of objectives. Some are clearly of first priority addressing immediate needs. Many will fill the vast knowledge gaps of the biology and ecology of palms. All of these proposed actions could help launch a permanent global effort to conserve palms.

a) **Produce conservation checklists of the Atlantic forest of Brazil and the forests of Irian Jaya and Papua New Guinea.**

The Atlantic Forest of Brazil is one of the most threatened forest ecosystems in the Americas. It has a rich palm diversity and numerous species of Unknown conservation status. This checklist would build upon recent field research in several Brazilian states and provide an overall understanding of the importance of Palmae.

The island of New Guinea represents the world's most extensive area of high palm diversity with almost nonexistent *in situ* conservation data. This checklist can be a counterpart to the systematic treatment of the Arecaceae for the *Flora Malesiana*, launched in 1995.

b) **Implement management plans for Endangered palms in Madagascar.**

Most of the palm species are threatened, and 20 possibly Extinct (Ex/E) in the Wild. These species should be given highest priority for re-collection, research on ecological requirements, *in situ* protection, and *ex situ* cultivation.

c) **Implement management plans for Endangered island palms in the Indian and Pacific Oceans.**

Palms on these islands are either threatened by invasive species, by direct exploitation, or by logging activities.

This commonality amongst these islands justifies a combined effort to prevent numerous extinctions, especially of monotypic genera. Promising palm conservation approaches in the Indian Ocean may have potential in the Pacific Ocean, and vice versa.

d) **Rescue other species.**

The following palms urgently need rescue actions; the development of appropriate approaches might serve as case studies:

i) *Corypha talieri*, Extinct in the Wild, from India;
ii) *Calamus pacystemonus*, Endangered and endemic to Sri Lanka, only recently refound and not under cultivation;
iii) *Roystonea stellata*, from Guantanamo, Cuba. Attempts to find this species in the field in 1990 were unsuccessful. Possibly Extinct in the Wild, but probably growing in a botanical garden in Cuba;
iv) *Salacca lophospatha*, known from two sites in Sabah. Possibly Extinct.

Palm Secretariat

An overall priority is the creation of an effective Secretariat for the Palm Specialist Group, which would provide a framework to support and coordinate various palm conservation actions. The extra effort required of this objective will be more than repaid in the benefits derived from sharing information and ideas among project implementers. It will also strengthen the network of the IUCN/SSC Palm Specialist Group and other palm specialists. The main tasks of the secretariat will be to:

a) In collaboration with WCMC, assume primary responsibility to refine and maintain a sound database of information about all palms, including *in situ* conservation status, occurrence in protected areas, status of cultivation, levels of utilization, and results of current and ongoing research;
b) Promote and facilitate exchange of information and knowledge between all institutions involved in palm conservation;
c) Provide reports and technical data needed to set priorities and implement palm conservation action (e.g. establishment and management of protected areas, cultivation practices, and reintroduction)

d) Promote and coordinate global palm conservation through an urgently needed meeting of the whole IUCN/SSC Palm Specialist Group;

e) Coordinate the reassessment of the conservation status of all palms, applying the new, quantitative IUCN Red List categories and criteria;

f) Coordinate the development of a species triage policy and procedure. Given the number of brink-of-extinction cases and limited feasible conservation actions, the difficult question arises as to which species should be given priority. A ranking procedure should take into account accurate and comparable *in situ* conservation data (based on the application of the revised IUCN Red List criteria), evolutionary uniqueness of a species, economic value, feasibility, etc.

Overview of recommendations made in this Action Plan

This section aims to summarize and group all recommendations given in this Action Plan into logical units. In addition, the maps (Figures 12.1 through 12.4) may serve as a quick reference for what is needed in different countries and regions.

Research

Research is one of the most important pillars of conservation. Much more research is needed in order to set a basis for assessments of conservation priorities, to develop urgently needed management plans for Endangered palms, to study poorly known areas and species, and to define the areas of highest palm diversity and their conservation needs.

1) Study palms of poorly known forests with high palm diversity.

See Figure 12.1.

2) Study threatened non-economic palms.

Palms which are described in more detail in one of the previous chapters are presented in Figure 12.1. Many more threatened palms need preliminary studies to set up conservation action.

3) Conduct taxonomic and ecological research.

a) New World genera needing revision: *Attalea, Bactris, Copernicia, Desmoncus, Geonoma, Roystonea*; for *Coccothrinax*, a comprehensive study including socioeconomics is recommended.

b) Old World genera needing revision: *Areca, Licuala, Pinanga, Salacca*, and, in combination with general research in this area, many genera of Papuasia.

c) National Floras of Venezuela, Malaysia, and the Philippines. Many other countries, especially in Indochina, are in need of national palm treatments, others are in progress (see Chapter 2). In the countries mentioned above, local specialists are ready to start work.

d) Floristic inventories of rattan palms are needed in Myanmar, Vietnam, Laos, Kampuchea, Sulawesi, the Moluccas, the Philippines, Irian Jaya, and Papua New Guinea. Publications appropriate for utilization by foresters should be encouraged.

4) Study threatened and underdeveloped economic palms.

See Chapter 4, Economic and Ornamental Palms.

In situ conservation

It is important to note that many of the research projects mentioned above will reveal a need for many more important and specific conservation actions belonging to various types.

5) Establish or strengthen protected areas.

Only a few larger protected areas which are extraordinarily important for palms can be proposed at present. However, the target of many recommendations are small scale habitat/species management areas, which are crucial for species conservation (see Figure 12.2).

6) Other legal regulations needed.

Palm and nature conservation in general should be promoted by legal measures, including options of financial incentives and support for appropriate projects. The specific measures recommended in this Action Plan are represented in Figure 12.2.

7) Specific conservation actions.

Specific physical improvements of habitat are an integral step towards recovery. See Figure 12.2.

Ex situ conservation

In spite of important restrictions, *ex situ* cultivation can play an important role in the conservation of Endangered palms. Besides conserving germplasm and providing sources for reintroductions (and for breeding programs of economic palms as well, see Chapter 4), such collections also constitute living laboratories for scientific studies of wild palms.

8) Establish living palm collections.

Besides big and well-managed palm collections (e.g. at Fairchild Tropical Garden, USA; Royal Botanic Gardens, Kew; Townsville Botanic Garden, Australia), it is important to establish or strengthen local botanic gardens in different regions of the world in order to initiate breeding programs for the most Endangered palms (see Figure 12.3).

9) Prepare reintroductions of Endangered species.

Make preparations to reintroduce several species throughout the original ranges of certain species of palms. See Figure 12.3.

10) Cultivate other threatened palms.

Cultivate certain species of threatened palms to reduce pressure on their wild populations. See Figure 12.3.

Economic and ornamental palms

Over-exploitation of wild palm populations takes place for three main products: rattan cane, palm hearts, and ornamental plants. There are many other palms threatened by unsustainable use and conservation management plans urgently need to be developed (see Figure 12.4).

11) Palms threatened by palm heart extraction.

Legal regulations are needed to protect the most Endangered populations, accompanied by development of sustainable harvest schemes and a program to supply palm hearts from cultivation.

12) Threatened ornamental palms.

More research is needed to develop efficient propagation in nurseries, and palm growers should be discouraged from buying wild grown individuals of these palm species.

13) Palms threatened by exploitation for timber, leaves, etc.

Some of these palms are widely distributed and are therefore not threatened by extinction on a global level. However, to maintain their existence and the benefits to the local people, more sustainable management has to be developed. Many endemic palms are at the brink of extinction.

14) Palms with high potential for domestication.

Breeding and domestication programs are necessary to protect the wild stands from over-exploitation and to maintain the whole range of genetic diversity of the following palms:

Americas:
a) macaúba (*Acrocomia aculeata*),
b) tucuma (*Astrocaryum vulgare*),
c) piaçava (*Attalea funifera*),
d) babaçu (*Attalea speciosa*, syn.: *Orbignya phalerata*),
e) carnaúba (*Copernicia prunifera*),
f) açai (*Euterpe oleracea, E. precatoria*),
g) juçara (*Euterpe edulis*),
h) buriti (*Mauritia flexuosa*),
i) patauá, bacaba, bacabi (*Oenocarpus* spp.),
j) licuri (*Syagrus coronata*).

Asia:
a) buri (*Corypha elata*),
b) kaong (*Arenga pinnata*),
c) sago (*Metroxylon sagu*),
d) nipa (*Nypa fruticans*),
e) salac (*Eleiodoxa conferta, Salacca affinis*),
f) rattans (*Calamus, Korthalsia, Daemonorops*).

Education and involvement of local people

Successful implementation of conservation actions such as the establishment of protected areas or reintroductions of palms within densely populated areas can only be achieved through the involvement of local people. In many cases, local people might benefit directly from the sustainable use of palm products, while in others, indirect benefits should be found or negotiated in return for the respect given to conservation issues.

Education plays an important role in conservation. New settlers, urban populations, or politicians rarely know the ecological and economic significance of palms, nor of the threats of menacing palms. Educational material should be widely distributed in schools and public campaigns. These educational tools should be produced in local languages, following the excellent examples of Malaysia (Kiew 1993) and Madagascar (Randrianasolo and Dransfield 1990). Planting of native palms as ornamentals, establishment of 'palm trails' in recreation areas or national parks, and educational programs in botanic gardens are other ways proposed to raise the profile of palms.

Implementation

The costs to carry out these proposed actions vary widely, depending on the nature of implementation. In many cases, the most favorable approach might be cooperation between existing organizations and research institutes, and the inclusion of palm projects in other aid and development projects and scientific expeditions.

However, some of the bigger projects will require more substantial funding, such as comprehensive research programs in specific areas, or the establishment of well-managed protected areas and *ex situ* breeding programs. Fortunately, many institutions are already involved in studies of major economic palms, but much more has to be done.

The proposed Secretariat of the Palm Specialist Group should enhance the process of implementation by coordinating projects, exchanging information (e.g. by means of a newsletter), and by helping with fundraising activities.

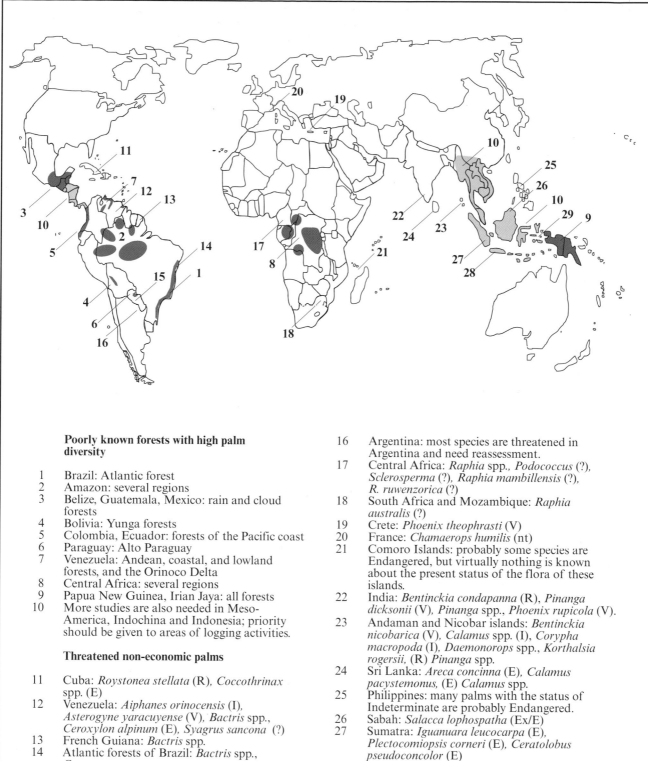

Poorly known forests with high palm diversity

1   Brazil: Atlantic forest
2   Amazon: several regions
3   Belize, Guatemala, Mexico: rain and cloud forests
4   Bolivia: Yunga forests
5   Colombia, Ecuador: forests of the Pacific coast
6   Paraguay: Alto Paraguay
7   Venezuela: Andean, coastal, and lowland forests, and the Orinoco Delta
8   Central Africa: several regions
9   Papua New Guinea, Irian Jaya: all forests
10 More studies are also needed in Meso-America, Indochina and Indonesia; priority should be given to areas of logging activities.

Threatened non-economic palms

11 Cuba: *Roystonea stellata* (R), *Coccothrinax* spp. (E)
12 Venezuela: *Aiphanes orinocensis* (I), *Asterogyne yaracuyense* (V), *Bactris* spp., *Ceroxylon alpinum* (E), *Syagrus sancona* (?)
13 French Guiana: *Bactris* spp.
14 Atlantic forests of Brazil: *Bactris* spp., *Geonoma* spp.
15 Paraguay: *Butia campicola* (E)

16 Argentina: most species are threatened in Argentina and need reassessment.
17 Central Africa: *Raphia* spp., *Podococcus* (?), *Sclerosperma* (?), *Raphia mambillensis* (?), *R. ruwenzorica* (?)
18 South Africa and Mozambique: *Raphia australis* (?)
19 Crete: *Phoenix theophrasti* (V)
20 France: *Chamaerops humilis* (nt)
21 Comoro Islands: probably some species are Endangered, but virtually nothing is known about the present status of the flora of these islands.
22 India: *Bentinckia condapanna* (R), *Pinanga dicksonii* (V), *Pinanga* spp., *Phoenix rupicola* (V).
23 Andaman and Nicobar islands: *Bentinckia nicobarica* (V), *Calamus* spp. (I), *Corypha macropoda* (I), *Daemonorops* spp., *Korthalsia rogersii*, (R) *Pinanga* spp.
24 Sri Lanka: *Areca concinna* (E), *Calamus pacystemonus*, (E) *Calamus* spp.
25 Philippines: many palms with the status of Indeterminate are probably Endangered.
26 Sabah: *Salacca lophospatha* (Ex/E)
27 Sumatra: *Iguanuara leucocarpa* (E), *Plectocomiopsis corneri* (E), *Ceratolobus pseudoconcolor* (E)
28 Java: *Ceratolobus glaucescens* (E), *C. pseudoconcolor* (E)
29 Ambon Island: *Drymophloeus oliviformis* (E)

Figure 12.1 Research needed
(global conservation status of most species is given in brackets)

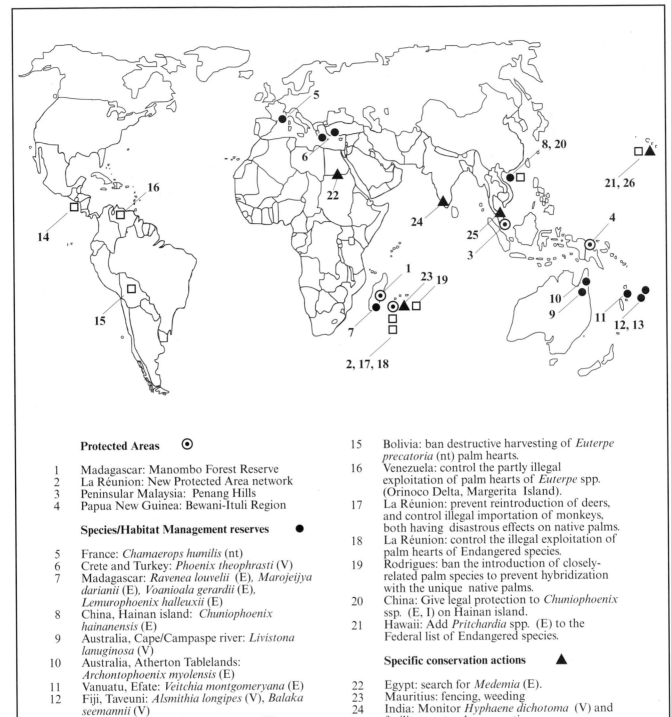

Protected Areas ⊙

1   Madagascar: Manombo Forest Reserve
2   La Réunion: New Protected Area network
3   Peninsular Malaysia: Penang Hills
4   Papua New Guinea: Bewani-Ituli Region

Species/Habitat Management reserves ●

5   France: *Chamaerops humilis* (nt)
6   Crete and Turkey: *Phoenix theophrasti* (V)
7   Madagascar: *Ravenea louvelii* (E), *Marojeijya darianii* (E), *Voanioala gerardii* (E), *Lemurophoenix halleuxii* (E)
8   China, Hainan island: *Chuniophoenix hainanensis* (E)
9   Australia, Cape/Campaspe river: *Livistona lanuginosa* (V)
10 Australia, Atherton Tablelands: *Archontophoenix myolensis* (E)
11 Vanuatu, Efate: *Veitchia montgomeryana* (E)
12 Fiji, Taveuni: *Alsmithia longipes* (V), *Balaka seemannii* (V)
13 Fiji, Viti Levu: *Cyphosperma tanga* (V)

Legal regulations needed □

14 Americas: *Chamaedorea* spp. (V, E) and other ornamental palms threatened by international trade should be monitored and a listing in Appendix II of the CITES convention should be proposed if necessary.

15 Bolivia: ban destructive harvesting of *Euterpe precatoria* (nt) palm hearts.
16 Venezuela: control the partly illegal exploitation of palm hearts of *Euterpe* spp. (Orinoco Delta, Margerita Island).
17 La Réunion: prevent reintroduction of deers, and control illegal importation of monkeys, both having disastrous effects on native palms.
18 La Réunion: control the illegal exploitation of palm hearts of Endangered species.
19 Rodrigues: ban the introduction of closely-related palm species to prevent hybridization with the unique native palms.
20 China: Give legal protection to *Chuniophoenix* ssp. (E, I) on Hainan island.
21 Hawaii: Add *Pritchardia* spp. (E) to the Federal list of Endangered species.

Specific conservation actions ▲

22 Egypt: search for *Medemia* (E).
23 Mauritius: fencing, weeding
24 India: Monitor *Hyphaene dichotoma* (V) and facilitate natural regeneration.
25 Peninsular Malaysia: Management of coastal palms (*Livistona saribus* (nt), *Phoenix paludosa* (nt))
26 Hawaii: Fence populations of Endangered species of *Pritchardia* and band stems against rats.

Figure 12.2 Protected areas, legislation, and other recommended conservation actions
(global conservation status of most species is given in brackets)

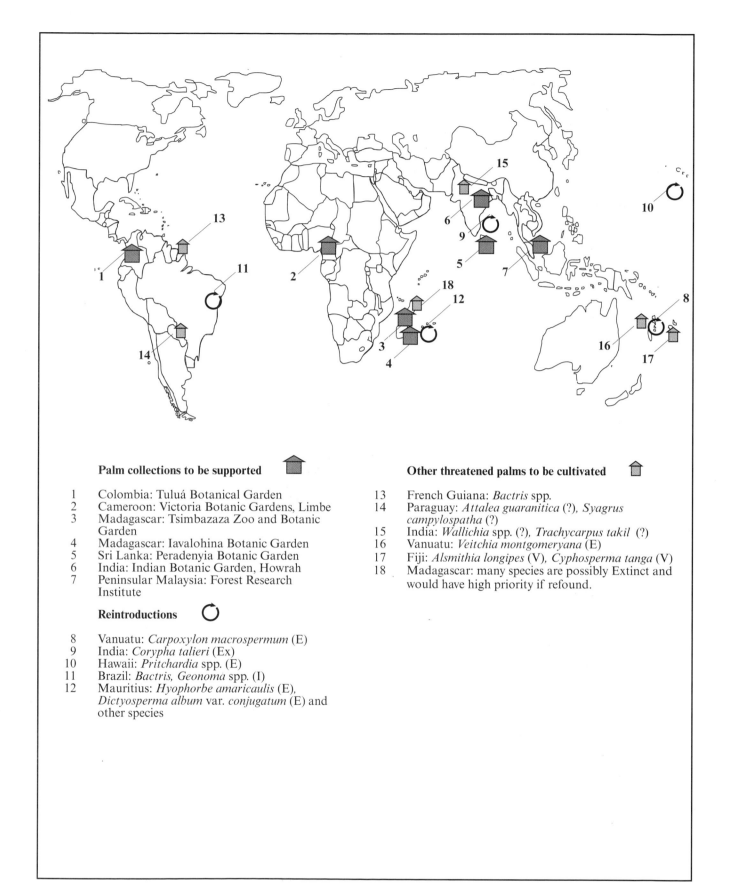

Palm collections to be supported 🏠

1 Colombia: Tuluá Botanical Garden
2 Cameroon: Victoria Botanic Gardens, Limbe
3 Madagascar: Tsimbazaza Zoo and Botanic Garden
4 Madagascar: Iavalohina Botanic Garden
5 Sri Lanka: Peradenyia Botanic Garden
6 India: Indian Botanic Garden, Howrah
7 Peninsular Malaysia: Forest Research Institute

Reintroductions ↻

8   Vanuatu: *Carpoxylon macrospermum* (E)
9   India: *Corypha talieri* (Ex)
10 Hawaii: *Pritchardia* spp. (E)
11 Brazil: *Bactris, Geonoma* spp. (I)
12 Mauritius: *Hyophorbe amaricaulis* (E), *Dictyosperma album* var. *conjugatum* (E) and other species

Other threatened palms to be cultivated 🏠

13 French Guiana: *Bactris* spp.
14 Paraguay: *Attalea guaranitica* (?), *Syagrus campylospatha* (?)
15 India: *Wallichia* spp. (?), *Trachycarpus takil* (?)
16 Vanuatu: *Veitchia montgomeryana* (E)
17 Fiji: *Alsmithia longipes* (V), *Cyphosperma tanga* (V)
18 Madagascar: many species are possibly Extinct and would have high priority if refound.

Figure 12.3 *Ex situ* conservation
(global conservation status of most species is given in brackets)

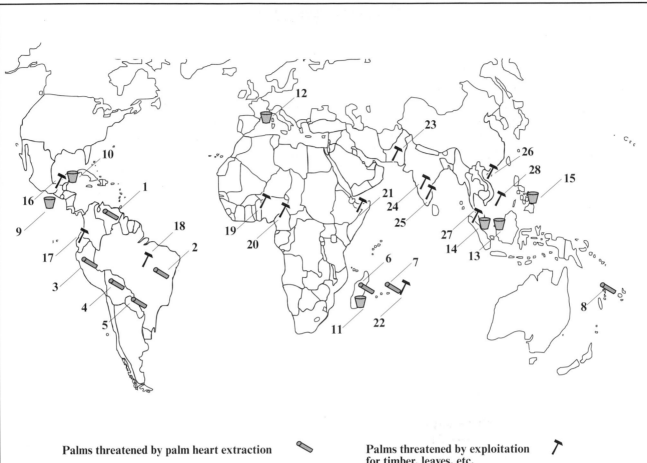

Palms threatened by palm heart extraction ⬤

1 Venezuela: *Euterpe oleracea* (nt) and *E. precatoria* (nt)
2 Brazil: *Euterpe* spp., *Attalea oleifera* (V)
3 Peru: *Euterpe* spp.
4 Bolivia: *Euterpe precatoria* (nt)
5 Paraguay: *Euterpe edulis* (V)
6 Madagascar: *Beccariophoenix madagascariensis* (E), *Dypsis decipiens* (E)
7 Mauritius and La Réunion: *Acanthophoenix rubra* (E), *Dictyosperma album* (E)
8 Vanuatu: *Veitchia montgomeryana* (E)

Threatened ornamental palms 🪣

9 Mexico, Americas: *Chamaedorea* spp. (E,V)
10 Mexico: *Pseudophoenix sargentii* (V)
11 Madagascar: *Marojejya darianii* (E), *Voanioala gerardii* (E)
12 France: *Chamaerops humilis* (nt)
13 Malaysia: *Johannesteijsmannia* spp. (E,V)
14 Peninsular Malaysia, Thailand: *Cyrtostachys renda* (nt)
15 Philippines: *Licuala spinosa* (nt)

Palms threatened by exploitation for timber, leaves, etc, 🔨

16 Southern Mexico: *Thrinax radiata* (nt), *Coccothrinax argentata* (nt)
17 Andean range: *Ceroxylon* spp. (V)
18 Brazil: *Syagrus coronata* (V)
19 West Africa: *Borassus aethiopum* (nt)
20 West Africa: rattans (*Eremospatha* (?) *Laccosperma* (?))
21 Somalia: *Livistona carinensis* (I), *Hyphaene* spp.
22 Rodrigues: *Latania verschaffeltii* (E)
23 Pakistan: *Nannorhops ritchiana* (?)
24 India: *Borassus flabellifer* (nt), *Caryota urens* (nt).
25 India: *Arenga wightii* (V)
26 China: *Chuniophoenix hainanensis* (E)
27 Malaysia: *Oncosperma tigillarum* (nt)
28 Asia (throughout): rattans (*Calamus* spp.; E,V)

Figure 12.4 Palms identified as threatened by economic or ornamental use
(global conservation status of most species is given in brackets)

References

Alam, M.K. 1990. *Rattans of Bangladesh.* Bangladesh Forest Research Institute, Chittagong.

Anon. 1991. *Endangered species and habitats of Thailand.* Ecological Research Department, Thailand. Inst. of Scientific and Technological Research. 239pp.

Ashton, P.S. and Gunatilleke, C.V.S. 1987. New light on the plant geography of Ceylon I – Historical plant geography. *Journal of Biogeography* 14:249–285.

Atkinson, P.J., Maunder, M. and Walter, K.S. 1995. *A reference list for plant re-introductions, recovery plans and restoration programmes.* Royal Botanic Gardens, Kew, U.K.

Bailey, L.H. 1942. Palms of the Seychelles. *Gentes Herbarum* 6(1):1–48.

Baldwin, M.F. (ed.) 1991. *Natural resources of Sri Lanka: conditions and trends.* Natural Resources Authority of Sri Lanka, Colombo.

Balick, M.J. 1988. Natural hybridization in neotropical palms. Pp.29–30 *in* Dransfield, J., Johnson, D. and Synge, H. *The palms of the New World: a conservation census.* IUCN-WWF Plants Conservation Programme, Pub. 2, Gland, Switzerland.

Balick, M.J. and Johnson, D. 1994. The conservation status of *Schippia concolor* in Belize. *Principes* 38(3):124–128

Barclay, C. 1974. A new locality of wild *Phoenix* in Crete. *Ann. Mus. Goulandris* 2:23–29.

Basu, S.K. 1991. India: Palm utilization and conservation. Pp.13–35 in Johnson, D. (ed.), *Palms for human needs in Asia.* Balkema, Rotterdam.

Basu, S.K. 1992. *Rattans (canes) in India: a monographic revision.* Rattan Information Centre, Forest Research Institute Malaysia, Kepong, Kuala Lumpur, Malaysia.

Basu, S.K. and Chakraverty, R.K. 1995. *A manual of cultivated palms in India.* Botanical Survey of India, Howrah.

Bates, D.M. 1987. The Robert and Catherine Wilson botanical garden at Las Cruces, Costa Rica. *Botanic Gardens Conservation News* 1(1):22–28.

Beccari, O. and Hooker, J.D. 1892. *The flora of British India.* 6:402–483.

Bernal, R.G. 1989. Endangerment of Colombian palms. *Principes* 33(3):113–128.

Bernal, R.G. and Alvarez, W.D. 1991. Preproposal for the creation of a national palm collection in Colombia. *Palms & Cycads* 33:5–7.

BGCI. 1994. Environmental education in Botanic gardens – guidelines for developing individual strategies. BCGI, Kew, U.K.

BGCI. 1995. A handbook for botanic gardens on the reintroduction of plants to the wild. Compiled by Akeroyd, J. and Wyse Jackson, P. BGCI, Kew, U.K.

BGCS. 1989. *The botanic gardens conservation strategy.* Botanical Gardens Conservation Secretariat. WWF and IUCN, Gland, Switzerland.

Borhidi, A. and Muñiz, O. 1983. *Catálogo de plantas Cubanas amenazadas o extinguidas.* Editorial Academia, Habana.

Bovi, M.L.A., Flores, W.C., Godoy Junior, G., Martins, A.L. de M., Spiering, S.H. 1994. Seed germination of progenies of *Bactris gasipaes*: percentage, speed and duration. In Dematté, M.E.S.P. (ed.). *Acta Horticulturae* 360:157–166.

Boydak, M. and Barrow, S. 1995. A new Locality for *Phoenix* in Turkey: Gölköy-Bödrum. *Principes* 39(3):117–122.

Brako L. and Zarucchi, J.L. 1993. *Catalogue of the flowering plants and gymnosperms of Peru.* Missouri Botanical Garden, Monographs in Systematic Botany 45, St. Louis.

Briggs, J.D. and Leigh, J.H. 1988. *Rare or threatened Australian plants.* Special Publication 14, Australian National Parks and Wildlife Service, Canberra.

Brown, G. 1988. Conserving a rare palm *Ptychosperma bleeseri* Burret, at Darwin Botanic Gardens, Northern Territory, Australia. *Botanic Gardens Conservation News* 1(3):14.

Brown, G. 1989. Darwin Botanic Garden, Northern Territories, Australia. *Botanic Gardens Conservation News* 1(4):49–53.

Castel-Branco, A.J.F. and Tordo, G.C. 1956. *Acerca do equilíbrio bioecológico dos povoamentos de 'cibes' Borassus spp. na Guiné Portuguesa.* Ministério do Ultramar, Lisboa.

Chand Basha, S. and Bhat, K.M. (eds) 1993. *Rattan management and utilisation.* Proceedings of the rattan (cane) seminar, India, 29–31 January 1992, Trichur. Kerala Forest Research Institute, India.

Corner, E.J.H. 1966. *The natural history of palms.* University of California Press, Berkeley.

Couturier, G. and Kahn, F. 1992. Notes of the insect fauna on two species of *Astrocaryum* (Palmae, Cocoeae, Bactridinae) in Peruvian Amazonia, with emphasis on potential pests of cultivated palms. *Bulletin de l'Institut Français d'Etudes Andines* 21:715–725.

de Granville, J.-J. 1990. Les palmiers de la Guyane française. *Bois et Forêts des Tropiques* 220:43–54.

de Granville, J.-J. 1992. Life forms and growth strategies of Guianan palms as related to their ecology. *Bulletin de l'Institut Français d'Etudes Andines* 21:533–548.

de Granville, J.-J. Checklist of the palms of the Guianas (in press).

de Zoysa, N. 1992. Tapping patterns of the kitul palm *Caryota urens* L. in the Sinharaja area, Sri Lanka. *Principes* 36(1):28–33.

de Zoysa, N.D. Palmae. In: Dassanayke, M.D. and Clayton, D. (eds), *A revised handbook to the flora of Ceylon*. Vol. 10. (in prep.)

de Zoysa, N.D., Gunatilleke, C.V.S and Gunatilleke, I.A.U.N. (unpublished). Comparative vegetation studies of undisturbed and selectively logged forest in the Sinharaja forest in Sri Lanka.

de Zoysa, N.D., Gunatilleke, C.V.S and Gunatilleke, I.A.U.N. 1986. Vegetation studies on a skid trail planted with mahogany in the Sinharaja MAB Reserve. *Sri Lanka Forester* 17:(3/4):142–156.

de Zoysa, N.D., Gunatilleke, C.V.S and Gunatilleke, I.A.U.N. 1988. Diversity of understorey vegetation in Sinharaja rain forest. *Sri Lanka Forester* 18(3/4):121–130.

de Zoysa, N.D., Gunatilleke, C.V.S and Gunatilleke, I.A.U.N. 1989. Vegetation studies of an abandoned shifting cultivation site in the Sinharaja rain forest, Sri Lanka. *Sri Lanka Forester* 19(1/2):3–16.

de Zoysa, N.D. and Vivekanandan, K. 1988. Recent progress in rattan research in Sri Lanka. In: Rao, A.N. and Vongkaluang, I. (eds), *Recent research on rattans*. Kasetsart University, Bangkok. Pp.25–32.

de Zoysa, N.D. and Vivekanandan, K. 1991. *The bamboo and rattan cottage industry in Sri Lanka: a livelihood in danger*. Forest Department of Sri Lanka, Battaramulla, Sri Lanka.

de Zoysa, N.D. and Vivekanandan, K. 1994. *Field guide to the rattans of Sri Lanka*. Forest Department of Sri Lanka, Battaramulla, Sri Lanka.

Dematté, M.E.S.P. (ed.). 1994. First international symposium on ornamental palms. *Acta Horticulturae* 360: 1–250.

Dickie J.B., Balick, M.J. and Linington, I.M. 1993. Studies on the practicality of *ex situ* preservation of palm seeds. *Principes* 37(2):94–98.

Dowe, J. 1989. *Palms of the South-West Pacific*. PACSOA, Milton, Australia.

Dowe, J. 1990. Ecological status and endangerment of Australian palms. *Palms & Cycads* 26:2–7.

Dowe, J. 1992. Extra-tropical palms: a statistical overview. *The Palm Enthusiast* 9(3):4–8.

Dowe, J. 1993. Palm conservation in The Palmetum, Townsville. *Danthonia* 2(2):1–3.

Dowe, J. and Hodel, D.R. 1994. A revision of *Archontophoenix* H. Wendl. and Drude (Arecaceae). *Austrobaileya* 4(2):227–244.

Dowe, J. and Uhl, N.W. 1989. *Carpoxylon macrospermum*. *Principes* 33(2):68–73.

Dransfield, J. 1979. *A manual of the rattans of the Malay Peninsula*. Forest Department, Malaysia.

Dransfield, J. 1984a. *The rattans of Sabah*. Forest Department, Sabah.

Dransfield, J. 1984b. The palm flora of Gunung Mulu National Park. In: Jermy, A.C. (ed.), *Studies on the flora of Gunung Mulu National Park, Sarawak*. Forest Department, Kuching, Sarawak. Pp.41–75.

Dransfield, J. 1988. *Beccariophoenix madagascariensis*. *Principes* 32(2):59–68.

Dransfield, J. 1992. *The rattans of Sarawak*. Royal Botanic Gardens, Kew, U.K.

Dransfield, J. 1995. Conservation of the Diversity of Indonesian Palms. Pp.77–84 *in* Suhirman *et al.* (eds), *Strategies for Flora Conservation in Asia. The Kebun Raya Bogor Conference Proceedings*. Kebun Raya, Bogor, Indonesia.

Dransfield, J. and Beentje, H. 1995. *Palms of Madagascar*. Royal Botanic Gardens, Kew, and The International Palm Society.

Dransfield, J. and Johnson, D. 1991. The conservation status of palms in Sabah (Malaysia). In: Johnson, D. (ed.), *Palms for human needs in Asia*. Balkema, Rotterdam. Pp.175–179.

Dransfield, J., Johnson, D. and Synge, H. 1988. *The palms of the new world: a conservation census*. IUCN-WWF Plants Conservation Programme, Pub. 2, Gland, Switzerland.

Dransfield, J. and Manokaran, N. (eds). 1993. *Plant resources of south-east Asia, No. 6, Rattans*. Pudoc, Wageningen, Netherlands.

Dransfield, J., Mogea, J.P., and Manokaran, N. 1989. Rattans. Pp.130–141 *in* Siemsonsma, J.S and Wulijarni-Soetjipto, N. (eds), *Plant resources of South-East Asia. Proceedings of the First PROSEA International Symposium*. Pudoc, Wageningen.

Du Puy, D. and B. and Randrianasolo, V. 1992. Some aspects of the palms of Madagascar, and their cultivation at the Parc de Tsimbazaza, Antananarivo. *Principes* 36(2):84–93.

Durán, R. 1995. *Pseudophoenix sargentii*: an Endangered palm species. *Principes* 39(4):219–224.

Everett, Y. (unpublished). The kitul palm: ethnobotany of *Caryota urens* in highland Sri Lanka. Department of Forestry and Resource Management, University of California, Berkeley.

Fernandes, H.Q.B. 1993. Native palms of Espírito Santo state, Brazil. In: Dematté, M.E.S.P. (ed.). 1994. *Acta Horticulturae* 360:95–111.

Fu, Li-Kuo (ed.) 1992. *China plant red data book*. Volume 1. Science Press, Beijing.

Galeano, G. 1991. *Las palmeras de la región de Araracuara*. Tropenbos 1, Bogotá.

Galeano, G. and Bernal, R. 1987. *Palmas del departamento de Antioquia: región occidental*. Universidad Nacional de Colombia, Bogotá.

Gamage, A.S., Ashton, P.M.S., Gunatilleke, C.V.S. and Gunatilleke, I.A.U.N. (unpublished). Feasibility studies on underplanting multiple use species in buffer zone pine plantation in Sinharaja.

Gemmill, C.E.C. Population genetics and phylogenetic systematics of the native Hawaiian palm genus *Pritchardia*. Ph.D. dissertation (in progress).

Gemmill, C.E.C., Ranker, T.A. and Ragone, D. 1993. Conservation genetics of the native Hawaiian palm genus *Pritchardia*. *Bulletin of the National Tropical Botanical Garden* 23:141–146.

Gibbons, M. and Spanner, T. W. 1995. *Nannorrhops ritchiana*, the Mazari palm, in Pakistan. *Principes* 39(24):177–182.

Glassman, S. 1972. *A revision of B. E. Dahlgren's index of American palms*. J. Cramer, Lehre.

Gottsberger, G. 1978. Seed dispersal by fish in the inundated regions of Humaitá, Amazônia. *Biotropica* 10:170–183.

Goulding, M. 1980. *The fishes and the forest*. University of California Press, Berkeley.

Green, M.J.B. 1992. Designing a minimum protected area network to conserve Sri Lanka's biological wealth. World Parks Congress on National Parks and Protected Areas, February 1992, Caracas, Venezuela.

Greuter, W. 1967. Beiträge zur Flora der Südägäis. 8. *Phoenix theophrasti*, die wilde Dattelpalme Kretas. *Bauhinia* 3:243–250.

Gunatilleke, C.V.S. and Gunatilleke, I.A.U.N. 1991. Threatened woody endemics of the wet lowlands of Sri Lanka and their conservation. *Biological Conservation* 55:17–36.

Gunatilleke, I.A.U.N. and Gunatilleke, C.V.S. 1990. Distribution of floristic richness in Sri Lanka. *Conservation Biology* 4(1):21–31.

Gunatilleke, I.A.U.N., Gunatilleke, C.V.S. and Abeygunawardena, P. 1993. Interdisciplinary research towards management of non-timber forest resources in lowland rain forests of Sri Lanka. *Economic Botany* 47(3):282–290.

Hahn, W. 1990. A synopsis of the Palmae of Paraguay. M.S. thesis, Cornell University, Ithaca, N.Y.

Hahn, W. and Gemmill, C.E.C.G. Low levels of plastid diversity in Hawaiian species of *Pritchardia* (in prep., draft available).

Henderson, A. 1995. *The palms of the Amazon*. Oxford University Press, New York.

Henderson, A. and Aubry, M. 1989. *Attalea crassispatha*, an endemic and endangered Haitian palm. *Principes* 33(2):88–90.

Henderson, A., Aubry, M., Timyan, J. and Balick, M. 1990. Conservation status of Haitian palms. *Principes* 34(3):134–142.

Henderson, A., Galeano, G. and Bernal, R. 1995. *Field guide to the palms of the Americas*. Princeton University Press, Princeton, New Jersey.

Hodel, D.R. 1982. In search of *Carpoxylon*. *Principes* 26(1):34–41.

Hodel, D.R. 1988. Letter to the editor. *Principes* 32(3):95,100

Hodel, D.R. 1992. *Chamaedorea palms: the species and their cultivation*. The International Palm Society, Allen Press, Lawrence, Kansas.

Hubbuch, C.E. 1989. *Attalea crassispatha* a rare palm from Haiti. *Botanic Gardens Conservation News* 1(5):55–56.

IUCN. 1980. *How to use the IUCN Red Data Book categories*. Threatened Plants Unit, IUCN, Kew.

IUCN. 1994. *IUCN Red List categories*. Gland, Switzerland.

IUCN. 1995. *Guidelines for re-introductions* (in press).

Jenhani, W. 1992. Ecological and genetic study of *Phoenix theophrasti* and *Phoenix canariensis* in Crete. 50 pp. (Chania, unpublished).

Johnson, D. 1988. Palms as multipurpose cash and subsistence tree crops. Pp.222–236 in Withington, D., MacDicken, K.G., Sastry, C.B. and Adamas, N.R. (eds), *Multipurpose tree species for small-farm use*. Winrock International, Arlington, Virginia.

Johnson, D. (ed.). 1991a. *Palms for human needs in Asia*. Balkema, Rotterdam.

Johnson, D. 1991b. The 'difficult' seeds: perspectives in palm germplasm conservation. *Mooreana* 1(2):25–32.

Johnson, D. 1992. *Additions and corrections to WCMC palm database by John Dowe* (in litt. to WCMC).

Johnson, D. 1994. The future of ornamental palms and the need for conservation. In: Demattê, M.E.S.P. (ed.). *Acta Horticulturae* 360:121–127.

Jumelle, H. and Perrier, H. 1945. Palmiers. 30. In: Humbert, H. (ed.), *Flore de Madagascar et des Comores*. Tananarive, Madagascar.

Kahn, F. and Castro, A. 1985. The palm community in a forest of central Amazonia, Brazil. *Biotropica* 17:210–216.

Kahn, F. and de Granville, J.-J. 1992. *Palms in forest ecosystems of Amazonia*. Springer Verlag, Ecological Studies 95, Berlin.

Kahn, F., Henderson, A., Brako, L., Hoff M. and Moussa, F. 1992. Datos preliminares a la actualización de la flora de Palmae del Perú: intensidad de herborización y riqueza de las colleciones. *Bulletin de l'Institut Français d'Etudes Andines* 10:170–183.

Kahn, F. and Mejía, K. 1990. Palm communities in wetland forest ecosystems of Peruvian Amazonia. *Forest Ecology and Management* 33/34:169–179.

Kahn, F. and Mejía, K. 1991. The palm communities of two terra firme forests in Peruvian Amazonia. *Principes* 35(1):22–26.

Kahn, F., Mejía K. and Castro, A. 1988. Species richness and density of palms in terra firme forests of Amazonia. *Biotropica* 20:266–269

Kahn, F., Mejía, K., Moussa, F. and Gómez, D. 1993. *Mauritia flexuosa*, la más acuática de las palmeras amazónicas. In: Kahn F., León B. and Young, K.R. (eds), Las plantas vasculares en las aguas continentales del Perú. *Travaux de l'Institut Français d'Etudes Andines* 75, Lima. Pp.287–308.

Kahn, F. and Millán, B. 1992. *Astrocaryum* (Palmae) in Amazonia, a preliminary treatment. *Bulletin de l'Institut Français d'Etudes Andines* 21:459–531.

Kahn, F. and Moussa, F. 1994a. Las palmeras del Perú. Colecciones, patrones de distribución, ecología, estatutos de conservación, nombres vernáculos, utilizaciones. *Travaux de l' Institut Français d'Etudes Andines 59*, Lima.

Kahn, F. and Moussa, F. 1994b. Diversity and conservation status of Peruvian palms. *Biodiversity and Conservation 3:227–241.*

Kiew, R. 1991. Palm utilization and conservation in Peninsular Malaysia. In: Johnson, D. (ed.), *Palms for human needs in Asia.* Balkema, Rotterdam. Pp.75–130.

Kiew, R. 1993. *Palma Malaysia.* Malayan Nature Society, Kuala Lumpur, Malaysia.

Leach, G.J., Dunlop, C.R. Barritt, M.J., Latz, P.K. and Sammy, N. 1992. Northern Territory plant species of conservation significance. *Northern Territory Botanical Bulletin* No. 13. Conservation Commission of the Northern Territory, Darwin.

Leigh J.H. and Briggs, J.D. 1992. *Threatened Australian plants: overview and case studies.* Australian National Parks and Wildlife Service, Canberra.

Leiva, A. 1988. The national botanic garden of Cuba. *Botanic Gardens Conservation News* 1(3):20–24.

Léon, H. 1939. Contribución al estudio de las palmas de Cuba. III. Género *Coccothrinax. Mem. Soc. Cubana Hist. Nat.* 13:107–156.

Liddle, D. 1993. An illusive palm. *Nature Territory* 3:43–45.

Lima, J.L.S. de. 1994. Ornamental palms native to northeastern Brazil and their geographic distribution. In: Demattê, M.E.S.P. (ed.). *Acta Horticulturae* 360:81–84.

Lippincott, C. 1992. Restoring Sargent's cherry palm on the Florida Keys. *Fairchild Tropical Garden Bulletin* 47(1):12–21.

Lippincott, C. 1995. Reintroduction of *Pseudophoenix sargentii* in the Florida Keys. *Principes* 39(1):5–13.

Loc, P.K. 1992. *Changes and complements proposed by Phan Ke Loc in the List of threatened plant species of Vietnam (in litt.* to WCMC).

Madulid, D.A. 1991. The Philippines: Palm utilization and conservation. Pp.181–225 *in* Johnson, D. (ed.), *Palms for human needs in Asia.* Balkema, Rotterdam..

Mansur-Azim, N. 1989. *A tentative list of species threatened in Bangladesh (in litt.* to WCMC).

Mathew, S.P. and Abraham, S. 1994. The vanishing palms of the Andaman and Nicobar islands, India. *Principes* 38(2):100–104.

Matthes, L.A.F. 1994. Palms used in Brazilian landscape planning. In: Demattê, M.E.S.P. (ed.). *Acta Horticulturae* 360:245–250.

Matthew, K. M. 1991. Notes on the distribution of *Bentinckia condapanna* on the Palni Hills in Peninsular India. *Principes* 35(3):139–141.

Meerow, A.W. 1992. *Betrock's guide to landscape palms.* Betrock Information Systems, Inc., Cooper City, Florida.

Mogea, J.P. 1991. Indonesia: Palm utilization and conservation. Pp. 37–73 *in* Johnson, D. (ed.), *Palms for human needs in Asia.* Balkema, Rotterdam.

Montmollin, B. de and Iatroù, G.A. 1995. Connaissance et conservation de la flore de l'île de Crète. *Ecologia mediterranea* 21:173–184.

Moon, A. 1824. Catalogue of indigenous and exotic plants of Ceylon.

Moore, H.E. Jr. 1957. *Veitchia. Gentes Herbarum* 8:483–536.

Moore, H.E. Jr. 1973. Palms in the tropical forest ecosystems of Africa and South America. Pp. 63–88 *in* Meggars, B.J., Ayensu, E.S., and Duckworth, W.D. (eds), *Tropical forest ecosystems in Africa and South America: a comparative review.* Smithsonian Institution Press, Washington, D.C.

Moore, H.E. Jr. 1979. Arecales. Pp.392–438 *in* Smith, A.C. (ed.), *Flora Vitiensis Nova.* Pacific Tropical Botanical Garden, Hawaii.

Moore, H.E., Jr. and Guého, L.J. 1984. *Flore des Mascareignes.* Palmiers (Fam. 189). Mauritius Sugar Industry Research Institute. Port Louis, Mauritius.

Moore, H.E. Jr., Phillips, R.H. and Vodonaivalu, V. 1982. Additions to the palms of Fiji. *Principes* 26(3):122–125.

Morakinyo, A. B. 1995. Profiles and pan-African distributions of the rattan species (Calamoideae) recorded in Nigeria. *Principes* 39(4):197–209.

Môro, J.R. 1994. A breeding program for *Bactris gasipaes* (pejibaye palm). In: Demattê, M.E.S.P. (ed.). *Acta Horticulturae* 360:135–139.

Moussa, F., Kahn, F., Henderson, A., Brako, L. and Hoff, M. 1992. Las palmeras en los valles principales de la Amazonia peruana. *Bulletin de l'Institut Français d'Etudes Andines* 21: 565–597.

Mughal, M.S. 1992. Spotlight on species: *Nannorrhops ritchiana.* Pakistan J. of Forestry 42(3):162–166.

Muñiz, O. and Borhidi, A. 1981. Palmas nuevas del género *Coccothrinax* Sarg. en Cuba. *Acta Bot. Acad. Sci. Hungaricae* 27: 439–454.

Muñiz, O. and Borhidi, A. 1982. Catálogo de las palmas de Cuba. *Acta Botanica Academiae Scientiarum Hungaricae* 28(3/4):309–345.

Murray, M.G., Green, M.J.B. and Walter, K.S. 1992. Status of plant and animal inventories for protected areas in the tropics. Report. WCMC, Cambridge, U.K.

Myers, N. 1993. Tropical forests: the main deforestation fronts. *Environmental Conservation* 20(1):9–16.

Ng, T.-T., Tie, Y.-L, and Kueh, H.-S., (eds). 1991. *Toward greater advancement of the sago industry in the '90s.* Proceedings of the fourth international sago symposium, August 6–9, 1990. Ministry of Agriculture and Community Development, Kuching, Sarawak, Malaysia.

Noblick, L.R. 1991. The indigenous palms of the state of Bahia, Brazil. Ph.D. diss., University of Illinois, Chicago.

Noblick, L. 1992. Reassessment of the garden's *Syagrus* collection. *Fairchild Tropical Garden Bulletin* 47(1): 31–35.

Obermeyer, A.A. and Strey, R.G. 1969. A new species of *Raphia* from northern Zululand and southern Mozambique. *Bothalia* 10(1):29–37.

Orellana, R., Ayora, N. and Lopez, C. 1988. *Ex situ* studies on five threatened species in the Yucatán Peninsula, Mexico. *Botanic Gardens Conservation News* 1(2):20–22.

Otedoh, M.O. 1982. A revision of the genus *Raphia* Beauv. (Palmae). *Journal of the Nigerian Institute for Oil Palm Research* 6(22):145–189.

Pearce, K.G. 1991. Palm utilization and conservation in Sarawak (Malaysia). Pp.131–173 *in* Johnson, D. (ed.), *Palms for human needs in Asia*. Balkema, Rotterdam.

Pearce, K.G. 1994. The palms of Kubah National Park, Matang, Kuching division. *Malayan Nature Journal* 48:1–36.

Pei S., Chen, S., and Tong, S. 1991. *Flora Reipublicae* (sic) *Popularis Sinicae* 13(1). Palmae. Science Press, Beijeng, China.

Pingitore, E.J. 1982. Rare palms in Argentinia. *Principes* 26(1):9–18.

Price, T. 1995. Community based management of Ron palm in Niger. *IUCN Forest Conservation Programme Newsletter* 21:9–10.

Puig, H., Riera, B. and Lescure, J.-P. 1990. Phytomasse et productivité. *Bois et Forêts des Tropiques* 220:25–32.

Purseglove, J.W. 1972. *Tropical crops: monocotyledons 2*. John Wiley and Sons, New York.

Quero, H. J. 1992. Current status of Mexican palms. *Principes* 36(4):203–216

Rajanaidu, N., Jalani, B.S., Rao, V. and Kushairi, A. 1993. New exotic palms for plantations. Pp.19–27 *in Proceedings 1991 PORIM international palm oil conference*. Vol. 1. PORIM, Kuala Lumpur, Malaysia..

Randrianasolo, V. and Dransfield J. 1990. *The Palms of Madagascar*. Tsimbazaza Botanical and Zoological Park/WWF (leaflet).

Ratnayake, P.D.K.C., Gunatilleke, C.V.S. and Gunatilleke, I.A.U.N. 1991. *Caryota urens* L. (Palmae): an indigenous multipurpose tree species in the wet lowlands of Sri Lanka. Pp.77–88 *in* Taylor, D.A. and MacDicken, K. (eds), *Research on multipurpose tree species*. Winrock International F/FRED, Bangkok.

Read, R. 1969. Notes on Ceylon palms gathered for the *Revised handbook to the flora of Ceylon* (unpublished material).

Renuka, C. 1992. *Rattans of the Western Ghats: a taxonomic manual*. Kerala Forest Research Institute, Peechi, Kerala, India.

Roux, J.-P. (ed.). 1995. *Livre Rouge de la flore menacée de France*. Tome I. Collection patrimoines naturels 20. Série Patrimoine génétique.

Russell-Smith, J. and Lucas, D. 1990. Notes on the natural distribution of *Ptychosperma bleeseri*. *Palms & Cycads* 26:8–10.

Scariot, A.O., Oliveira Filho, A.T. and Lleras, E. 1989. Species richness, density and distribution of palms in an eastern Amazonian seasonally flooded forest. *Principes* 33(4):172–179.

Strahm, W.A. (ed.). 1989. *Plant red data book for Rodrigues*. Koeltz Scientific Books, Koenigstein, Germany.

Stuessy, T.F., Sanders, R.W. and Matthei, O.R. 1983. *Juania australis* revisited in the Juan Fernandez Islands, Chile. *Principes* 27(2):71–74.

Subhadrabandhu, S. and Sdodee, S. (eds) 1995. Fifth International Sago Symposium. *Acta Horticulturae* 389.

Tan, C.F. 1992. *Prospects for rattan planting and a field manual for rattan cultivation in the South Pacific*. South Pacific Forestry Development Programme, Port Vila, Vanuatu.

Thin, N.N. 1992. *List of palms rare and endangered species of Indochina* (*in litt.* to WCMC).

Thomas, M.B. and McDonald, W.J.F. 1987. Rare and threatened plants of Queensland. Information Series QI87003. Queensland Department of Primary Industries, Brisbane.

Threatened Plant Unit. 1983. *List of rare, threatened and endemic plants in Europe*. European Committee for the conservation of Nature and natural Resources. Council of Europe. Strasbourg.

Thulin, M. 1995. *Flora of Somalia*. Royal Botanic Gardens, Kew, U.K.

Thwaites, G.H.K. 1864. *Enumeratio plantarum zeylaniae*. Dulau, London.

Tim Penulis. 1992. *18 varietas salak*. Penebar Swadaya, Jakarta, Indonesia.

Timyan, J.C. and Reep, S.F. 1994. Conservation status of *Attalea crassispatha* (Mart.) Burret, the rare and endemic oil palm of Haiti. *Biological Conservation* 68:11–18.

Trimen, H. 1885. Remarks on the composition, geographical affinities and origin of the flora of Ceylon. *Journal of the Royal Asiatic Society* (Ceylon branch) 9:139–159.

Trimen, H. 1898. *A handbook to the flora of Ceylon*. Dulau, London.

Tucker, R. 1989. The Townsville Palmetum, Queensland, Australia. *Botanic Gardens Conservation News* 1(5): 40–44.

Tucker, R. 1990. The Palmetum: its objectives and development. *Principes* 34(2):86–93.

Tuley, P. 1995. *The palms of Africa*. Trendrine Press, Cornwall.

Turland, N.J., Chilton, L. and Press, J.R. 1993. *Flora of the cretan area – annotated checklist and atlas*. The Natural History Museum, London.

Uhl, N.W. and Dransfield, J. 1987. *Genera palmarum: a classification of palms based on the work of Harold E. Moore, Jr.* The L.H. Bailey Hortorium and the International Palm Society, Allen Press, Lawrence, Kansas.

UN Economic Commission for Europe. 1991. *European Red List of Globally Threatened Animals and Plants.* 439 pp. UN Sales No. E.91.II.E.34.

Valois, A.C.C. 1994. Genetic resources of palms. In: Demattê, M.E.S.P. (ed.). *Acta Horticulturae* 360:113–120.

Ven, L.B. van der. 1994. Comments on production and commercialization of ornamental palms. In: Demattê, M.E.S.P. (ed.). *Acta Horticulturae* 360:241–242.

Vovides, A.P. and Bielma, M.A.G. 1994. A study of the *in situ* situation of four species of threatened understorey palms of the genus *Chamaedorea* in the wild in the state of Veracruz, Mexico. *Principes* 38(2):109–113.

Wan Razali, W. M., Dransfield, J. and Manokaran, N. (eds). 1992. *A guide to the cultivation of rattan.* Malayan Forest Record 35. Forest Research Institute Malaysia, Kepong, Kuala Lumpur, Malaysia.

Wang, X. and Yang, Z. The plants in China – an Action Plan for their conservation. IUCN/SSC (in prep.).

Watt, G. 1883–1889. *Dictionary of economic products of India.* Calcutta. Reprint 1972, Jeyyed Press, Delhi.

Wightman, G. 1992. Integrated plant conservation programs in the Top End of the Northern Territory and the future role of the Darwin Botanic Gardens. Pp.61–65 *in* Butler, G., Meredith, L. and Richardson, M. (eds). *Conservation of rare or threatened plants in Australasia.* Australian National Parks and Wildlife Service.

Williams, J.T. 1991. *Research needs for bamboo and rattan to the year 2000.* Tropical Tree Crops Program, International Fund for Agricultural Research, Arlington, Virginia.

Wyse Jackson, P.S., Cronk Q.C.B. and Parnell J.A.N. 1990. Notes on a critically endangered palm from Mauritius, *Hyophorbe amaricaulis* Mart. *Botanic Gardens Conservation News* 1(6):24–26.

Zizka, G. 1991. Flowering plants of Easter Island. *Palmengarten* 3.

Definitions of the IUCN Red List
conservation categories[1]

Extinct (Ex). Taxa which are no longer known to exist in the wild after repeated searches of their type localities and other known or likely places.

Endangered (E). Taxa in danger of extinction and whose survival is unlikely if the causal factors continue operating. Included are taxa whose numbers have been reduced to a critical level or whose habitats have been so drastically reduced that they are deemed in immediate danger of extinction.

Vulnerable (V). Taxa believed likely to move into the Endangered category in the near future if the causal factors continue operating. Included are taxa of which most or all the populations are decreasing because of over-exploitation, extensive destruction of habitat or other environmental disturbance; taxa with populations that have been seriously depleted and whose ultimate security is not yet assured; and taxa with populations that are still abundant but are under threat from serious adverse factors throughout their range.

Rare (R). Taxa with small world populations that are not at present Endangered or Vulnerable, but are at risk. These taxa are usually localized within restricted geographical areas or habitats or are thinly scattered over a more extensive range.

Indeterminate (I). Taxa known to be Extinct, Endangered, Vulnerable or Rare, but where there is not enough information to say which of the four categories is appropriate.

Insufficiently Known (K). Taxa that are suspected but not definitely known to belong to any of the above categories because of a lack of information.

Not threatened (nt). Taxa that are not in any of the above categories.

No Information or Unknown (?). Taxa for which there is no information.

Note: In addition to the categories above, occasionally "hybrid" categories are used, such as Ex/E (probably Extinct) or E/V (near Endangered).

[1] These are the old categories (IUCN 1980). The revised categories, not generally referred to in this Action Plan, may be found in *IUCN Red List Categories* (IUCN 1994).

Appendix 2

Highly endangered palms

2A By region

The global conservation status of all species is Endangered, if not stated otherwise. Palms marked with '+' belong to monotypic genera, those marked with '*' are endemic. See Appendix 2B for more information about distribution, synonyms, author name, and conservation status.

Caribbean
Florida (1)
 Sabal miamiensis (Ex/E) *
Bermuda (1)
 Sabal bermudana *
Cuba (3)
 Coccothrinax borhidiana *
 C. crinita ssp. *crinita* *
 Thrinax ekmaniana *
Dominican Republic (1)
 Pseudophoenix ekmanii *
Haiti (2)
 Attalea crassispatha *
 Copernicia ekmanii *
Puerto Rico (1)
 Gaussia attenuata *

Meso-America
Mexico (5)
 Brahea edulis *
 Chamaedorea glaucifolia *
 C. klotzschiana
 C. metallica *
 C. tuerckheimii
Guatemala (3)
 Chamaedorea brachypoda
 C. tenerrima *
 C. tuerckheimii
Honduras (1)
 Chamaedorea brachypoda
Belize (1)
 Schippia concolor *
Nicaragua (1)
 Reinhardtia koschnyana
Costa Rica (7)
 Chamaedorea amabilis
 C. brachyclada
 C. pumila (incl. *C. minima*) *
 C. sullivaniorum
 C. undulatifolia *
 Cryosophila cookii *
 Reinhardtia koschnyana
Panama (7)
 Chamaedorea amabilis
 C. brachyclada
 C. correae *
 C. sullivaniorum
 C. verecunda *
 Cryosophila kalbreyeri
 Reinhardtia koschnyana

South America
Bolivia (1)
 Parajubaea torallyi *
Brazil (5)
 Allagoptera arenaria *
 Bactris soeiroana *
 Itaya amicorum + *
 Lytocaryum weddelianum *
 (including *L. insigne*)
 Syagrus leptospatha *
Colombia (15)
 Aiphanes leiostachys *
 A. parvifolia *
 Attalea amygdalina *
 (incl. *A. victoriana*)
 A. colenda
 Ceroxylon alpinum ssp. *alpinum*
 C. sasaimae
 Chamaedorea amabilis
 C. sullivaniorum
 Cryosophila kalbreyeri
 Geonoma chlamydostachys *
 Phytelephas schottii
 P. tumacana *
 Reinhardtia koschnyana
 Wettinia fascicularis *
 W. microcarpa *
Ecuador (2)
 Ceroxylon alpinum ssp. *ecuadorense* *
 Attalea colenda
Paraguay (1)
 Butia campicola (=*Syagrus c.*) *
Peru (1)
 Attalea tessmannii *
Venezuela (2)
 Ceroxylon alpinum ssp. *alpinum*
 Phytelephas schottii

Africa and Indian Ocean islands
Sudan (2)
 Medemia abiadensis *
 M. argun
Egypt (1)
 Medemia argun
Comoro Islands(1)
 Ravenea hildebrantii *
Madagascar (84)
 Beccariophoenix madagascariensis + *
 Borassus sambiranensis *
 Dypsis spp. * (69 species, see Appendix 2B)

Lemurophoenix halleuxii + *
Marojejya darianii *
Masoala kona *
Orania trispatha (=*Halmoorea t.*) *
Ravenea albicans *
R. julietiae *
R. lakatra *
R. latisecta *
R. louvelii (=*Louvelia madagascariensis*) *
R. nana *
R. xerophila *
Satranala decussilvae + *
Voanioala gerardii + *
Mauritius (7)
Dictyosperma album var. *album*
D. album var. *conjugatum* *
Hyophorbe amaricaulis *
H. lagenicaulis *
H. vaughanii *
Latania loddigesii *
Tectiphiala ferox + *
Réunion (2)
Latania lontaroides *
Dictyosperma album var. *album*
Rodrigues (2)
Dictyosperma album var. *aureum* *
Hyophorbe verschaffeltii *
Latania verschaffeltii *

Asia
India (1)
Corypha taliera (Ex) *
Sri Lanka (7)
Areca concinna *
Calamus delicatulus *
C. ovoideus *
C. pachystemonus *
C. radiatus *
C. zeylanicus *
Loxococcus rupicola + *
China (1)
Chuniophoenix hainanensis *
Thailand (1)
Pinanga adangensis
Peninsular Malaysia (22)
Arenga retroflorescens *
Calamus endauensis *
C. minutus *
C. moorhousei *
C. padangensis *
C. pulaiensis *
C. radulosus *
C. senalingensis *
C. setulosus *
Daemonorops oligophylla *
Iguanura corniculata *
Johannesteijsmannia lanceolata *
J. magnifica *
Licuala corneri *
L. kemamanensis *
L. moyseyi *
L. ridleyana *
Maxburretia rupicola *
Pinanga acaulis *
P. adangensis
P. cleistantha *

Plectocomia dransfieldiana *
Sabah (4)
Calamus hepburnii *
Nenga gajah
Salacca lophospatha (Ex/E) *
S. multiflora *
Sarawak (14)
Areca abdulrahmanii *
A. ahmadii *
A. andersonii *
A. brachypoda *
A. chaiana *
A. dayung *
A. jugahpunya *
A. klingkangensis *
A. subacaulis *
Calamus conjugatus *
Daemonorops unijuga *
Iguanura chaiana *
Pogonotium moorei *
Licuala orbicularis *
Kalimantan (1)
Licuala hallieriana *
Sumatra (3)
Ceratolobus pseudoconcolor
Iguanura leucocarpa *
Nenga gajah
Java (3)
Ceratolobus glaucescens *
C. pseudoconcolor
Pinanga javana *
Moluccas (1)
Drymophloeus oliviformis *

Australia and South-west Pacific islands
Australia (2)
Ptychosperma bleeseri *
Archontophoenix myolensis *
New Caledonia (3)
Cyphophoenix nucele *
Kentiopsis oliviformis + *
Lavoixia macrocarpa + *
Vanuatu (3)
Carpoxylon macrospermum + *
Veitchia montgomeryana *
V. spiralis *
Fiji (4)
Neoveitchia storckii + *
Veitchia filifera *
V. pedionoma *
V. petiolata *

Pacific
Hawaii (8)
Pritchardia affinis *
P. aylmer-robinsonii *
P. kaalae *
P. munroi *
P. napaliensis *
P. remota *
P. schattaueri *
P. viscosa *
Easter Island
Paschalococos disperta + (Ex) *

Highly endangered palms

2B By genus

Genus/Species (+ = monotypic)[1]	World Conservation Status[2]	Distribution
Aiphanes *leiostachys* Burret	E	Colombia
A. parvifolia Burret	E	Colombia
Allagoptera *arenaria* (Gomes) Kuntze	E	Brazil
Archontophoenix *myolensis* Dowe	E	Australia
Areca *abdulrahmanii* J. Dransf.	E	Sarawak
A. ahmadii J. Dransf.	E	Sarawak
A. andersonii J. Dransf.	E	Sarawak
A. brachypoda J. Dransf.	E	Sarawak
A. chaiana J. Dransf.	E	Sarawak
A. concinna Thwaites	E	Sri Lanka
A. dayung J. Dransf.	E	Sarawak
A. jugahpunya J. Dransf.	E	Sarawak
A. klingkangensis J. Dransf.	E	Sarawak
A. subacaulis (Becc.) J. Dransf.	E	Sarawak
Arenga *retroflorescens* H. Moore & Meijer	E	Sabah
Attalea *colenda* Balslev & A. Henderson	E	Colombia (E), Ecuador (?)
A. crassispatha (Mart.) Burret	E	Haiti
A. tessmannii Burret	E	Peru
A. amygdalina Kunth (incl. *A. victoriana* Dugand)	E	Colombia
Bactris *soeiroana* in ed. Noblick	E	Brazil
Beccariophoenix *madagascariensis* Jum. & Perrier+	E [CR]	Madagascar
Borassus *sambiranensis* Jum. & Perrier	E	Madagascar
Brahea *edulis* Watson	E	Mexico
Butia *campicola* (Barb. Rodr.) Noblick (= *Syagrus c.*)	E	Paraguay
Calamus *conjugatus* Furt.	E	Sarawak
C. delicatulus Thwaites	E	Sri Lanka
C. endauensis J. Dransf.	E	Pen. Malaysia
C. hepburnii J. Dransf.	E	Sabah
C. minutus J. Dransf.	E	Pen. Malaysia
C. moorhousei Furt.	E	Pen. Malaysia
C. ovoideus Thwaites ex Trimen	E	Sri Lanka
C. pachystemonus Thwaites	E	Sri Lanka
C. padangensis Furt.	E	Pen. Malaysia
C. pulaiensis Becc.	E	Pen. Malaysia
C. radiatus Thwaites	E	Sri Lanka
C. radulosus Becc.	E	Pen. Malaysia
C. senalingensis J. Dransf.	E	Pen. Malaysia
C. setulosus J. Dransf.	E	Pen. Malaysia
C. zeylanicus Becc.	E	Sri Lanka
Carpoxylon *macrospermum* H.A. Wendl. & Drude +	E	Vanuatu
Ceratolobus *glaucescens* Blume	E	Java
C. pseudoconcolor J. Dransf.	E	Java (E), Sumatra (E)
Ceroxylon *alpinum* Bonp. ssp. *alpinum*	E	Colombia (E), Venezuela (E)
C. alpinum Bonp. ssp. *ecuadorense* Galeano	E	Ecuador
C. sasaimae Galeano	E	Colombia
Chamaedorea *amabilis* H.A. Wendl. ex Dammer	E	Costa Rica (E), Panama (E), Colombia (E)
C. brachyclada H.A. Wendl.	E	Costa Rica (E), Panama (E)
C. brachypoda Standley & Steyerm.	E	Guatemala (E), Honduras (E)
C. correae Hodel & Uhl	E	Panama
C. glaucifolia H.A. Wendl.	E	Mexico
C. klotzschiana H.A. Wendl.	E	Mexico
C. metallica Cook ex H. Moore	E	Mexico
C. pumila H.A. Wendl. ex Dammer (incl. *C. minima* Hodel)	E	Costa Rica

Genus/Species (+ = monotypic)[1]	World Conservation Status[2]	Distribution
C. sullivaniorum Hodel & Uhl	E	Costa Rica (E), Panama (E), Colombia (E)
C. tenerrima Burret	E	Guatemala
C. tuerckheimii (Dammer) Burret	E	Guatemala (E), Mexico E)
C. undulatifolia Hodel & Uhl	E	Costa Rica (E)
C. verecunda Grayum & Hodel	E	Panama
Chuniophoenix *hainanensis* Burret	E	China (Hainan Is.)
Coccothrinax *borhidiana* Muñiz	E	Cuba
C. crinita Becc. ssp. *crinita*	E	Cuba
Copernicia *ekmanii* Burret	E	Haiti
Corypha *taliera* Roxb.	Ex	India
Cryosophila *cookii* Bartlett	E	Costa Rica
C. kalbreyeri (Dammer ex Burret) Dahlgren	E	Colombia (E), Panama (E)
Cyphophoenix *nucele* H. Moore	E	New Caledonia
Daemonorops *oligophylla* Becc.	E	Pen. Malaysia
D. unijuga J. Dransf.	E	Sarawak
Dictyosperma *album* H.A. Wendl. & Drude ex Scheffer+		
var. *album*	E	Mauritius (E), Reunion (E)
var. *aureum* Balf. f.	E	Rodrigues
var. *conjugatum* Moore & Guého	E	Mauritius
Drymophloeus *oliviformis* (Giseke) Miq.	E	Moluccas
Dypsis *acaulis* J. Dransf.	EX/E	Madagascar
D. ambanjae Beentje (incl. *Phloga sambiranensis* Jum.)	EX/E	Madagascar
D. ambilaensis J. Dransf.	E EN	Madagascar
D. ambositrae Beentje	E CR	Madagascar
D. ampasindavae Beentje (incl. *Neodypsis loucoubensis* Jum.)	E CR	Madagascar
D. angusta Jum.	E EN	Madagascar
D. angustifolia (H. Perr.) Beentje & J. Dransf.	E EN	Madagascar
D. anovensis J. Dransf.	EX/E	Madagascar
D. antanambensis Beentje	E EN	Madagascar
D. aquatilis Beentje	E EN	Madagascar
D. (=Chrysalidocarpos) arenarum (Jum.) Beentje & J. Dransf.	E CR	Madagascar
D. (=Neodypsis) basilonga (Jum. & Perr.) Beentje & J. Dransf.	E EN	Madagascar
D. beentjei J. Dransf.	E EN	Madagascar
D. bejofo Beentje	E EN	Madagascar
D. (=Neophloga) betamponensis (Jum.) Beentje & J. Dransf.	EX/E	Madagascar
D. boiviniana Baill.	E EN	Madagascar
D. bosseri J. Dransf.	EX/E	Madagascar
D. brevicaulis (Guillaumet) Beentje & J. Dransf.	E CR	Madagascar
D. (=Neodypsis) canaliculata (Jum.) Beentje & J. Dransf.	EX/E	Madagascar
D. canescens (Jum. & Perr.) Beentje & J. Dransf.	EX/E	Madagascar
D. caudata Beentje	E CR	Madagascar
D. (=Neodypsis) ceracea (Jum.) Beentje & J. Dransf.	EX/E	Madagascar
D. (=Neophloga) commersionana (Baill.) Beentje & J. Dransf.	E CR	Madagascar
D. cookei J. Dransf.	E EN	Madagascar
D. (=Chrysalidocarpos) decipiens (Becc.) Beentje & J. Dransf.	E EN	Madagascar
D. (=Neophloga) digitata (Becc.) Beentje & J. Dransf.	E CR	Madagascar
D. dransfieldii Beentje	E EN	Madagascar
D. elegans Beentje	E CR	Madagascar
D. eriostachys J. Dransf.	E EN	Madagascar
D. faneva Beentje	E EN	Madagascar
D. fanjana Beentje	E EN	Madagascar
D. furcata J. Dransf.	EX/E	Madagascar
D. glabrescens (Becc.) Becc.	E EN	Madagascar
D. hovomantsina Beentje	E CR	Madagascar
D. ifanadianae Beentje	E CR	Madagascar
D. (=Neophloga) integra (Jum.) Beentje & J. Dransf.	E CR	Madagascar
D. intermedia Beentje	E CR	Madagascar
D. interrupta J. Dransf.	E CR	Madagascar
D. laevis J. Dransf.	E CR	Madagascar
D. lanuginosa J. Dransf.	EX/E	Madagascar
D. (=Neodypsis) ligulata (Jum.) Beentje & J. Dransf.	EX/E	Madagascar
D. (=Neophloga) lutea (Jum.) Beentje & J. Dransf.	E EN	Madagascar

Genus/Species (+ = monotypic)[1]	World Conservation Status[2]	Distribution
D. mahia Beentje	E CR	Madagascar
D. (=*Neophloga*) *mangorensis* (Jum.) Beentje & J. Dransf.	E CR	Madagascar
D. mirabilis J. Dransf.	E EN	Madagascar
D. moorei Beentje	E EN	Madagascar
D. (=*Neodypsis*) *nauseosa* (Jum. & Perr.) Beentje & J. Dransf.	E CR	Madagascar
D. (=*Chrysalidocarpos*) *nossibensis* (Becc.) Beentje & J. Dransf.	E CR	Madagascar
D. oropedionis Beentje	E CR	Madagascar
D. ovobontsira Beentje	E CR	Madagascar
D. (=*Neophloga*) *pervillei* (Jum.) Beentje & J. Dransf.	EX/E	Madagascar
D. plurisecta Jum.	EX/E	Madagascar
D. (=*Neophloga*) *poivreana* (Baill.) Beentje & J. Dransf.	E CR	Madagascar
D. psammophila Beentje	E CR	Madagascar
D. pulchella J. Dransf.	EX/E	Madagascar
D. ramentacea J. Dransf.	E CR	Madagascar
D. remotiflora J. Dransf.	EX/E	Madagascar
D. (=*Chrysalidocarpos*) *sahanofensis* (Jum. & Perr.) Beentje & J. Dransf.	E EN	Madagascar
D. saintelucei Beentje	E CR	Madagascar
D. sanctaemariae J. Dransf.	E CR	Madagascar
D. scandens J. Dransf.	E CR	Madagascar
D. (=*Neophloga*) *simianensis* (Jum.) Beentje & J. Dransf.	E EN	Madagascar
D. singularis Beentje	E CR	Madagascar
D. soanieranae Beentje	EX/E	Madagascar
D. (=*Neodypsis*) *tanalensis* (Jum. & Perr.) Beentje & J. Dransf.	EX/E	Madagascar
D. tenuissima Beentje	E EN	Madagascar
D. tokoravina Beentje	E EN	Madagascar
D. trapezoidea J. Dransf.	E CR	Madagascar
D. tsaravotsira Beentje	E EN	Madagascar
Gaussia *attenuata* (Cook) Becc.	E	Puerto Rico
Geonoma *chlamydostachys* Galeano	E	Colombia
Hyophorbe *amaricaulis* Mart.	E	Mauritius
H. lagenicaulis (L. Bailey) H. Moore	E	Mauritius
H. vaughanii L. Bailey	E	Mauritius
H. verschaffeltii H.A. Wendl.	E	Rodrigues
Iguanura *chaiana* Kiew	E	Sarawak
I. corniculata Becc.	E	Pen. Malaysia
I. leucocarpa Blume	E	Sumatra
Itaya *amicorum* H. Moore +	E	Brazil (E), Peru (E)
Johannesteijsmannia *lanceolata* J. Dransf.	E	Pen. Malaysia
J. magnifica J. Dransf.	E	Pen. Malaysia
Kentiopsis *oliviformis* (Brongn. & Gris) Brongn. +	E	New Caledonia
Latania *loddigesii* Mart.	E	Mauritius
L. lontaroides (Gaertner) H. Moore	E	Reunion
Lavoixia *macrocarpa* H. Moore +	E	New Caledonia
Lemurophoenix *halleuxii* J. Dransf. +	E	Madagascar
Licuala *corneri* Furt.	E	Pen. Malaysia
L. hallieriana Becc.	E	Kalimantan
L. kemamanensis Furt.	E	Pen. Malaysia
L. moyseyi Furt.	E	Pen. Malaysia
L. orbicularis Becc.	E	Sarawak
L. ridleyana Becc.	E	Pen. Malaysia
Loxococcus *rupicola* H.A. Wendl. & Drude +	E	Sri Lanka
Lytocaryum *weddelianum* (H.A. Wendl.) Tol. (incl. *L. insigne* (Hort. ex Drude) Tol.	E	Brazil
Marojejya *darianii* J. Dransf. & Uhl	E CR	Madagascar
Masoala *kona* Beentje	E EN	Madagascar
Maxburretia *rupicola* (Ridl.) Furt.	E	Pen. Malaysia
Medemia *abiadensis* H.A. Wendl.	E	Sudan
M. argun (Mart.) Wurtt. ex H.A. Wendl.	E	Egypt (E), Sudan (E)
Nenga *gajah* J. Dransf.	E	Sabah (E), Sumatra (E)
Neoveitchia *storckii* (H.A. Wendl.) Becc. +	E	Fiji
Orania (=*Halmoorea*) *trispatha* (J. Dransf. & Uhl) Beentje & J. Dransf.	E CR	Madagascar
Parajubaea *torallyi* (Mart.) Burret	E	Bolivia

Genus/Species (+ = monotypic)[1]	World Conservation Status[2]	Distribution
***Paschalococos** disperta* J. Dransf. +	Ex	Easter Island
***Pelagodoxa** henryana* Becc. +	E	Marquesas
***Phytelephas** schottii* H.A. Wendl.	E	Colombia (E), Venezuela (E)
P. tumacana Cook	E	Colombia
***Pinanga** acaulis* Ridl.	E	Pen. Malaysia
P. adangensis Ridl.	E	Thailand (E), Pen. Malaysia (E)
P. cleistantha J. Dransf.	E	Pen. Malaysia
P. javana Blume	E	Java
***Plectocomia** dransfieldiana* Madulid	E	Pen. Malaysia
***Pogonotium** moorei* J. Dransf.	E	Sarawak
***Pritchardia** affinis* Becc.	E	Hawaii
P. aylmer-robinsonii H. St.John	E	Hawaii
P. kaalae Rock	E	Hawaii
P. munroi Rock	E	Hawaii
P. napaliensis H. St.John	E	Hawaii
P. remota Becc.	E	Hawaii
P. schattaueri Hodel	E	Hawaii
P. viscosa Rock	E	Hawaii
***Pseudophoenix** ekmanii* Burret	E	Dominican Republic
***Ptychosperma** bleeseri* Burret	E	Australia
***Ravenea** albicans* Jum. (=*Louvelia a.*)	E EN	Madagascar
R. hildebrantii C. D. Bouché	E EN	Comoro
R. julietiae Beentje	E EN	Madagascar
R. lakatra Jum. (= *Louvelia l.*)	E EN	Madagascar
R. latisecta Jum.	E EN	Madagascar
R. louvelii Jum. & Perr. (= *Louvelia madagascariensis*)	E EN	Madagascar
R. nana Beentje	E EN	Madagascar
R. xerophila Jum.	E EN	Madagascar
***Reinhardtia** koschnyana* (H.A. Wendl. & Dammer) Burret	E	Costa Rica (E), Nicaragua (E), Panama (E), Colombia (E)
***Sabal** bermudana* L. Bailey	E	Bermuda
S. miamiensis Zona	Ex/E	USA
***Salacca** lophospatha* J. Dransf. & Mogea	Ex/E	Sabah
S. multiflora Mogea	E	Pen. Malaysia
***Satranala** decussilvae* Beentje & J. Dransf.+	E EN	Madagascar
***Schippia** concolor* Burret +	E	Belize
***Syagrus** leptospatha* Burret	E	Brazil
***Tectiphiala** ferox* H. Moore +	E	Mauritius
***Thrinax** ekmaniana* (Burret) Borhidi & Muñiz	E	Cuba
***Veitchia** filifera* (H.A.Wendl.) H. Moore	Ex/E	Fiji
V. montgomeryana H. Moore	E	Vanuatu
V. pedionoma (A.C. Smith) H. Moore	E	Fiji
V. petiolata (Burret) H. Moore	E	Fiji
V. spiralis H. A. Wendl.	E	Vanuatu
***Voanioala** gerardii* J. Dransf. +	E CR	Madagascar
***Wettinia** fascicularis* (Burret) H. Moore & J. Dransf.	E	Colombia
W. microcarpa (Burret) R. Bernal	E	Colombia

Remarks:

[1] The following 13 American palms, listed provisionally as synonyms of variable and more widespread species in Henderson (1995), also deserve special attention. These are endangered populations, mostly isolated or at the margin of the species' range, and may be elevated to valid species or subspecies after more thorough taxonomic study in the future:

Aiphanes pachyclada Burret (Colombia), *Attalea burretiana* Bondar (Brazil), *Catoblastus andinus* Dugand (Colombia), *C. sphaerocarpus* (Burret) Burret (Colombia), *Ceroxylon mooreanum* Galeano & Bernal (Colombia), *Chamaedorea tenella* H.A. Wendl. (Costa Rica, Guatemala, Mexico), *Copernicia humicola* León and *C. occidentalis* León (Cuba), *Euterpe cuatrecasana* Dugand (Colombia), *Mauritiella pacifica* Dugand (Colombia and Equador), *Prestoea simplicifrons* (Burret) Denevers & Henderson (Colombia), *Syagrus acaulis* (Drude) Becc. (Brazil), *S. lilliputiana* (Barb. Rodr.) Becc. (Paraguay).

[2] Conservation Status:

Ex	Extinct
Ex/E	Possibly Extinct
E	Endangered
E CR	Critically Endangered Madagascar
E EN	Endangered in Madagascar

The division of Critically Endangered and Endangered according to the new IUCN Red List Categories (IUCN 1994) was only made for the palms of Madagascar (see Dransfield and Beentje 1995).

Endemic palms with
Unknown conservation status[1,2]

Actinorhytis *poamau* Becc. — Solomon Is.

Aiphanes *disticha*
  (Wallace ex Regel) Burret — Colombia

A. eggersii Burret — Ecuador

A. leiospatha Burret — Colombia

Areca *caliso* Becc. — Mindanao

A. congesta Becc. — PNG (E. Sepik Dist.)

A. costata Kurz — Old World

A. jobiensis Becc. — Irian Jaya (Ansus; Japen Is.)

A. laxa Buch.-Ham. — Andamans

A. ledermanniana Becc. — PNG (E. Sepik Dist.)

A. montana Ridl. — Pen. Malaysia

A. multifida Burret — PNG (C. Dist.)

A. nannospadix Burret — PNG (Gulf Dist.)

A. niga-solu Becc. — Solomon Is.

A. novo-hibernica Becc. — Bismarck Arch. (New Ireland)

A. oxycarpa Miq. — Sulawesi (N.)

A. rechingeriana Becc. — Solomon Is.

A. rheophytica J. Dransf. — Sabah

A. rostrata Burret — PNG (C. Dist.)

A. solomonensis Burret — Solomon Is.

A. torulo Becc. — Solomon Is.

A. warburgiana Becc. — Irian Jaya

Arenga *gracilicaulis* F. Bailey — PNG (N. Dist.)

Astrocaryum *echinatum* Barb. Rodr. — Brazil

A. kewense Barb. Rodr. — Brazil

A. pygmaeum Drude — Brazil

A. trachycarpum Burret — Ecuador

A. weddellii Drude — Brazil

Attalea *(Orbignya) eichleri* Drude — Brazil

A. exigua Drude — Brazil

Bactris *bradei* Burret — Brazil

B. faucium Mart. — Bolivia

B. gracilior Burret — Costa Rica

B. infesta Mart. — Bolivia

B. vulgaris Barb. Rodr. — Brazil

Balaka *pauciflora*
  (H. Wendl.) H. Moore — Fiji (Ovalau)

Barcella *odora* (Trail) Drude — Brazil

Borassus *heineana* Becc. — PNG (E. Sepik Dist.)

Brassiophoenix *drymophloeoides*
  Burret — PNG (C. Dist.)

B. schumannii (Becc.) Essig — PNG (NE.)

Calamus *acidus* Becc. — Sulawesi+

C. aggregatus Burret — Myanmar

C. albus Pers. — Moluccas+

C. altiscandens Burret — PNG (W. Dist.)

C. amphibolus Becc. — Sulawesi+

C. anomalus Burret — PNG (Calamus Dist.)

C. arfakianus Becc. — Irian Jaya (Arfak Mts.)

C. arugda Becc. — Mindanao

C. austro-guangxiensis
  Pei & Chen — Guangxi (Shangsi, Shiwandashan)

C. balansaeanus Becc.
  var. *castaneolepis* (Wei) Pei & Chen — Guangxi

C. barbatus Zippelius — Irian Jaya (S. Coast)

C. batanensis (Becc.) Baja-Lapis — Philippines (Batan & Sabtang Is.)

C. bengkulensis Becc. — Sumatra+

C. billitonensis Becc. — Sumatra+

C. boniensis Becc. — Sulawesi

C. cawa Blume — Moluccas+

C. compsostachys Burret — China

C. congestiflorus J. Dransf. — Sabah (Nabawan; Sapa Payau For. Res.)

C. delessertianus Becc. — India (S.)

C. depauperatus Ridl. — Irian Jaya

C. didymocarpus Warb. — Sulawesi+

C. diepenhorstii Miq.
  var. *exulans* Becc. — Philippines

C. diepenhorstii Miq.
  var *major* J. Dransf. — Sabah (near Lahad Datu)

C. dimorphacanthus Becc.
  var. *benguetensis* Baja-Lapis — Luzon (Benguet)

C. distichus Ridl.
  var. *shangsiensis* Pei & Chen — Guangxi

C. divaricatus Becc.
  var. *contrarius* J. Dransf. — Sarawak

Calamus *dransfieldii* Renuka — Kerala

C. egregius Burret — Hainan Is.

C. elopurensis J. Dransf. — Sabah (E. Lowlands)

C. equestris Willd. — Moluccas+

C. erectus Roxb.
  var. *birmanicus* Becc. — Yunnan

C. faberi Becc. var.
  brevispicatus (Wei) Pei & Chen — Guangdong

C. feanus Becc.
  var. *medogensis* Pei & Chen — Xizang Zizhiqu

C. fissijugatus Burret — Sumatra+

C. flagellum var.
  furvifurfuraceus Pei & Chen — Yunnan

C. gamblei Becc. — Tamil Nadu (Nilgiri Hills)

C. gogolensis Becc. — PNG (Madang Dist.)

C. halmaherensis Burret — Moluccas

C. hookerianus Becc. — India+ (Coromandel Coast)

C. humboldtianus Becc. — Irian Jaya

C. hypoleucus Kurz — Myanmar

C. insignis Griff.
  var. *longispinosus* J. Dransf. — Pen. Malaysia+

C. interruptus Becc. — Irian Jaya

C. kandariensis Becc. — Sulawesi+

C. karnatakensis
  Renuka & Lakshmana — Karnataka

C. kerrianus Becc. — Thailand

C. kingianus Becc. — Assam

C. klossii Ridl. — Irian Jaya

C. latisectus Burret — Sumatra+

C. leiocaulis Becc. — Sulawesi+

C. leiospathus Barlett — Sumatra+

C. leptostachys Becc. — Sulawesi

C. leucotes Becc. — Myanmar

C. macrorrhynchus Burret — China

C. macrosphaerion Becc.	Sulawesi+
C. mayrii Burret	Irian Jaya
C. melanacanthus Mart.	Myanmar
C. merrillii Becc.	
var. *nanga* Becc.	Mindanao
C. mesilauensis J. Dransf.	Sabah (Mt. Kinabalu)
C. microcarpus Becc.	
var. *diminutus* Becc.	Luzon
var. *longiocrea* Baja-Lapis	Luzon
C. microsphaerion Becc.	
var. *spinosior* Becc.	Palawan
C. moszkowskianus Becc.	Irian Jaya
C. multispicatus Burret	China
C. nambariensis Becc.	
var. *alpinus* Pei & Chen	Yunnan
var. *menglongensis* Pei & Chen	Yunnan
var. *nambariensis*	Assam
var. *xishuangbannaensis* Pei & Chen	Yunnan
var. *yingjiangensis* Pei & Chen	Yunnan
C. obovoideus Pei & Chen	Yunnan+
C. opacus Blume	Sumatra+
C. orthostachys Furt.	Sulawesi+
C. pachystachys Warb.	Sulawesi+
C. palembanicus Becc.	Sumatra+
C. palustris Griff.	
var. *longistachys* Pei & Chen	Yunnan
C. papuanus Becc.	Irian Jaya
C. paucijugus Becc.	Sulawesi+
C. paulii J. Dransf.	Sarawak
C. pedicellatus Becc.	Sulawesi
C. pilosissimus Becc.	Irian Jaya
C. platyacanthoides Merr.	Hainan Is.
C. platyacanthus Warb. ex Becc.	
var. *mediostachys* Pei & Chen	Yunnan (Mangla; Yaoqu)
C. polydesmus Becc.	Myanmar
C. prattianus Becc.	Irian Jaya
C. pseudomollis Becc.	Sulawesi+
C. psilocladus J. Dransf.	Sarawak
C. pulchellus Burret	Hainan Is.
C. pulcher Miq.	Borneo
C. ramulosus Becc.	Luzon
C. rhabdocladus Burret	
var. *globulosus* Pei & Chen	Yunnan
var. *rhabdocladus*	China
C. rheedei Griff.	Kerala (Malabar)
C. rhytidomus Becc.	Kalimantan
C. rubiginosus Ridl.	Borneo
C. rudentum Lour.	Vietnam
C. rumphii Blume	Moluccas+
C. sabalensis J. Dransf.	Sarawak
C. salicifolius Becc.	Vietnam
C. schaeterianus Burret	Sumatra+
C. scleracanthus Becc.	Sulawesi+
C. serrulatus Becc.	Irian Jaya
C. siphonospathus Mart.	
var. *farinosus* Becc.	Luzon
var. *oligolepis* Becc.	Luzon
var. *polylepis* Becc.	Luzon
var. *siphonospathus*	Luzon
C. spinulinervis Becc.	Borneo
C. steenisii Furt.	Irian Jaya
C. sumbawaensis Burret	Lesser Sunda Is.+
C. tapa Becc.	Borneo
C. tetradactyloides Burret	Hainan Is.
C. timorensis Becc.	Lesser Sunda Is.+
C. tolitoliensis Becc.	Sulawesi+

C. travancoricus Beddome	Kerala (Malabar)
C. viridissimus Becc.	Mindanao
C. wailong Pei & Chen	Yunnan
C. walkeri Hance	China
C. yunnanensis Pei & Chen	
var. *densiflorus* Pei & Chen	Yunnan
var. *intermedius* Pei & Chen	Yunnan
var. *yunnanensis*	Guangxi
C. zebrinus Becc.	Irian Jaya
C. zollingeri Becc.	Sulawesi+
Calyptrocalyx *albertisianus* Becc.	PNG (W. Dist.)
C. (Paralinospadix) amischa Burret	PNG (C. Dist.)
C. angustifrons Becc.	PNG (E. Sepik Dist.)
C. archboldianus Burret	PNG (C. Dist.)
C. arfakiana comb. nov. ined.	Irian Jaya
C. bifurcatus Becc.	PNG (E. Sepik Dist.)
C. caudiculata comb. nov. ined.	Irian Jaya
C. clemensiae Burret	PNG (Morobe Dist.)
C. elegans	
Becc. ex Schumann & Lauterb.	PNG (Madang Dist.)
C. flabellata comb. nov. ined.	Irian Jaya
C. (P.) forbesii (Ridl.)Burret	PNG (Calyptrocalyx Dist.)
C. geonomiformis comb. nov. ined.	Irian Jaya
C. (P.) hollrungii (Becc.) Burret	PNG (Morobe Dist.)
C. (P.) julianetii (Becc.) Burret	PNG (Calyptrocalyx Dist.)
C. lauterbachianus Becc.	PNG (Morobe Dist.)
C. laxiflorus Becc.	PNG (W. Sepik Dist.)
C. (P.) lepidota Burret	PNG (W. Dist.)
C. (P.) merrilliana Burret	PNG (W. Dist.)
C. (P.) micholitzii (Ridl.) Burret	PNG
C. (P.) microspadix (Becc.) Burret	PNG (E. Sepik Dist.)
C. moszkowskianus Becc.	Irian Jaya
C. multifida comb. nov. ined.	Irian Jaya
C. polyphyllus Becc.	PNG (E. Sepik Dist.)
C. (P.) pusilla (Becc.) Burret	PNG (Milne Bay Dist.)
C. schlechteranus Becc.	PNG (Madang Dist.)
C. (P.) schlechteri (Becc.) Burret	PNG (Madang Dist.)
C. schultzianus Becc.	PNG (E. Sepik Dist.)
C. stenophyllus Becc.	PNG (Morobe Dist.)
C. (P.) stenoschista Burret	PNG (Calyptrocalyx Dist.)
Ceroxylon *utile* (Karsten) H. Wendl.	Colombia
C. ventricosum Burret	Ecuador
Chamaedorea *macrospadix* Oersted	Costa Rica
C. plumosa Hodel	Chiapas+
Chuniophoenix *nana* Burret	Vietnam
Clinostigma *collegarum* J. Dransf.	Bismarck Arch. (New Ireland)
C. ponapensis Becc.	Caroline Is.
C. vaupelii (Burret) Burret	Western Samoa (Savaii)
Corypha *griffithiana* Becc.	Myanmar
C. martiana Becc. ex Hoof.f.	Myanmar
Cryosophila *macrocarpa* R. Evans	Colombia+
Cyrtostachys *brassii* Burret	PNG (C. Dist.)
C. compsoclada Burret	PNG (N. Dist.)
C. glauca H. Moore	PNG (Morobe Dist.)
C. ledermanniana Becc.	PNG (E. Sepik Dist.)
C. loriae Becc.	PNG (Cyrtostachys Dist.)
C. microcarpa Burret	PNG (W. Dist.)
C. peekeliana Becc.	Bismarck Arch. (New Ireland)
C. phanerolepis Burret	PNG (Morobe Dist.)
Daemonorops *aruensis* Becc.	Moluccas+
D. bakauensis Becc.	Sumatra+
D. banggiensis J. Dransf.	Sabah
D. binnendijkii Becc.	Sumatra+
D. calapparia Blume	Moluccas, New Guinea+
D. confusa Furt.	Sumatra
D. forbesii Becc.	Sumatra+

D. horrida Burret	Sumatra+
D. kurziana Hook.f.	Andamans
D. lamprolepis Becc.	Sulawesi+
D. lamprosphaerion Becc.	Sulawesi+
D. longispinosa Burret	Sumatra+
D. megalocarpa Burret	Sumatra+
D. microcarpa Burret	Sumatra+
D. mirabilis Mart.	Borneo
D. mollis (Blanco) Merr.	Philippines
D. nigra (Rumph.) Blume	Moluccas+
D. oligolepis Becc.	Mindanao
D. pachyrostris Becc.	Borneo
D. palembanica Blume	
var. *bangkana* Becc.	Sumatra+
var. *palembanica*	Sumatra+
D. pedicellaris Becc.	Mindanao
D. plagiocycla Burret	Sumatra+
D. riedeliana Becc.	Sulawesi+
D. robusta Warb.	Sulawesi+
D. schlechteri Burret	Sulawesi+
D. schmidtiana Becc.	Thailand
D. serpentina J. Dransf.	Sabah
D. singalana Becc.	Sumatra+
D. stenophylla Becc.	Sumatra+
D. trichroa Miq.	Sumatra+
D. uschdraweitiana Burret	Sumatra+
***Desmoncus** phoenicocarpus*	
Barb. Rodr.	Brazil
***Drymophloeus** beguinii*	
(Burret) H. Moore	Moluccas+
D. bifidus Becc.	Irian Jaya
D. leprosus Becc.	Irian Jaya
D. litigiosus (Becc.) H. Moore	Irian Jaya
D. oninensis (Becc.) H. Moore	Irian Jaya
D. porrectus (Burret) H. Moore	Moluccas+
***Eugeissona** ambigua* Becc.	Kalimantan
***Euterpe** broadwayae*	
Becc. ex Broadway	Tobago
E. longevaginata Mart.	Bolivia
***Geonoma** epetiolata* H. Moore	Panama
G. gastoniana Glaziou ex Drude	Brazil
G. tenuissima H. Moore	Ecuador (Los Rios Prov.)
G. trigona	
(Ruiz Lopez & Pavon) Gentry	Peru (Pasco)
***Goniocladus** petiolatus* Burret	Fiji (Viti Levu)
***Gronophyllum** affine*	
(Becc.) Essig & Young	Irian Jaya
G. apricum Young	PNG (W. Sepik Dist.)
G. cyclopensis Essig & Young	Irian Jaya
G. flabellatum (Becc.) Essig & Young	Irian Jaya
G. gibbsianum (Becc.) H. Moore	Irian Jaya
G. gracile (Burr.) Essig & Young	PNG (W. Dist.)
G. kjellbergii Burret	Sulawesi
G. ledermannianum (Becc.) H. Moore	PNG (E. Sepik Dist.)
G. leonardii Essig & Young	PNG (C. Dist.)
G. luridum Becc.	Irian Jaya
G. mayrii (Burret) H. Moore	Irian Jaya
G. micranthum	
(Burr.) Essig & Young	Irian Jaya
G. microcarpum Scheffer	Moluccas (Seram)
G. microspadix Burret	Sulawesi (Linkobale)
G. montanum (Becc.) Essig & Young	Irian Jaya
G. oxypetalum Burret	Moluccas (Pulau Mangoeli)
G. pleurocarpum	
(Burret) Essig & Young	PNG (Madang Dist.)
G. procerum (Blume) H. Moore	Irian Jaya

G. rhopalocarpum	
(Becc.) Essig & Young	PNG (Morobe Dist.)
G. sarasinorum Burret	Sulawesi (Posso Lake)
G. selebicum (Becc.) Becc.	Sulawesi (Kandari)
***Guihaia** argyrata*	
(Lee & Wei) Lee, Wei & J. Dransf.	China
***Gulubia** longispatha* Becc.	PNG (E. Sepik Dist.)
G. moluccana (Becc.) Becc.	Moluccas
G. palauensis	
(Becc.) H. Moore & Fosb.	Palau
G. valida Essig	PNG (W. Sepik Dist.)
***Heterospathe** annectens* H. Moore	Louisiade Arch. (Rosel Is.)
H. arfakiana (Becc.) H. Moore	Irian Jaya
H. brassii (auth.?)	Solomon Is.
H. brevicaulis Fernando	Luzon (Aurora Prov.)
H. cagayanensis Becc.	Luzon
H. clemensiae (Burret) H. Moore	PNG (Morobe Dist.)
H. delicatula H. Moore	PNG (Milne Bay Dist.)
H. dransfieldii Fernando	Palawan (Puerto Princesa)
H. elegans (Becc.) Becc.	PNG (Madang Dist.)
H. glabra (Burret) H. Moore	Irian Jaya
H. kajewskii Burret	Solomon Is.+
H. ledermanniana Becc.	PNG (W. Sepik Dist.)
H. lepidota H. Moore	PNG (N. Dist.)
H. micrantha (Becc.) H. Moore	Irian Jaya
H. muellerana (Becc.) Becc.	PNG (C. Dist.)
H. obriensis (Becc.) H. Moore	PNG (C. Dist.)
H. parviflora Essig	Bismarck Arch. (New Britain)
H. pilosa (Burret) Burret	Irian Jaya
H. pulchra H. Moore	D'Entrecasteaux (Fergusson Is.)
H. ramulosa Burret	Solomon Is.+
H. salomonensis Becc.	Solomon Is.+
H. scitula Fernando	Luzon (Camarines Norte Prov.)
H. sensisi Becc.	Solomon Is.+
H. sibuyanensis Becc.	Philippines (Sibuyan)
H. sphaerocarpa Burret	PNG (N. Dist.)
H. trispatha Fernando	Luzon
H. versteegiana Becc.	Irian Jaya
***Hydriastele** beccariana* Burret	Irian Jaya
H. carrii Burret	PNG (C. Dist.)
H. geelvinkiana (Becc.) Burret	Irian Jaya (Miosnow Is.)
H. kasesa (Lauterb.) Burret	Bismarck Arch. (New Ireland)
H. lepidota Burret	PNG (W. Dist.)
H. rostrata Burret	Moluccas+
H. variabilis (Becc.) Burret	Irian Jaya
***Hyospathe** macrorhachis* Burret	Ecuador
***Hyphaene** benadirensis* Becc.	Somalia (S.)
H. dankaliensis	
Becc. var.*subcompressa* Becc.	Ethiopia
H. doreyi Furt.	Angola
H. incoje Furt.	Mozambique
H. megacarpa Furt.	Mozambique
H. migiurtina Chiov.	Somalia (NE.)
H. nodularia Becc.	Ethiopia
H. pleuropoda Becc.	Somalia (S.)
H. santoana Furt.	Guinea-Bissau
***Iguanura** prolifera* Kiew	Kalimantan
***Korthalsia** angustifolia* Blume	Kalimantan (S.& C.)
K. brassii Burret	PNG (W. Dist.)
K. concolor Burret	Sabah
K. merrillii Becc.	Palawan
K. scaphigeroides Becc.	Mindanao (incl. Basilian Is.)
***Laccosperma** laurentii*	
(De Wild.) J. Dransf.	Cameroon
L. majus (Burret) J. Dransf.	Bioko
L. robustum (Burret) J. Dransf.	Cameroon

Licuala acuminata Burret	Borneo
L. angustiloba Burret	PNG (W. Dist.)
L. anomala Becc.	Irian Jaya
L. aruensis Becc.	Moluccas+
L. bacularia Becc.	Irian Jaya
L. bellatula Furt.	Irian Jaya
L. bracteata Gagnepain	Vietnam
L. brevicalyx Becc.	Irian Jaya
L. concinna Burret	PNG (W. Dist.)
L. debilis Becc.	Irian Jaya
L. distans Ridl.	Thailand
L. ferruginoides Becc.	Sumatra+
L. flavida Ridl.	Irian Jaya
L. gjellerupii Becc.	Irian Jaya
L. grandiflora Ridl.	Irian Jaya
L. insignis Becc.	Irian Jaya
L. klossii Ridl.	Irian Jaya
L. leprosa Dammer ex. Becc.	PNG (Sepik Riv.)
L. leptocalyx Burret	Irian Jaya (Waigeo)
L. linearis Burret	PNG (C. Dist.)
L. macrantha Burret	PNG (Gulf Dist.)
L. malayana Becc.	Pen. Malaysia+
L. merguensis Becc.	Myanmar
L. micholitzii Ridl.	Sarawak
L. micrantha Becc.	PNG (W. Sepik Dist.)
L. montana Dammer & Lauterb.	PNG (Madang Dist.)
L. moszkowskiana Becc.	Irian Jaya
L. naumanii Burret	Solomon Is.+
L. naumonensis Becc.	Irian Jaya
L. oninensis Becc.	Irian Jaya
L. pachycalyx Burret	Irian Jaya
L. parviflora Dammer ex. Becc.	PNG (E. Sepik Dist.)
L. paucisecta Burret	PNG (C. Dist.)
L. peekelii Lauterb.	Bismarck Arch. (New Ireland)
L. penduliflora Zippelius	Irian Jaya
L. petiolulata	
Becc. var. kanepiensis Becc.	Kalimantan+
L. platydactyla Becc.	PNG (E. Sepik Dist.)
L. polyschista Lauterb. & Schumann	PNG (Madang Dist.)
L. pulchella Burret	Irian Jaya
L. radula Gagnepain	Vietnam
L. rumphii Blume	Moluccas+
L. simplex	
(Schumann & Lauterb.) Becc.	PNG (Madang Dist.)
L. steinii Burret	Irian Jaya
L. tanycola H. Moore	Irian Jaya
L. telifera Becc.	Irian Jaya
L. thoana Saw & J. Dransf.	Pen. Malaysia
L. tomentosa Burret	Vietnam
L. veitchii Wats.	Borneo
Linospadix albertissima (Becc.) Burret	PNG (W. Dist.)
L. angustisecta (Becc.) Burret	PNG (C. Dist.)
L. canina (Becc.) Burret	Irian Jaya
L. elegans Ridl.	PNG (W. Sepik Dist.)
L. longicruris (Becc.) Burret	PNG (W. Sepik Dist.)
Livistona beccariana Burret	Louisiade Arch. (Rossel Is.)
L. brassii Burret	PNG (W. Dist.)
L. crustacea Burret	PNG (W. Dist.)
L. melanocarpa Burret	PNG (W. Dist.)
L. merrillii Becc.	Luzon
L. rotundifolia (Lam.) Mart.	
var. mindorensis Becc.	Mindoro
Lytocaryum hoehnei (Burret) Toledo	Brazil (Atlantic For.)
Metroxylon sagu Rottb.	
f. micranthum (Blume) Rauwerdink	PNG
f. sagu	Mindanao

Oncocalamus wrightianus Hutch.	Nigeria (S.)
Oncosperma gracilis Becc.	Luzon (Biliran)
Orania archboldiana Burret	PNG (W. Dist.)
O. aruensis Becc.	Moluccas+
O. brassii Burret	PNG (C. Dist.)
O. clemensiae Burret	PNG (Morobe Dist.)
O. decipiens Becc. var. decipiens	Mindoro
O. disticha Burret	PNG (C. Dist.)
O. lauterbachiana Becc.	PNG (Madang Dist.)
O. macropetala	
Schumann & Lauterb.	PNG (Madang Dist.)
O. micrantha Becc.	PNG (Madang Dist.)
O. palindan (Blanco) Merr.	
var. sibuyanensis (Becc.) Merr.	Philippines (Sibuyan)
O. paraguanensis Becc.	Palawan
O. regalis Zippelius	Irian Jaya
O. rubiginosa Becc.	Luzon
Phoenix abyssinica Drude	Ethiopia
P. atlantica A. Chev.	Cape Verde Is.
P. caespitosa Chiov.	Somalia (NE.)
P. pusilla Gaertner	India
Pholidocarpus ihur Blume	Sulawesi+
P. sumatranus Becc.	Sumatra+
Physokentia avia H. Moore	Bismarck Arch. (E. New Britain Dist.)
P. insolita H. Moore	Solomon Is.
P. whitmorei H. Moore	Solomon Is.
Phytelephas aequatorialis Spruce	Ecuador
Pinanga acuminata	
(Burret) J. Dransf.	Borneo
P. arundinacea Ridl.	Borneo
P. batanensis Becc.	Philippines (Batan)
P. bicolana Fernando	Luzon+
P. cucullata J. Dransf.	Sarawak (Serian Dist.)
P. densiflora Becc.	Sumatra+
P. gracillima Merr.	Borneo
P. grandis Burret	Sumatra+
P. griffithii Mart.	Meghalaya (Khasi Hills)
P. hexasticha Scheffer	Myanmar
P. hookeriana Becc.	Meghalaya (Khasi Hills; Nuclow; Chura)
P. hymenospatha Hook.f.	Myanmar
P. insignis Becc.	
var. leptocarpa Becc.	Negros
var. loheriana Becc.	Luzon
P. latisecta Blume	Sumatra+
P. paradoxa (Griff.) Scheffer	Pen. Malaysia, Sumatra+
P. paucisecta (Burret) J. Dransf.	Borneo
P. punicea (Miq.) Merr.	
var. papuana (Becc.) Burret	Irian Jaya (Andai)
P. rupestris J. Dransf.	Sarawak (Bako Nat. Pk.)
P. sinii Burret	Guangxi
P. ternatensis Scheffer	Moluccas+
P. variegata Becc. var. concolor Becc.	Kalimantan+
Plectocomia bractealis Becc.	India
P. microstachys Burret	Hainan Is.
Plectocomiopsis paradoxus Becc.	Myanmar
Pritchardia pacifica Seemann	
var.marquisensis F. Brown	Marquesas
var. pacifica	Tonga
Ptychococcus albertisianus	
Becc.ex Martelli	PNG (W. Dist.)
P. archboldianus Burret	PNG (W. Dist.)
P. arecinus Becc.	Irian Jaya
P. elatus Becc.	PNG
P. guppyanus (Becc.) Burret	Solomon Is.+

P. kraemerianus (Becc.) Burret   Bismarck Arch. (Muliama, New Ir. Dist.)

P. paradoxus Becc.   Irian Jaya

Ptychosperma *ambiguum* (Becc.) Becc.   Irian Jaya

P. buabe Essig   PNG (NW. Sepik Riv. basin)

P. burretianum Essig   D'Entrecasteaux (Normanby Is.)

P. caryotoides Ridl.   PNG

P. furcatum (Becc.) Becc.   PNG

P. hosinoi (Kanehira) H. Moore & Fosb.   Caroline Is. (Ponape)

P. keiense (Becc.) Becc.   Moluccas+

P. ledermanniana Becc.   Caroline Is. Ponape; Kusaie)

P. lineare (Burret) Burret   PNG (SE.)

P. mambare (F. Bailey) Becc.   PNG (C.E. coast)

P. microcarpum (Burret) Burret   PNG

P. palauense (Kanehira) H. Moore & Fosb.   Palau

P. pullenii Essig   PNG (Coastal foothills)

P. ramosissimum Essig   Louisiade Arch. (Rossel Is.)

P. sanderanum Ridl.   PNG (Milne Bay Dist.)

P. streimannii Essig   PNG (Kuriva For. Res.)

P. tagulense Essig   Louisiade Arch. (Sudest Is.)

P. vestitum Essig   PNG (C. Sepik Riv. Bas.)

P. waitianum Essig   PNG (SE.)

Raphia *gentiliana* De Wild.   Zaire

R. hookeri G. Mann & H. Wendl.
    var. *rubrifolia* Otedoh   Nigeria

R. laurentii De Wild.   Zaire

R. monbuttorum Drude
    var. *monbuttorum*   Sudan (Equatorial)
    var. *mortehanii* (De Wild.) Otedoh   Zaire

R. rostrata Burret   Angola (Cabinda)

R. sese De Wild.   Zaire

R. textilis Welw.   Angola

R. vinifera P. Beauv.
    var. *nigerica* Otedoh   Nigeria

Rhapis *excelsa* (Thunb.) Henry   Sichuan

R. filiformis Burret   China

R. gracilis Burret   China

R. humilis Blume   China

R. macrantha Gagnepain   Vietnam

R. multifida Burret   China

R. robusta Burret   Guangxi

R. subtilis Becc.   Laos

Rhopaloblaste *brassii* H. Moore   Irian Jaya

R. ceramica (Miq.) Burret   Moluccas+

R. dyscrita H. Moore   PNG (Morobe Dist.)

R. ledermanniana Becc.   PNG (E. Sepik Dist.)

R. sp. aff. *ceramica* (Miq.) Burret   PNG (W. Sepik Dist.)

Sabal *gretheriae* Quero   Yucatan (Chiquila, Quintana Roo)

S. pumos (Kunth) Burret   Mexico

Salacca *magnifica* Mogea   Borneo

S. siamensis Mogea, ined.   Thailand

Siphokentia *beguinii* Burret   Moluccas+

S. pachycarpus Burret   Moluccas+

Sommieria *affinis* Becc.   Irian Jaya

S. elegans Becc.   Irian Jaya (Vogelkop Pen.)

S. leucophylla Becc.   Irian Jaya

Syagrus *campylospatha* (Barb. Rodr.) Becc.   Paraguay

S. cardenasii Glassman   Bolivia

Wallichia *chinensis* Burret   Guangxi

W. siamensis Becc.   Thailand

---

[1] + Distribution possibly incomplete

[2] Remarks:
This list does not include some species now considered to be synonyms of variable and more widespread species (listed below), although some may get ranked as true species following a modern taxonomic revision: *Attalea butyracea* (Central America), *A. phalerata* (South America), *Attalea* spp. (incl. *Orbignya, Scheelea*), *Bactris setulosa* (Central America), *Bactris setosa* (South America), *Bactris* spp., *Ceroxylon* spp. (Colombia), *Copernicia* spp. (Cuba), *Desmoncus orthacanthos* (South and Central America), *D. polyacanthos* (South America), *Euterpe catinga* (South America), *Euterpe precatoria* (South and Central America), *Geonoma pohliana* (Brazil), *Hyphaene coriacea* (Somalia), *Pinanga capitata* (Borneo), *Prestoea acuminata* (South and Central America), *Prestoea carderi* (South America), *Prestoea* spp. (South America), *Roystonea regia* (Central America), *Wettinia* spp. (incl. *Catoblastus*) and some others.

Citations of selected palm Floras (since 1900) and other references

THE AMERICAS
Regional Floras

Flora of the Guianas (Guyana, Surinam, French Guiana). 1985+. Univ. Utrecht, Neth. and Smithsonian. Inst., Wash., DC. Palmae to be scheduled.

Flora of the Lesser Antilles – Leeward and Windward Islands. 3. Read, R.W. 1979. Palmae. Arn. Arb. Harv. Univ., Jamaica Plain, MA: 320–368.

Flora Mesoamericana. 1980+. Miss. Bot. Gard., St. Louis MO and Nat. Aut. Univ. Mex. (UNAM), Mexico. Palmae to be scheduled.

Flora Neotropica. 1968+. 53. *Arecaceae Part 1. Introduction and Iriarteinae.* Henderson, A. 1990. New York Bot. Gard., NY. 101 pp.

Borchsenius, F.K. & Bernal, R. *A Monograph of Aiphanes (Palmae).* In press.

Subregional Floras

(Bahamas) *Flora of the Bahama Archipelago* (incl. Turks and Caicos). Correll, D.S. & Correll, H.B. 1982. Palmae. Cramer, Vaduz, Liechtenstein:250–265.

(Bolivia) *Sinopsis de las Palmeras de Bolivia.* Balslev, H. & Moraes, M. 1989. *AAU Reports* 20. Bot. Inst. Aarhus U. and Herb. Nac. de Bol., La Paz. 107 pp.

(Brazil) *Flora Brasilica.* 1940+. Inst. Bot. Sec. Agri., São Paulo. Palmae status unknown.

(Cayman Islands) *Flora of the Cayman Islands.* Procter, G.R. 1984. Palmae. *Kew Bull.* Add. Ser. 11:219–224.

(Colombia) *Flora of Colombia.* 1982+. Inst. Cien. Nat., Univ. Nac., Bogotá. Palmae status unknown.

(Costa Rica) *Flora Costaricensis.* 1971+. Field Mus. Nat. Hist., Chicago. Palmae (Fam. 17) schedule unknown.

(Cuba) *Flora de Cuba.* 1. León, H. 1946. Palmaceae. Cultural, La Habana:236–269.

(Ecuador) *Flora of Ecuador.* 1973+. Dept. Syst. Bot. Univ. Goteborg and Sect. Bot., Riksm., Stockholm. Palmae scheduled 1996.

(French Guiana) *Flore de la Guyane Française.* 1. Lémee, A. 1955. Palmiers. Libr. Lechevalier, Paris:198–236.

(Guatemala) *Flora of Guatemala.* 1. Standley, P.C. & Steyermark, J.A. 1958. Palmae. *Fieldiana Bot.* 24(1):196–299.

(Haiti) *Flore d'Haiti.* Barker, H.D. & Dardeau, W.S. 1930. Phoenicales. Serv. Tech. Depart. de L'Agri. et L'Enseig. Prof., Port-au-Prince: 36–42.

(Jamaica) *Flowering Plants of Jamaica.* Read, R.W. 1972. Palmae (Arecaceae). Univ. West Indies, Mona, Jamaica:73–76.

(Nicaragua) *Flora of Nicaragua Manual.* 1977+. Miss. Bot. Gard. and Herb. Nac. Nicar., Univ. Centroamer. Palmae not yet scheduled.

(Panama) *Flora of Panama.* 2(2). Palmaceae. Bailey, L.H. 1943. *Ann. Miss. Bot. Gard.* 30:337–396.

(Paraguay) *Flora del Paraguay.* 1983+. Geneva Herb., Switz. Palmae. Hahn, W.J. In process.

(Peru) *Flora of Peru.* 1(2). MacBride, J.F. 1960. Palmae. *Bot. Series: Field Mus. Nat. Hist.* 13:321–418.

(Peru) *Las Palmeras del Peru.* Kahn, F. & Moussa, F. 1994. Mémoires de l'Inst. Fran. Etud. And., Lima. 181 pp.

(Puerto Rico) *Flora of Puerto Rico and Adjacent Islands: A Systematic Synopsis.* Liogier, A.H. & Martorell, L.F. 1982. Palmae (checklist). Edit. Univ. P. Rico, Río Piedras:222–223.

(Surinam) *Flora of Suriname* 5(1). Palmae. Wessels Boer, J.G. 1965. E.J. Brill, Leiden. 172 pp.

(Trinidad and Tobago) *Flora of Trinidad and Tobago* 1928+. Agriculture, Lands and Fisheries, Trinidad and Tobago. Palm status unknown.

(United States) *Vascular Flora of the Southeastern United States* 1980+. Univ. N. Carolina, Chapel Hill NC. Palmae. Read, R.W. Publication schedule undetermined.

(Venezuela) *Contributions to the Flora of Venezuela.* Steyermark, J.A. 1951. Palmae. *Fieldiana: Bot.* 28(1):71–92; 1957, Palmae. *Fieldiana: Bot.* 28(4):809–814.

Other References

(Brazil) *Flora Brasiliensis.* Drude, O. 1882. Palmae. 3(2):251–610.

(Costa Rica) *Flora of Costa Rica.* 1. Standley, P.C. 1937. Palmae. *Fieldiana Bot.* 18(1):107–128.

(Cuba) Catálogo de las Palmas de Cuba. Muñiz, O. & Borhidi, A. 1982. *Acta Bot. Acad. Sci. Hung.* 28(3–4):309–345.

(Dominica) *Flora of Dominica (BWI).* 1. Hodge, W.H. 1954. Palmae. *Lloydia* 17(1):149–154.

AFRICA, MADAGASCAR and INDIAN OCEAN
Regional Floras

Flora of Southern Africa (South Africa, Lesotho, Swaziland, Namibia, Botswana). 1963+. Bot. Res. Inst., Pretoria. Palmae, Vol 2, schedule unknown.

Flora of Tropical East Africa (Kenya, Uganda, Tanzania). Dransfield, J. 1986. Palmae, Balkema, Rotterdam. 56 pp.

Flora of West Tropical Africa (West Africa south of 18°N and west of Lake Chad and Fernando Po). Russell, T.A. 1968. Palmae. 3(1):159–168. Crown Agents, London.

Flora Zambesiaca (Zambia, Zimbabwe, Botswana, Malawi, Mozambique, Caprivi Strip). 1960+. Crown Agents, London. Palmae (Fam. 198), schedule unknown.

Flore d'Afrique Centrale (Zaire, Rwanda, Burundi). 1972+. Jard. Bot. Nat. de Belgique, Meise. Palmae status unknown.

Subregional Floras

(Angola) *Conspectus Florae Angolensis.* 1937+. Junta Invest. Cien. Ultr., Lisbon. Palmae status unknown.

(Cameroon) *Flore du Cameroun* 1963+. Min. Enseig. Sup. Rech. Sci., Yaounde and Mus. Nat. Hist. Nat., Paris. Palmae status unknown.

(Central African Republic) *Catalogue de la Flore de L'empire Centrafricaine.* 1980+. ORSTOM, Paris. Palmae status unknown.

(Gabon) *Flore du Gabon.* 1961+. Mus. Nat. Hist. Nat., Paris. Palmae status unknown.

(Guinea-Bissau) *Flora da Guiné Portuguesa.* 1972+. Min. Ultr., Lisboa. Palmae status unknown.

(Indian Ocean) *Flore des Mascareignes* (La Réunion, Maurice, Rodrigues). Moore, H.E. Jr. & Guého, L.J., 1984. Palmiers (Fam. 189). Sugar Ind. Res. Inst., Mauritius, Port Louis. 34 pp.

(Madagascar) *Flore de Madagascar et des Comores.* Jumelle, H. & Perrier, H. 1945. Palmiers (Fam. 30), Tananarive, Madagascar. 186 pp.

(Mozambique) *Flora de Moçambique.* 1969+. Junta Invest. Cien. Ultr., Lisboa. Palmae status unknown.

(Namibia) *Prodromus einer Flora von Sudwestafrica.* Friedrich-Holzhammer, M. 1967. Arecaceae (Part 161), Cramer, Lehre, Germany. 2 pp.

(Rwanda) *Flore du Rwanda, Spermatophytes.* 1978. Ann. Mus. Roy. Afr. Centr., Tervuren, Belgium. Palmae status unknown.

(São Tomé and Principe) *Flora de S. Tomé e Principe.* 1972+. Junta Invest. Cien. Ultr., Jard. e Mus. Agri. Ultr., Lisboa. Palmae status unknown.

(Seychelles) *Flowering Plants of Seychelles.* Robertson, S.A. 1989. Palmae (Fam. 187). Royal Botanic Gardens, Kew, U.K.:244–255.

(Somalia) *Flora of Somalia 4.* Thulin, M. 1995. Royal Botanic Gardens, Kew, U.K.

Other References

(Southern Africa) *The Indigenous Palms of Southern Africa.* Wein, H. 1969. Howard Timmins, Capetown. 62 pp.

ASIA and OCEANIA
Regional Floras

Flore du Cambodge, du Laos et du Viet Nam. 1960+. Mus. Nat. Hist. Nat., Paris. Palmae status unknown.

Flora Malesiana. (Brunei, Indonesia, Malaysia, PNG, Philippines, Pacific, Australasia). 1948+. Flora Malesiana Found., Leiden, Netherlands. Palmae: a team project, to begin 1995, to be completed 2000.

The Palm Flora of New Guinea and the Bismarck Archipelago. Essig, F.B. 1977. Bot. Bull. 9, Off. For., Div. Bot., Lae, PNG. 53 pp.

Subregional Floras

(Australia) *Flora of Australia.* 1981+. Bur. Flora and Fauna., Canberra. Palmae, Vol. 39, schedule unknown.

(Bangladesh) *Flora of Bangladesh.* 1972+. Bangl. Agr. Res. Coun., Dhaka. Palmae status unknown.

(Bhutan) *Flora of Bhutan.* 3(1). Noltie, H. J. 1994. Arecaceae (Fam. 234). Royal Botanic Gardens, Edinburgh, U.K.:408–431.

(China) *Flora Reipublicae (sic) Popularis Sinicae.* 13(1). Palmae. Pei S., *et al.* 1991. Science Press, Beijeng. 172 pp.

(Fiji) *Flora Vitiensis Nova.* Vol. 1. Palmae. (Fam. 39). Moore, H.E. Jr. Nat. Trop. Bot. Gard., Kauai, HI:392–438.

(Hawaii) *The Manual of the Flowering Plants of Hawai'i.* 2. Read, R.W. & Hodel, D.R. 1990. Arecaceae (Fam. 120). Univ. Hawaii Press and Bish. Mus., Honolulu HI:1360–1375.

(India) *Flora of India.* 1978+. Bot. Soc. India, Howrah. Palmae status unknown.

(New Caledonia) *Flore de la Nouvelle-Calédonie et Dépendances.* 1967+. Mus. Nat. Hist. Nat., Paris. Palmae schedule unknown.

(Pakistan) *Flora of Pakistan.* Malik, K.A. 1984. Palmae (Fam. 153). Pak. Agr. Res. Coun., Islamabad. 33 pp.

(Papua New Guinea) *Handbooks of the Flora of PNG* 1978+. Melbourne Univ. Press, Melbourne. Palmae status unknown.

(Philippines) *Flora of the Philippines* 1990+. Botanical Research Institute of Texas, Ft. Worth and Philippine National Museum, Manila. Palmae schedule not yet established.

(Sri Lanka) *A Revised Handbook of the Flora of Ceylon* 1980+. Amerind Pub. Co., New Delhi, India. Palmae to be completed in 1996 by Neela de Zoysa.

(Taiwan) *Flora of Taiwan.* 5. Li, H.-L. 1978. Palmae. Epoch Pub., Taipei:784–794.

(Thailand) *Flora of Thailand* 1970+. Appl. Sci. Res. Corp. and Thai. Inst. Sci. Tech. Res., Bangkok. Palmae scheduled for 1995 by J. Dransfield and A. Barfod.

Other References

(Australia) *Palms in Australia.* Jones, D. 1984. Reed, Frenchs Forest NSW. 278 pp.

(India) *Palms of British East India.* Griffith, W. 1850. Charles A. Serrao, Calcutta. 182 pp.

(India) *Flora of British India* (India, Bangladesh, W. Tibet, S. Burma, Malay Pen.). 6. Beccari, O. & Hooker, J.D. 1894. Palmae. L. Reeve, London:402–483.

(India) *Palms of India.* Mahabale, T.S. 1982. Maharashtra Assoc. Cult. Sci., Pune. 245 pp.

(India, Sri Lanka) *Palms of British India and Ceylon.* Blatter, E. 1926. Oxford Univ. Press, London. 600 pp.

(Indochina) *Flore Générale de L'Indo-Chine* (Vietnam, Laos, Kampuchia, E. Thailand). Gagnepain, F. 1937. Palmiers. Manon et Cie, Paris:946–1056.

(Indonesia) *Palem Indonesia.* Sastrapradja, S. *et al.* 1978. Lembaga Biologi Nasional, Bogor. 120 pp.

(Malay Peninsula) *The Flora of the Malay Peninsula.* 5. Palmae. Ridley, H.N. 1925. Palmaceae. Reeve, London:1–72.

(Malaya) *Palms of Malaya.* Whitmore, T.C. 1973. Oxford Univ. Press, London. 132 pp.

(Micronesia) *A Geographical Checklist of Micronesian Monocotyledonae.* Fosberg, F.R. *et al.* 1987. Palmae. *Micronesica* 20(1/2):80–89.

(Myanmar) Enumeration of Burmese Palms. Kurz, S. 1874. *Jol. Asia. Soc. Bengal* 63(2):191–217.

(New Caledonia) The Indigenous Palms of New Caledonia. Moore, H.E. Jr. & Uhl, N.W. 1984. *Allertonia* 3(5):313–402.

(Philippines) *Guide to Philippine Flora and Fauna.* 4. Guzman, E.D. de & Fernando, E.S. 1986. Palms. Min. Nat. Res., Manila:145–233.

(Polynesia) *Flora of Southeastern Polynesia* (Marquesas, Gambier, Pitcairn, Tuamotus, Tubuai). Monocotyledons I. Brown, F.B.H. 1931. Palmae. *Bull. Bish. Mus. Hawaii* 84:117–128.

(Solomon Islands) *Palms of the Solomon Islands.* Dowe, J.L. (ed.) 1989. Palm & Cycad Soc. Austr., Milton, Qld. 56 pp.

(Southwest Pacific) *Palms of the South-West Pacific.* Dowe, J.L. 1989. Palm & Cycad Soc. Austr., Milton, Qld. 198 pp.

(Thailand) *Flora of Thailand.* 1. Suvatti, C. 1978. Palmae. Roy. Inst. Bangkok:332–345.

Appendix 5

Contacts

(Ch), Dr, Michael J., BALICK, Director & Philecology Curator, The New York Botanical Garden, Inst. of Economic Botany, 200 Street & Southern Blvd., Bronx, 10458, New York, U S A, 1/718/8178763, 1/718/2201029, mbalick@NYBG.ORG

Dr, Henrik, BALSLEV, Sarmiento de Gamboa 383 y Darwin, Quito, Ecuador, 593/2/434884, 593/2/434884, hbalslev@pi.pro.ec

Dr, Anders S., BARFOD, Assistant Professor, Botanical Institute, Nordlandsvej 68, Risskov, DK-8240, DENMARK, 45/89/423188, 45/89/424747

(M), Dr, Shyamal K., BASU, Advisor, The Agri-Horticultural Society of India, 1 Alipore Road, Calcutta, 700 027, INDIA, 91/33/4791713,

(M), Prof., David M., BATES, Professor of Botany, L.H. Bailey Hortorium, 462 Mann Library, Cornell University, Ithaca, 14853-4301, NY, U S A, 1/607/2553155, 1/607/2557979, dmb15@cornell.edu

(M), Dr, Henk, BEENTJE, Senior Scientific Officer, Royal Botanic Gardens, Kew, Richmond, Surrey, TW9 3AE, UNITED KINGDOM, 44/181/3325210, 44/181/3325278, h.beentje@rbgkew.org.uk

(M), Dr, Juan Jose, CASTILLO M., Director of Herbarium, Facultad de Agronomia, Universidad de San Carlos, Zona 12, Apartado Postal 1545, Guatemala City, 01901, GUATEMALA, 502/2/769794, 502/2/769770,

(M), Dr, Robin, CHAZDON, Associate Professor, University of Connecticut, U-42, Department of Ecology &, Evolutionary Biology, Storrs, 06269-3042, CT, U S A, 1/860/4864057, 1/860/4864320, chazdon@uconnvm.uconn.edu

(M), Dr, Charles R., CLEMENT, Researcher, INPA - National Research Institute for Amazonia, C.P. 478, Manaus, 69011-970, AM, BRAZIL, 55/92/6423300, 55/92/6421845, cclement@cr-am.rnp.br

Dr, Lidio, CORADIN, EMBRAPA/CENARGEN, C.P. 10-2372, Brasilia, D.F., 70.000, BRAZIL,

(M), Dr, Jean-Jacques, DE GRANVILLE, Directeur de Recherches, ORSTOM, Laboratoire de Botanique, B.P. 165, Cayenne Cedex, 97323, FRANCE, 33/594299283, 33/594319855,

Dr, Darlene, DE MASON, Department of Botany & Plant Science, University of California, Riverside, 92521, CA, U S A,

(M), Dr Ms, Neela, DE ZOYSA, Research Associate, Harvard University, Arnold Arboretum, 22 Divinity Avenue, Cambridge, 02138, MA, U S A, 1/617/4962380, 1/617/4959484, g6487ndezo@umbsky.cc.umb.edu

(M), Prof. Dr., Maria Esmeralda S. P, DEMATTE, Associate Professor, FCAV-UNESP, Dept. de Horticultura, Rodovia Carlos Tonanni, km 5, Jaboticabal, SP, 14870-000, BRAZIL, 55/16/3232500, 55/16/3224275,

(M), Mr, John Leslie, DOWE, Botanic Collections Officer, Townsville Botanic Gardens, P.O. Box 1268, Townsville, 4810, Queensland, AUSTRALIA, 61/77/220455, 61/77/253290,

Dr, John, DRANSFIELD, Senior Principal Scientific Officer, Royal Botanic Gardens, Kew, Herbarium, Richmond, TW9 3AE, Surrey, UNITED KINGDOM, 44/181/3325225, 44/181/3325278, J.dransfield@rbgkew.org.uk

Dr, Frederick B., ESSIG, Department of Biology, University of South Florida, 4202 East Fowler Avenue, LIF 169, Tampa, 33620, FL, U S A,

Dr, Randall, EVANS, Department of Botany, Field Museum of Natural Hist., Roosevelt Rd. at Lake Shore Dr, Chicago, 60605, IL, U S A,

Dr, H.Q.B., FERNANDES, Museu de Biologia Mello Leitao, Inst. Brasileiro do Patrimonio, Cultural, Santa Teresa, ES, 29650-000, BRAZIL,

(M), Dr, Edwino, FERNANDO, Dept. of Forest Biological Sciences, University of the Philippines, College of Forestry, Los Baños College, Laguna, 4031, PHILIPPINES, 63/94/2773, 63/94/3673, esf@mudspring.vplb.edu.ph

(M), Dr, Jack B., FISHER, Director of Research, Fairchild Tropical Garden, 11935 Old Cutler Rd., Miami, 33156, FL, USA, 1/305/6652844, 1/305/6658032,

(M), Dr, Gloria, GALEANO, Instituto de Ciencias Naturales, Univ. Nacional de Colombia, Apartado 7495, Bogota, COLOMBIA, 57/1/3694262,

(M), Dr, William, HAHN, Visiting Scientist, Smithsonian Institution, Lab. of Molecular Systematics, MRC-534, Washington, 20560, DC, U S A, 1/301/2383444, 1/301/2383059, hahn@onyx.si.edu

(M), Dr, Andrew, HENDERSON, Associate Curator, Institute of Systematic Botany, New York Botanical Garden, Bronx, 10458, NY, U S A, 1/718/8178973, 1/718/2201029, ahenderson@nybg.org

(M), Dr, Donald R., HODEL, Environmental Horticulturist, University of California, Cooperative Extension, 2615 S. Grand Avenue, Suite 400, Los Angeles, 90007, CA, U S A, 1/213/7444881, 1/213/7457513, drhodel@ucdavis.edu

(M), Mr, Charles, HUBBUCH, Director of Curators, Fairchild Tropical Garden, Fairchild Research Building, 11935 Old Cutler Road, Miami, 33156, FL, U S A, 1/305/6652844, 1/305/2535463, CHubbuch@AOL.COM

Mr, Anthony K., IRVINE, Rainforest Ecologist, Tropical Forest Research Centre C.S.I.R.O., Wildlife and Ecology Division, P.O. Box 780, Atherton, 4883, Queensland, AUSTRALIA, 61/70/918830, 61/70/913245, tony.irvine@tfrc.csiro.au

Dr, Alan R., JOHNSON, Old World Coordinator, Station Biologique de la Tour du Valat, Le Sambuc, Arles, 13200, FRANCE, 33/90/972013, 33/90/972019,

(DCh), Dr, Dennis V., JOHNSON, Consultant, P.O. Box 4522, Pocatello, 83205-4522, Idaho, U S A, 1/208/2328090, djohn37@aol.com

Dr, Francis, KAHN, Director of Research, ORSTOM, C.P. 09747, Brasilia, D.F., 70001.970, BRAZIL, 55/61/2485323, 55/61/2485378, orstom@cnpq.br

Dr, Phan, KE LOC, University of Hanoi, Department of Botany, Thuong Dinh, Dond Da, Hanoi, VIETNAM,

(M), Prof. Dr., Mohammad Salar, KHAN, Honorary Adviser, Bangladesh National Herbarium, BARC Complex, Farm Gate, Dhaka, 1215, BANGLADESH, 8802/311273, 8802/813032,

Prof., Ruth, KIEW, University Lecturer/Prof. of Bot., Agricultural University of Malaysia, Dept. of Biology, Universiti Pertanian Malaysia, UPM Serdang, 43400, Selangor, MALAYSIA, 60/3/9486101, 60/3/9483745,

M., Jean-Yves, LESOUEF, Curator, Conservatoire Botanique National de Brest, 52 Allee du Bot, Brest, 29200, FRANCE, 33/98418895, 33/98415721,

(M), Dr, Domingo, MADULID, Scientist III (Curator), National Museum, Botany Division, P.O. Box 2659, Manila, PHILIPPINES, 63/2/476887, 63/2/5300288, 6363376@mcimail.com

(M), Dr, Navaratnam, MANOKARAN, Director, Div. of Envi. Sciences, Forest Research Institute Malaysia, Kepong, Selangor, Kuala Lumpur, 52109, MALAYSIA, 60/3/6302100, 60/3/6367753, nmano@frim.gov.my

Dr, Kember, MEJIA, IIAP, Apartado Postal 784, Iquitos, PERU,

(M), Dr, Johanis P., MOGEA, Head, Division of Botany, R & D Centre for Biology, Indonesian Inst. of Sciences, Herbarium Bogoriense, Jalan Raya Juanda No. 22, Bogor, 16122, INDONESIA, 62/251/322035, 62/251/325854,

Dr, Jorge, MORA URPI, Universidad de Costa Rica, Ciudad Univer. Rodrigo Facio, San Jose, COSTA RICA,

(M), Dr, Monica, MORAES RAMIREZ, Researcher, Herbario Nacional de Bolivia, Casilla 10077, Correo Central, La Paz, BOLIVIA, 591/2/792416, 591/2/391176, monica@palma.bo

Ing., Celio, MOYA LOPEZ, Grupo de Recursos Naturales, Ministerio de la Cien, Aptdo. 52, Sancti Spiritus, CP 60200, CUBA,

Dr, Onaney, MUÑIZ, Instituto de Geografia, Ministerio del Ambiente, Capitolio Nacional, Industria esquina San Jose, Habana Vieja, Ciudad Habana, CUBA,

Mr, John, NEWBY, Director, Africa & Madag. Progr., WWF International, Avenue du Mont Blanc, Gland, 1196, SWITZERLAND, 41/22/3649111, 41/22/364238, john.newby@wwf_int.ch

(M), Dr, Larry, NOBLICK, Collections Development Manager, The Montgomery Foundation, Inc., 11901 Old Cutler Road, Miami, 33156, FL, USA, 1/305/6673800, 1/305/6615984, 103067.377@compuserve.com

(M), Dr, Rajanaidu, NOOKIAH, Head, Plant Scien. & Biotechn. Unit, Palm Oil Research Institute of Malaysia, PORIM, P.O. Box 10620, Kuala Lumpur, 50720, MALAYSIA, 60/3/8259155, 60/3/8259446, rnaidu@porim.gov.my

Dr, Edward E., OJOMO, NIFOR Coconut Substation, P.O. Box 222, Badagry, Lagos State, NIGERIA,

(M), Dr, Katharine, PEARCE, Lecturer, Universiti Pertanian Malaysia, Serdang, 43400, Selangor, MALAYSIA, 60/3/9486101, 60/3/9432514

Dr, Henrik Borgtoft, PEDERSEN, Botanical Institute, Nordlandsvej 68, Risskov, DK-8240, DENMARK,

Dr., Jean-Pierre, PROFIZI, B.P. 2820, Brazzavile, CONGO,

(M), Prof., Francis, PUTZ, Professor and Senior Associate, University of Florida/CIFOR, Department of Botany, P.O. Box 118526, Gainesville, 32611-8526, FL, USA, 1/352/3921486, 1/352/3923993, fep@botany.ufl.edu

(M), Dr, Hermilo J., QUERO, Researcher, Jardin Botanico, UNAM, Instituto de Biologia, Ciudad Universitaria, Apartado Postal 70-614, Mexico, D.F., 04510, MEXICO, 52/5/6229056, 52/5/6229046, quero@servidor.unam.mx

Dr, Robert W., READ, Botanist Emeritus, Smithsonian Institute, Quest End, 272 Rose Apple Lane, Naples, 33961, FL, USA, 1/813/7931074,

(M), Dr, C., RENUKA, Scientist, Kerala Forest Research Institute, Peechi, Trichur, 680 653, Kerala, INDIA, 91/487/782061, 91/487/782249,

(M), Mr, Paul, TULEY, General Secretary, Tropical Agriculture Association (UK), 49 Mount Place, The Mount, Guildford, GU2 5HU, Surrey, UNITED KINGDOM,

Dr, Natalie W., UHL, L.H. Bailey Hortorium, Cornell University, 467 Mann Library, Ithaca, 14853, NY, USA,

Mr, Bertrand, VON ARX, 2064 Trinity Valley Road, Lumby BC 2G0 V0E, CANADA,

Dr, Isara, VONGKALUANG, Kasetsart University, Faculty of Forestry, Bangkok, 10900, THAILAND,

(M), Dr, Scott, ZONA, Palm Biologist, Fairchild Tropical Garden, 11935 Old Cutler Road, Miami, 33156, FL, USA, 1/305/6652844, 1/305/6658032, zonas@servax.fiu.edu

Other contacts:

Susan ABRAHAM, Department of Botany, University of Kerala, Trivandrum, Kerala, India

Rodrigo G. BERNAL, Instituto de Ciencias Naturales, Univ. Nacional de Colombia, Apartado 7495, Bogota, COLOMBIA, rbernal@ciencias.campus.unal.edu.co

Miguel A. GARCIA BIELMA
Instituto de Ecología A. C., Apartado 63, 91000, Xalapa, Veracruz, Mexico

Michael FERRERO, Flecker Botanic Gardens Cairns, P.O.Box 359, Cairns QLD 4870, 61/70/502482, 61/70/321183

Francis FRIEDMANN, Laboratoire de Phanérogamie, Museum National d'Histoire Naturelle, 16, rue de Buffon, 75005 Paris, France

Dr Maria Luisa GARCIA, Centro Nacional de Conservacion de Recursos Fitogeneticos (CNCRF), Callejon La Ceiba, El Limon, Apdo. 4661, Aerugo, 2101–A, Venezuela, Fax: 043/831932

Dr Chrissen E.C. GEMMILL, Dept. EPO Biology, University of Colorado, Campus Box 334, Boulder CO 80309, 303/492/0780, 303/492/8699, gemmill@spot.colorado.edu

Dr David H. LORENCE, National Tropical Botanical Garden, P.O.Box 340, Lawai, Kauai, Hawaii 97665, USA, 808/332/7324, 808/332/9765

Sam P. MATHEW, Tropical Botanic Garden and Research Institute, Palode, Trivandrum, Kerala, India

Dr Judas Tadeu DE MEDEIROS-COSTA, Univ. Federal de Pernambuco, Rua Ambrósia Machado, 178, Iputinga, 50670-010, Recife, PE, Brazil

Dr Bertrand DE MONTMOLLIN, biol conseils s.a., rue de la Serre 5, CH-2000 Neuchâtel, Switzerland, 41/38/255024, 41/38/255290

Andrew B. MORAKINYO, 27 Seville Street, Brighton, East Sussex, BN2 3AR, UK.

Sven NEHLIN, Asocacíon Venezolana de Palmas (AVEPALMAS), Fundacíon LA SALLE, Edif. OCEI, piso 6, Moriperez, Caracas, Venezuela, snehlin@dino.conicit.ve

Dr Leng Guan SAW, Forest Research Institute Malaysia, Kepong, Selangor, Kuala Lumpur, 52109, MALAYSIA, sawlg@frim.gov.my

Suliana SIWATIBU, Foundation for the Peoples of the South Pacific (FSP), P.O.Box 951, Port Vila, Vanuatu, 678/22915, 678/24510

Fred W. STAUFFER, Fundacion Instituto Botanico de Venezuela, Apdo. 2156, Caracas, 1010-A, Venezuela, ,Fax 02/662908, 73000.561@compuserve.com

Dr Wendy STRAHM, Species Survival Programme, IUCN – The World Conservation Union, Rue Mauverney 28, CH-1196 Gland, Switzerland, 41/22/9990157, 41/22/9990015, was@hq.iucn.org

Andrew P. VOVIDES, Instituto de Ecología A. C., Apartado 63, 91000, Xalapa, Veracruz, Mexico, vovidesa@sun.ieco.conacyt.mx